Caring for Our Own

Caring for Our Own

Why There Is No Political Demand for New American Social Welfare Rights

Sandra R. Levitsky

OXFORD
UNIVERSITY PRESS

OXFORD
UNIVERSITY PRESS

Oxford University Press is a department of the University of Oxford.
It furthers the University's objective of excellence in research, scholarship,
and education by publishing worldwide.

Oxford   New York
Auckland   Cape Town   Dar es Salaam   Hong Kong   Karachi
Kuala Lumpur   Madrid   Melbourne   Mexico City   Nairobi
New Delhi   Shanghai   Taipei   Toronto

With offices in
Argentina   Austria   Brazil   Chile   Czech Republic   France   Greece
Guatemala   Hungary   Italy   Japan   Poland   Portugal   Singapore
South Korea   Switzerland   Thailand   Turkey   Ukraine   Vietnam

Oxford is a registered trademark of Oxford University Press
in the UK and certain other countries.

Published in the United States of America by
Oxford University Press
198 Madison Avenue, New York, NY 10016

Cataloging-in-Publication Data on file with the Library of Congress

ISBN 978-0-19-999312-3 (hbk); 978-0-19-999313-0 (pbk)

9 8 7 6 5 4 3 2 1
Printed in the United States of America
on acid-free paper

For Greta

CONTENTS

ACKNOWLEDGMENTS

Finishing a book is much harder than starting a book. One arrives at the end with a feeling of accomplishment, but also a profound sense of indebtedness.

My list of debts begins with graduate school. My intellectual interests lie at the intersection of law and political sociology, and I was fortunate to work with faculty in the Department of Sociology at the University of Wisconsin-Madison who not only value interdisciplinarity but also in many respects embody the best of this approach to research. I arrived in graduate school with a law degree, and under Mark Suchman's mentorship began the process of learning how to think like a social scientist rather than a lawyer. Mark is one of the most intellectually supple thinkers I have met in sociology, demonstrating a rare adeptness at and appreciation for both quantitative and qualitative methods—and a working knowledge of a staggering range of substantive areas. My work has benefited enormously from his energy, his ideas, and his sheer enthusiasm for scholarship.

Pam Oliver represents, in my mind, everything that is superlative about the Wisconsin Sociology Department, especially the commitment to the spirited exchange of ideas and to high-caliber sociological research. I learned as much from *observing* Pam—teaching, presenting, chairing—as I did from our substantive discussions over my research. Myra Marx Ferree repeatedly pushed my work beyond where I could have imagined it could go, only to seem unfazed when I observed how thoroughly my work was transformed by her suggestions. Howie Erlanger played an important role in shaping the socio-legal foundations of my work, and in sharpening and clarifying the presentation of my writing. KT Albiston, whose substantive work is perhaps closest to my own, served not only as an intellectual role model and insightful critic, but also as a professional mentor, sharing her experiences as a professor with an honesty and openness that I have always deeply appreciated.

This book also benefited along the way from the generous feedback of sociologists in southern California, where I did the fieldwork for the project: David Meyer, David Snow, Francesca Polletta, and the other participants of the UC-Irvine Social Justice and Social Movement Seminar, as well as Kevin Riley, Daisy Rooks, Gabe Raley, and Rene Almeling, all graduate students at the time in the UCLA Sociology Department who welcomed me into their dissertation writing group during my sojourn in Los Angeles.

One of the most difficult moments in transforming an interdisciplinary dissertation into a book was identifying my primary audience. As I struggled with this, I received some invaluable advice from my friend Scott Barclay: "Remember who showed you the love." And with this, I need to thank my intellectual family: the law and society community. At the top of this list are a handful of scholars who have served, more than anything, as intellectual role models. Everyone can point to two or three pieces of scholarship that proved transformative in their intellectual and professional trajectories. For me that inspiration was found in the work of Michael McCann, Susan Silbey, Patricia Ewick, and Austin Sarat. The ideas in this book would not exist without their contributions to socio-legal studies, and I would probably be a practicing attorney today if I hadn't been inspired by their work during my last year in law school. Scott Barclay and Anna Marshall are the closest to professional guardian angels I could ever imagine. What began as a casual invitation to a miniconference on cause lawyering in Los Angeles has turned into a steady stream of professional guidance, support, and friendship. I also owe a special thanks for the ideas, conversations, jokes, debates, reviews, coffees, meals, and email exchanges I have had with other members of the law and society community that nourished both me and this book project along the way: Caroline Lee, Lynn Jones, Steve Boutcher, Mary Nell Trautner, Scott Cummings, Laurie Edelman, Cal Morrill, Laura Beth Nielson, Anna Kirkland, Robin Stryker, Carroll Seron, George Lovell, Becky Sandefur, Rachel Best, and Liz Holzer. I am also grateful to everyone in the Law & Society Association's Law & Social Movements Collaborative Research Network for their consistently helpful feedback over the years.

I have been lucky to begin my professional career at the University of Michigan, which provided a nurturing and vibrant intellectual home. I am particularly grateful for the contributions of Margaret Somers, Howard Kimeldorf, Renee Anspach, Karin Martin, and Kiyo Tsutsui, who all read my manuscript from beginning to end and offered comments that significantly deepened the analysis in the book.

Over the course of working on this book, I had the opportunity to present earlier versions of chapters at various institutions, including Brown University, Ohio State University, the University of Michigan, the University of Minnesota, the University of California, Berkeley, and the University of Chicago. I am grateful to those audiences for their interest and their many excellent suggestions.

Both the Social Science Research Council (SSRC) and the National Science Foundation (NSF) provided generous support for the research in this book, through, respectively, the SSRC Philanthropy and the Nonprofit Sector Dissertation Fellowship, and an NSF Doctoral Dissertation Improvement Grant from the Law and Social Sciences Program.

My editor at Oxford University Press, James Cook, was supportive of this project from an early stage and was unfailingly helpful through the process of revising and editing the book. I am particularly grateful for his prescience in sending the manuscript to four anonymous reviewers who provided some of the most insightful feedback I ever received on the project.

Portions of Chapter 4 were published in *Law & Society Review* 42 (2008):551–590. I am grateful to Wiley-Blackwell for allowing me to reprint this material.

The challenge of sustaining me during the process of writing this book fell overwhelmingly to my family, and I need to thank them for their own unique contributions. My mother, Carol Levitsky, the quintessential Jewish mother, has never stopped reminding me to balance work with other things in life that nourish the body and soul. My father and stepmother, David Levitsky and Barbara Strupp, both hard scientists who routinely ask questions about alternative hypotheses as a matter of casual dinner conversation, have long modeled for me a life driven by intellectual curiosity. My sister and closest friend, Susie Roselle, provided me with the sustenance of really hard laughter. My brother, Steve Levitsky, my younger siblings, Mike and Sarah, and all of the partners and kids who round out my large, loud family—I am grateful to have had them all along for the ride. I also want to acknowledge the support of my partner's family: Ray and Clarice Krippner, Leah Krippner, Paul Goddard, Margot Canaday, and Rachel Spector.

I cannot imagine having finished this book (or graduate school, for that matter) without the friendship of Shauna Morimoto, with whom I began my training at Wisconsin. Our coffee and wine and dessert dates in Madison—and ASA dates since Madison—have been such a lifeline and source of joy over all these years.

Which brings me to Greta, to whom I dedicate this book. It is impossible to separate Greta's intellectual contributions to this book from the other kinds of life contributions that made this book possible. Greta read every word of this manuscript in all of its versions, from dissertation to book. She engaged me in conversations over dinner and washing dishes that produced some of the best ideas in the book. She demonstrated for me in her own work the power of rigorous scholarship and the importance of pursuing answers to genuinely important questions, and if I ever doubted the caliber or direction of my own research, she showered me with her irrepressible Midwestern optimism. But Greta also gave birth to our baby girl, Esme. There is no single thing that has transformed my life more than that one act. The tedium of writing the final draft of this book was greatly ameliorated by the sounds of baby laughter and Grover imitations, by feeding ducks, making pancakes, riding trikes, and playing in a world where suitcases become boats, pillows become trains, and stuffed animals become family. It is one thing to intellectualize about family beliefs in caring for our own; it is quite another to experience the emotional pull of care provision first hand.

Finally, I want to thank the caregivers, social workers, and activists who gave up their scarce time to participate in this study and who tolerated my quiet observations in their support groups over so many months. All qualitative researchers, I think, hope to do justice to the stories of their participants, and I have made every endeavor to do so in this case. When I made my goodbyes to one support group at the end of this study, a longstanding member of the group joked that he expected me to write something now that would transform the long-term health care system in the United States. We had a good laugh over this, and then an elderly Latina woman, new to the support group, leaned over and whispered to me in all seriousness, "*I really need that.*" This book is really my attempt to figure out why the conversation about long-term care reform has not yet emerged in American political discourse beyond a whisper.

Caring for Our Own

CHAPTER 1

Introduction

A t fifty-nine years old, Susanna did not expect to find herself working full time and caring for both of her ailing parents on her own. Susanna's father and mother have both been diagnosed with Alzheimer's disease and live in a house down the block from her in a lower middle-class suburb outside of Los Angeles. The two children Susanna raised as a single mother are grown and have moved away. Two of her brothers unexpectedly passed away, and her only remaining sibling lives across the country. During the work week, Susanna hires someone to stay with her parents for four hours a day. She cannot afford to hire additional in-home assistance, so her parents are left alone in the afternoon until she returns from work at 5:00 p.m. After work, she cooks them dinner, checks their mail, administers their medications, and does any shopping they require. On the weekends, she is their full-time caregiver—bathing them, dressing them, assisting them with many of the basic activities of daily living. Susanna routinely uses all of her vacation leave caring for her parents, and on at least one occasion required a three-week leave of absence from work. She pays for virtually all of her parents' care on her own. Her parents' modest Social Security and pension checks cover their mortgage and utilities, but little else. Medicare does not cover all of their medications, nor does it pay for their in-home care assistance, and their income is just above the cutoff line to qualify for long-term care assistance under California's Medicaid program. Diagnosed with pre-diabetes, Susanna is concerned that her vision has been getting blurry, but she has not had time to see a doctor. She recently had a root canal, but hasn't had time to pick up her antibiotics. She describes herself as "super stressed" and perpetually exhausted. And yet, reflecting on her circumstances, she observes, "If not me, then who?... I look at my parents, and they did everything for me when I was growing up. It's just my turn.

I just never thought I'd do it all alone. I never thought I'd do it both at the same time."

If care provision for society's most vulnerable has historically been understood to be a family responsibility (Harrington 2000), the particular kinds of struggles that Susanna has confronted in caring for her parents—the geographic dispersion of family, the level of care required by her parents, the strains on her income, job, and physical and mental health—are relatively new phenomena. Over the course of the past several decades, the massive entry of women into the paid labor force, changing family structures, and the aging of the population have all produced social welfare needs that are satisfied neither by traditional social arrangements nor by existing social welfare policy.

In the United States, existing social welfare policies were designed for an earlier era, when men served as the primary breadwinners for the family and women provided care for the young, the sick, and the old "for free" in the home (Huber and Stephens 2006). The architects of the American welfare state did not anticipate a world where women participate in the paid labor force at rates equal to or exceeding men,[1] where family forms have been reconfigured, and where changes in health care and living standards have dramatically extended the life expectancy of the average citizen. In 1975, 47% of mothers with children under eighteen participated in the U.S. labor market. By 2009 that number had risen to more than 71%.[2] The percentage of U.S. households headed by a single parent has nearly doubled since 1970.[3] The population aged eighty-five and older—who tend to require very high levels of care—is currently the fastest growing segment of the older population (Folbre and Nelson 2000; Rubin 2001). In 1970, there were just 1.4 million Americans over the age of eighty-five; today it is approximately 6.1 million. By 2050, there are predicted to be as many as 20.9 million baby boomers over the age of eighty-five (Gonyea 2005). The average American couple today has more parents living than children (Smith 1999).[4] Women now spend more years providing care for elderly parents than they do for dependent children (Smith 1999). As a result of these and other trends, contemporary families find themselves struggling with the need for elder care, child care, assistance with single parenthood, and health and economic security (Bonoli 2006).

---

1. During the Great Recession, the number of women in the paid labor market surpassed the number of men for the first time in American history (Rampell 2010).

2. *BLS Reports*. U.S. Bureau of Labor Statistics. Report 1040, February 2013.

3. http://www.census.gov/newsroom/releases/archives/families_households/cb07-46.html, retrieved August 6, 2010.

4. The average American couple has more than two parents living today and typically has fewer than two children (Smith 1999).

One of the most striking characteristics of these social welfare trends is how stubbornly their underlying social arrangements have persisted in the face of changing social conditions. Despite women's dramatically increased participation in the labor market, for example, American women still provide 80% of child care, two-thirds of elder care, and do more than two-thirds of housework (National Alliance for Caregiving and AARP 2009; Williams 2000). Similarly, norms about what it means to be a "good worker"—requiring, in effect, that employees commit themselves full time to their jobs without interruption for childrearing or other family commitments—persist despite increases in both women's labor force participation and parenting commitments from men (Albiston 2005). For most people, these norms represent taken-for-granted expectations for how we should maintain our social welfare. Not only do they remain unchallenged by the public, they remain largely unseen.

Because of the durability of these social practices, values, and norms, many American families find themselves on uncertain new terrain: they continue to hold deep normative commitments to existing social welfare arrangements, even as shifting demographic, economic, and sociopolitical realities have made it difficult for them to live up to these commitments on their own. For years, reform advocates have been calling for new social policies in the United States to offset the risks posed by these long-term trends: flexible work arrangements, paid family leave, tax credits, caregiving stipends, extended school days, state-subsidized home care, respite care, child care, adult day care, and other supportive services.[5] But most reform advocates concede that no matter how striking the social risks posed by new social needs, the United States is unlikely to expand public provision without significant public demand for state intervention (Abel 1990; Daly and Rake 2003; Gornick and Meyers 2003; Harrington 2000; Stone 2000). So where is the "groundswell of public support" (Williams and Boushey 2010:61), the social movement for new social policy which many commentators predicted in the face of these growing unmet needs (Hochschild 1997)? By most accounts, it has never materialized. Even as the economic strains and psychological stresses on families have intensified, the American public has shown little appetite for translating their private family dilemmas into political demands for new social policies (Gornick and Meyers 2003).

For social scientists, this gap between growing unmet social welfare needs and existing social policy presents a rare opportunity to observe the effects of unmet need on the ideology of family responsibility for social

---

5. This literature is far too expansive to cite in its entirety, but a few representative examples include Gornick and Meyers (2003), Williams (2000), Jacobs and Gerson (2004), and Harrington Meyer and Herd (2007).

welfare provision. Theory suggests that if families are unable to provide adequate care for their own, they should reevaluate the taken-for-granted beliefs and values which construct practices such as long-term care or child care as exclusively a family responsibility. *How then does the ideology of family responsibility for social welfare persist even in the face of well-documented unmet need?*

The answer, this book argues, lies in a better understanding of how individuals imagine solutions to the new social welfare problems they confront in their everyday lives. The ideology of family responsibility for care provision is by all accounts the dominant understanding of social welfare provision in the United States. Challenges to that ideology do not simply emerge whole cloth in response to contemporary crises in care, nor does the dominant ideology merely give way in the face of unmet need. The experiences individuals have seeking solutions to unmet needs may highlight the limitations of taken-for-granted social rules and practices, and in some cases, suggest the possibility of alternative social arrangements. Existing social services and social welfare policies in this regard provide key resources for imagining alternative social arrangements for care. But discontent with unmet needs and awareness of alternative social arrangements do not alone produce demands for new social policy. The political imagination requires a way of integrating new solutions to unmet needs with more familiar ways of thinking and talking about social welfare provision. This synthesis, referred to here as *discursive integration*,[6] produces new understandings of social welfare provision but rarely does it displace the belief in the family as the primary guarantor of health security. Understanding the role of existing social welfare policies in the process of grievance construction as it relates to both facilitating and obstructing the development of oppositional understandings of care provision is critical to seeing how Americans reproduce the dominant ideology of family responsibility even in the face of unmet need.

IDEOLOGY OF FAMILY RESPONSIBILITY

The ideology of family responsibility, sometimes referred to as the ideology of "familism" or "familialism" (Barrett and McIntosh 1982; Dalley 1988),

---

6. In earlier work (2008), I referred to this concept as *discursive assimilation*. My colleague Howard Kimeldorf observed that assimilation almost always suggests that the new is being assimilated into the old, or that the old has the power to absorb, neutralize or co-opt the new. This downplays the possibilities of oppositional understandings emerging from the combination of the old and the new. Given the evidence of counterhegemonic understandings of care provision that emerged in this study, I have since changed the term to *discursive integration*.

refers to a particular set of norms and beliefs about who should be responsible for the care of society's dependent members. Ideology is conceived here not as a single all-encompassing schema that determines how people think and act, but as a process by which meaning is constructed, reinforced, and in some cases transformed (Ewick and Silbey 1999). In this view, ideology shapes social life not by controlling people's thoughts, but by being utilized as a form of sense making. For ideology to be reproduced, it has to be "lived, worked out, and worked on. It has be invoked and applied and challenged" (Ewick and Silbey 1999:1037). Thus, when adult children care for their aging parents as a way of reciprocating the care that they received growing up, they reproduce the ideology of family responsibility (Ungerson 1987). When a daughter takes care of her mother the way her mother cared for her grandmother, she reproduces the ideology of family responsibility. The ideology of family responsibility is constituted by social norms portraying the family as a cohesive unit based on mutual responsibility and affection (Dalley 1988) where women should—and do—carry most of the burden and cost of caring. Caring for family members is understood as a natural or inherent moral obligation, superior to any other form of care, such as paid home health care or institutional care.

Norms about the "naturalness" of family responsibility for care are so pervasive in western societies that it's very hard for people to imagine the social organization of care in any other way. Asked to explain why they are caring for their relatives, many people will simply make reference to their family relationship (e.g., "I'm her daughter." or "He's my husband.") and see no need for explanation or elaboration (Walker 1991). So powerful are these normative beliefs in the obligation to care for family, that even adult children who feel they owe no debt to their parents—who, for example, grew up abused by a violent or alcoholic parent—nevertheless still feel an obligation to provide care, or express guilt if they fail to do so (Abel 1991; Walker 1991).

The belief that family should bear the primary burden of care provision has two corollaries in public policy (Montgomery 1999). First, the government should provide public services and benefits only in cases where there is no family or after family resources have been exhausted. In other words, state resources should not be provided for people who "ought" to be relying on support from their families (Finch 1989). Second, only the minimal amount of support should be provided in order to reinforce—and avoid weakening—family-based care.

Social scientists and historians have amassed wide-ranging empirical evidence that family care patterns are not, in fact, a reflection of an inherent or natural moral imperative. The "naturalness" of family care, for example, is undermined by the reality that some people do not provide care for their relatives (Finch 1989). Indeed there are many laws that are designed to coerce families to take on their "natural" responsibilities. The consistency and patterning of family care suggests not a biological imperative, but a coherent ideology underlying these practices (Dalley 1988). Feelings of "duty," "obligation," and "responsibility" are not natural feelings; they are prescriptive concepts, rooted in a particular view of the moral order of the social world (Finch 1989)

Historically, care has been provided both in and out of the household, as unpaid family labor or as paid labor in the market. Janet Finch's (1989) review of historical evidence on family care provision finds that in the early industrial period, for example, when conditions of poverty were especially harsh, family relationships were highly utilitarian; relatives offered support only if there was a possibility of mutual benefit. Anything short of that would have been considered an unaffordable luxury. Hendrik Hartog's 2012 study of inheritance and old age from the mid-nineteenth to the mid-twentieth century reinforces this. Contrary to the view of family as naturally fulfilling their obligations to family, Hartog finds that inheritance was routinely used by older people as an inducement to persuade—or coerce—family or others to care for them in old age.

The particular balance of state and family care has varied across time and place, reflecting not just a society's beliefs, but also its political system, economic structure, and cultural practices. That balance is often reflected in and reinforced by the laws and policies of that society (Finch 1989; Glenn 2010; Montgomery 1999; Walker 1991). In the United States, contemporary care practices have been shaped by a long line of legal policies—dating back to English Poor Laws in the sixteenth century—legitimizing and reinforcing the primacy of family responsibility. Recognizing that a sense of family obligation does not develop in a vacuum and that families do not always fulfill their natural obligations towards each other, British policymakers enacted legislation to ensure that people do not abandon their responsibilities to care for family (Finch 1989). Today, twenty-two states in the United States retain filial responsibility laws on the books, which designate certain family members as responsible for the care of older parents and effectively coerce them into assuming their "proper" responsibilities (Montgomery 1999). The state has also sought to encourage families to care for their relatives through incentives, such as tax allowances for those caring for dependents.

But law and social policy have most powerfully influenced the reproduction of the ideology of family responsibility through their capacity to grant and withhold services and subsidies. As Alan Walker (1991) has observed, the influence of social policy on family care provision lies in the assumptions it makes about the nature and availability of family assistance in rationing care. For example, a number of federal programs, such as the Veterans Health Administration, subsidize personal care services for chronically ill or disabled adults. The largest of these is Medicaid, which authorized states in 1975 to exercise a Personal Care Services Option for eligible Medicaid beneficiaries. More than thirty states exercised this option on the rationale that public funding of home- and community-based services prevented or prolonged institutionalization, which is far more costly (Glenn 2010:115–118). But Medicaid contains one important limitation on reimbursement for services: it will not reimburse "legally responsible relatives" for care provision. The refusal to pay family caregivers for services that the state would otherwise pay professionals to do reflects (and arguably reinforces) normative assumptions that family members are supposed to give care for free, on the basis of love and affection and reciprocity (Glenn 2010). Similarly, the dramatic shift in medical care provision from hospitals into the home over the last thirty years, discussed in Chapter 2, has been premised on the assumption that there exists a reserve army of family caregivers that can be drawn upon to provide for free those services that were once the sole prerogative of medical professionals (Dalley 1988; Glazer 1993).

To be clear, the argument here is not that there is something inherently wrong with embracing values about the importance of caring for dependent family members or that family caregivers are suffering from false consciousness in adhering to such beliefs. There are good reasons for believing in and enacting many of the values that lie at the heart of ideology of family responsibility. Membership in a family is unlike that of any other social group. With the exception of adopted children, most people do not have to become a member of a family; they are born into it, and in most cases remain in it no matter what else happens in their life. In every other social group membership can be revoked or withdrawn. Our social world derives shape and meaning from having a set of relationships marked by such commitments and obligations (Finch 1989). Chronically ill and disabled adults really do want to be cared for in familiar surroundings and to remain in the community, and many—although not all—would prefer to be cared for by family rather than strangers. Family caregivers derive real satisfaction from perceiving themselves as fulfilling their duties to family (Donelan et al. 2002), and as the next chapter elaborates, they often experience positive emotional rewards from doing so.

The point is that the uncritical reproduction of the ideology of family responsibility has produced a number of adverse consequences. First, the ideology depends on—and reinforces—gender, race, and class inequalities. The assumption that family members should take care of their own is really an assumption that women should take care of their own (Dalley 1988; Glenn 2010; Harrington Meyer and Herd 2007; Hooyman and

Gonyea 1995). It is gender, not kin ties, that determines who assumes the caregiving role in any family. This explains why daughters-in-law are usually third in line after spouses and daughters to become a family caregiver, rather than sons (Montgomery and Kosloski 2001; Walker 1991). Some men do take on caregiving responsibilities, but they tend to do so only when a female family member is unavailable. Gender shapes how men and women enact their caregiving role—what they do, how much they do, how they experience care provision. It structures the consequences of caregiving with regard to financial, emotional, and physical health, lost opportunities, and the lack of freedom to make choices that are important to their own well-being (Hooyman and Gonyea 1995). By ignoring the gendered aspects of caregiving, policymakers fail to acknowledge the inequity in this distribution of labor (Abramovitz 1996). Family labor, to the extent that it is recognized at all, tends to be viewed as free labor, and as a result, the size of the sacrifices involved in women's caregiving typically goes unrecognized.

The uncritical promotion of the ideology of family responsibility for care also reinforces race and class inequalities in at least two ways. First, low-income and minority groups tend to bear an unequal share of the burden and costs of care. The prevalence of chronic illness and level of disability are significantly greater among low-income and minority groups (Hayward et al. 2000; House et al. 1990). These factors tend to place greater demands on minority family caregivers, who also have more competing work and family obligations. Low-income and minority employees tend to lack the financial resources to hire help and are more likely to be employed in positions that offer less flexibility (Glazer 1993; Merrill 1997). Second, when care provision is done as paid work, it is not only gendered, but racialized (Boris and Klein 2012; Duffy 2011; Glenn 2000; Hooyman and Gonyea 1995). The people who perform care work in institutionalized settings or as home health aides are overwhelmingly women of color, many of them recent immigrants. As Evelyn Nakano Glenn (2000:86) has observed, "When care work is done by people who are accorded little status and respect in the society by reason of race, class, or immigrant status, it further reinforces the view of caring as low-skilled 'dirty work.'" The devaluation of care work then rationalizes low wages and lack of benefits in paid care work.

In addition to reinforcing gender, race, and class inequalities, a second consequence of the uncritical reproduction of the ideology of family responsibility is the consignment of many people to care in families that are not equipped physically, emotionally, or economically to provide the best quality care. Despite the widespread belief that family care is the best care, not all family-provided care is actually in the best interest of dependent family members. Family members, for example, do not automatically know how to care for chronically ill adults. To paraphrase Rhonda Montgomery

(1999:402), just as the ability to give birth does not automatically make one a good parent, family ties do not automatically make one a good caregiver. There is ample evidence that not only can care provision provoke conflict, anger, and resentments within families (Abel 1991), but that this can lead to emotionally and physically abusive care (Hooyman and Gonyea 1995; Wolf 1996).

Finally, and most relevant to the subject of this book, the uncritical reproduction of the ideology of family responsibility has played a key role in minimizing public demand for new social policies that might ameliorate contemporary strains on care provision. As Rhonda Montgomery (1999) has observed, one of the most powerful means to maintain support for existing policies is to assert their congruence with public choice. *We "choose" to take care of our own in this country, and therefore there is no need for policy reform.* But of course "choice" implies alternatives, and the American social welfare system provides few, if any, alternatives to family care provision. As long as Americans understand family responsibility for care provision as "natural" or "normal," the state can maintain the impression that nonintervention is both acceptable and justified (Walker 1991).

Governments clearly have a vested interest in shaping how people should think about their family responsibilities. The estimated economic value of family's unpaid contributions to long-term care in the United States is more than $450 billion a year (Feinberg et al. 2011). During times of sharp fiscal constraints, governments have been known to place a stronger emphasis on family support in the interests of reducing public expenditures (Crowther 1982). Many policymakers claim that increasing state intervention would weaken family ties, and that expanded social welfare programs will trigger a rapid growth of demand for services as families start "coming out of the woodwork" to claim public benefits for work they have always performed "for free" (Hooyman and Gonyea 1995). Not only do these assumptions have little support in empirical research, but researchers have found that state nonintervention is much more likely to strain family care relationships (Clark 1993; Hooyman and Gonyea 1995; Miller et al. 2009; Walker 1991). Caregivers of chronically ill adults who receive some help in the form of in-home assistance, day care, or other community services are less likely to suffer the physical and mental effects of stress and are more likely to keep their family members at home compared to people who do not receive assistance. Research has also shown families continue to be extensively involved in caregiving responsibilities even when formal services are also used.

All of these concerns have contributed to the persistence of the status quo in American social policy even as social forces are dramatically changing the landscape of contemporary care provision. Today, many families simply cannot meet the needs of dependent relatives on their own, and yet American social policies have not adjusted to offset or address their unmet needs. Jacob Hacker (2004) refers to changes in social welfare needs that occur without significant changes in the structure of social policy as "drift."[7] The primary characteristic of drift, he argues, is that it seems to occur outside the immediate control of policymakers, as if it were natural or inadvertent. Whereas many welfare state scholars imply that drift is an apolitical process (Armingeon and Bonoli 2006; Bonoli et al. 2000; Huber and Stephens 2001; Pierson 2001a)—after all, who can control the aging of the population?—the emergence of the gap between what American families need and what existing social policies provide, Hacker argues, is often mediated by politics. In the context of growing social welfare risks, opponents of expanded state provision don't have to orchestrate major policy reforms; they simply have to block policy interventions designed to ameliorate those new risks. And in the case of care needs, they need only to continue to extol the virtues of family-provided care.

But if the contemporary care crisis can be traced in part to policy drift, it is notable that families too have failed to respond to unmet needs by demanding social policy reform. The inability or unwillingness to adjust family care norms in the face of unmet needs could be characterized as "family drift." Ultimately, the ideology of family responsibility reinforces itself by preventing demand for social services and benefits (Walker 1991). The goal of this book is to identify how this happens, and under what conditions beliefs about family responsibility are questioned, rejected, or reimagined by family caregivers in ways that point toward new solutions to the growing long-term care crisis.

LEGAL CONSCIOUSNESS AND THE STUDY OF LAW IN EVERYDAY LIFE

The theoretical underpinnings for this book lie in two approaches to studying the dynamics of social change: the socio-legal literature on legal consciousness and the political sociology literature on social movements and political mobilization. While research on political mobilization seems like an obvious starting point for the inquiry here, the reasons for focusing on law and legal consciousness are less evident and therefore require some explication. One of the key arguments of this book is that law and social policy play a pivotal role in reinforcing the ideology of family responsibility,

---

7. For a related argument see Erin Kelly (2010) and her theory regarding "failure to update."

not only by communicating a particular set of values and norms, but also by rendering those values material: existing social welfare policies serve as important institutional resources that shape how, and to what extent, individuals formulate political grievances and justify a greater role in social welfare provision. While political sociologists have a long history of study-ing the concepts of ideology and hegemony (e.g., Anderson 1977; Barker 1990; Gramsci 1971; Mann 1986; Williams 1982), the particular role of legal concepts such as "rights" or "entitlements" or "filial responsibility" in legitimating or contesting dominant ideologies has been the particular domain of socio-legal scholars.

The concept of hegemony is most famously traced to Gramsci's study of the production, reproduction, and mobilization of popular consent (1971). Gramsci himself did not have a lot to say about law, but notably, he located hegemony at the intersection of state and civil society, where he also located law (Hunt 1990). Law was seen in Gramsci's view as a consti-tutive force, not merely a coercive one. Most law does not actually have to do with the physical powers of the state, but instead focuses on enabling a particular way of life: it legitimizes certain relationships, authorizes cer-tain social practices, and produces particular social institutions (Litowitz 2000). Characterizing law as "educational," Gramsci saw one of law's effects in society as portraying a specific mode of life as "legal"—or approved by the state (Litowitz 2000). In this regard, Gramsci could be characterized as an early proponent of social constructionism in socio-legal studies.

Social constructionism emerged in law and society scholarship as a criti-cal response to a long tradition of "gap" studies in the social sciences. Up until the 1980s, law and society scholars had been studying the gap between what laws on the books say and what they do in action—or between what the law promises and what it actually delivers. These studies repeatedly proved the existence of this gap, but they failed to explain the durability of the dominant legal ideology in the face of such persistent disparities (Sarat and Silbey 1988). Why do people acquiesce to a legal system that promises equal treatment, but that systematically reproduces inequality? In the 1980s, socio-legal scholars began to look at this question in a funda-mentally different way: instead of interpreting the gap between "law on the books" and "law in action" as a problem, law and society scholars sought to think about how the gap might actually contribute to the power and dura-bility of existing legal and political arrangements (Ewick and Silbey 1999; Sarat and Silbey 1988). Rather than focus on the failures of social policy, researchers turned their attention to all the ways in which law *is* effective, so effective, in fact, that we no longer notice its presence in everyday life (Sarat and Silbey 1988; Silbey and Sarat 1989). The power of law, these authors argued, lies in its ability to inscribe itself in the most mundane, the most hidden forms of day-to-day behavior. The places where law is hardest to see, and where it is hardest to differentiate from the social norms by which people structure their everyday lives, is where law derives its hegemonic power (Silbey 2005):

> We pay our bills because they are due; we respect our neighbors' property because it is theirs. We drive on the right side of the road (in most nations) because it is prudent. We rarely consider through what collective judgments and procedures we have defined "coming due," "theirs," or "prudent driving." If we trace the source of these meanings to some legal institution or practices, the legal origin is fixed so far away in time and place that circumstances of their invention have been long forgotten. As a result, contracts, property, or traffic rules seem not only necessary but natural and inevitable parts of social life. (Ewick and Silbey 1998:15)

By helping to constitute the way people behave routinely, these scholars observed, law not only legitimates particular norms and values, but it actually masks any alternatives. By shaping what becomes ordinary practice, dominant legal ideology makes it difficult to even imagine how life could be structured in any other way.

The project of unmasking the power and durability of the dominant legal ideology, these theorists argued, requires a deliberate shift away from the study of policy shortcomings and toward the study of law in everyday life (Sarat and Silbey 1988; Silbey and Sarat 1989). By leaving the state behind and looking at how ordinary people construct their local worlds, we might not only illuminate the hidden power of legal ideology, but be better positioned to observe strategies of resistance that seek to challenge the underlying bases of that ideology.

The focus of this book closely tracks that of the original legal consciousness thinkers: *How do we explain the durability of the ideology of family responsibility—and the absence of demand for new social policy—even in the face of unmet needs?* But this book departs from the socio-legal literature on legal consciousness in one important way: whereas the early calls to study legal consciousness insisted on turning away from the study of state policy in order to explore the cultural dimensions of law in everyday life (Sarat and Silbey 1988), the analysis of this book focuses very explicitly on the role of state policy in structuring how individuals imagine solutions to new social problems. The call for the study of law in everyday life has produced a voluminous literature that seeks to understand law from the "bottom up," both in particular sites of social action—such as government offices (Sarat 1990; White 1990), workplaces (Albiston 2005; Bumiller 1988; Marshall 2003; McCann 1994), and street corners (Nielsen 2004)—and among particular groups of citizens (e.g., the poor (Gilliom 2001), the working class (Merry

1990), working women (Marshall 2005; Quinn 2000), the disabled (Engel and Munger 2003), or gay men and lesbians (Hull 2006)). And it is here, steeped in the symbols, stories, meanings, and norms people draw on in crafting solutions to their everyday problems, that law and society scholars may have taken Sarat and Silbey's advice to leave the state behind too literally. The micro-level analyses that have come to dominate the study of law and society are rarely connected to the macro-level politics that shape them. If we are serious about studying the political imagination—both how citizens imagine solutions to the problems they face and how they construct strategies of resistance to dominant social practices—then we need to identify the resources with which they formulate solutions and devise strategies of resistance (see Perrin 2006). And if we do this, we may find that one of the most significant resources for the political imagination is state policy itself.

Recently socio-legal scholars have more directly engaged with the relationship between law and social policy and legal and political consciousness: Michael McCann's 1994 study of the pay equity movement; Charles Epp's 2009 study of campaigns to reform policing, sexual harassment, and playground safety; and Steven Teles's 2008 analysis of the emergence of the conservative legal movement all explore the ways in which macro-level legal and political conditions shape legal consciousness and political strategy. Yet it is notable that each of these studies focuses on social movements, activists, and other stakeholders as the primary objects of analysis. These are actors who, to varying degrees, are already participating in organized political action. Here we are concerned with why people are not participating in organized political action, people who, in most cases, cannot even imagine why political action might be necessary.

The analysis here follows a long line of cultural theorists who have suggested that in any given time and place, individuals have a limited repertoire of cultural resources from which they can draw in formulating beliefs and strategies of action (Sewell 1992; Swidler 1986). These resources include all the conventions, rules, meanings, and practices that form the "toolkit" (Swidler 1986) of skills and strategies from which people draw in responding to the world around them. The policies produced by legislatures and the decisions rendered by courts offer particular interpretations of problems and solutions which, once stamped with the legitimacy of the state, individuals absorb as noteworthy and tuck away in their cultural repertoire for future use (Ferree 2003). Later, when called upon to imagine a solution to a new social problem, individuals draw on these tools in shaping their strategies of action. Given the potential influence of state policy on the political imagination, then, this book places the relationship between everyday experiences and social policy at the center of analysis.

Key to this idea of a toolkit is the notion that individuals not only use these cultural resources in the situation in which they first learned to use them, but they can transpose or extend them to new situations (Sewell 1992). The consequences of such transpositions are neither predictable nor uniform, but they hold out the possibility of challenging existing social institutions by altering the social rules and practices which constitute them (Hunt 1990; Sewell 1992). Notably, virtually all socio-legal scholars who study the durability of hegemonic norms and practices return again and again to this possibility of counterhegemony and resistance (Ewick and Silbey 1992; Ewick and Silbey 1995; Hunt 1990; Merry 1990; Sarat and Silbey 1988; Scott 1990): if law's power is exerted in everyday, taken-for-granted social practices, then resistance too exists in these everyday acts, for resistance always exists side by side with power (Ewick and Silbey 1998; Foucault 1978). This approach to thinking about social change suggests that oppositional beliefs or practices do not necessarily come from outside the operation of hegemonic social structures, but arise from within (Steinberg 1999). To paraphrase Alan Hunt (1990), all struggles to challenge institutionalized norms and practices begin on old ground. "[C]ounterhegemony is not some purely oppositional project conceived of as if it were constructed 'elsewhere,' fully finished and then drawn into place, like some Trojan horse of the mind, to do battle with the prevailing hegemony." Counterhegemony starts from "where people are at" (Hunt 1990:313). It involves the reworking and the refashioning of those elements which are constitutive of the dominant ideology in ways that ultimately transcend the dominant ideology (see also Sewell 1992).[8]

But the line between reworking the elements of the dominant ideology and reinforcing the dominant ideology is a fine one. As others have observed, the risk of co-optation is real (Hunt 1990). McCann (1994), Epps (2009), Teles (2008), and many others (e.g., Crenshaw 1988; Scheingold 1974; Williams 1987) have documented the power and possibility of relying on the language of rights and rights strategies to effect reform, but also the very real constraints inherent to relying on law and litigation as tools for social change. The presence of multiple, even conflicting views of the dominant ideology often serves to protect that ideology from radical critique (Ewick and Silbey 1999). If ideology were singularly conceived and consistent, then it would be vulnerable to challenge whenever personal experience seems to contradict it. The complexity and contradictions that exist

---

8. Hunt (1990) uses the case of labor rights to illustrate this: labor unions began with the traditional elements of individual rights—freedom of speech, freedom of association—and constructed from them the notion of collective rights, now institutionalized, if still contentiously, in American law.

within a given ideology provide individuals with a variety of interpretations of their personal experiences, most of which are consistent with, and therefore supportive of, the dominant ideology (Silbey 2005:350).

What remains unknown—and relatively unstudied—are the conditions that mediate between resistance and co-optation in these cases. Under what conditions do families struggling with new social needs reimagine the ideology of family responsibility for social welfare provision—and under what conditions do they merely reinforce it? What prevents counterhegemonic understandings of new social welfare needs from developing into political demand for alternative social arrangements? This book draws on two concepts to help answer these questions: politicization and discursive integration. The concept of politicization is in many ways very similar to the socio-legal understanding of resistance, but is intended to reestablish the important connection between everyday experiences, ideologies of social welfare, and the policies of the state. Discursive integration seeks to understand at a cognitive level exactly how individuals imagine solutions to their social welfare problems that either reinforce or challenge the status quo.

POLITICIZATION

As with many concepts in the social sciences, researchers have deployed the term *politicization* generously, in wide-ranging contexts, and somewhat imprecisely. Some refer to the politicization of issues (Haines 1979; Hay 2007; Starr and Immergut 1987), while others refer to the politicization of people (Frease 1975). Some analyze politicization at a cultural or discursive level (Fraser 1989; Somers and Block 2005), while others focus on individual-level politicization (Taylor and Whittier 1992). Depending on what one seeks to explain, of course, justifications can be made for all of these conceptualizations of the term, and so some explication is necessary for the particular usage employed here. This book seeks to illuminate the conditions under which individuals confronted by new and unmet needs come to challenge taken-for-granted assumptions about social welfare provision. "Politicization" in this context refers specifically to the process by which individuals come to (1) view longstanding "private" needs or interests as matters of legitimate public deliberation and decision making, (2) imagine solutions to their unmet needs or interests—what this book refers to as *grievance construction*—and (3) make claims to an official agency or other perceived responsible party for action (see Haines 1979; Hay 2007). The term is conceptualized here not as a stable or static entity, but as a continuum, constantly developed in concrete social action, as certain opportunities and ideational and institutional resources become available (Mansbridge 2001). At its most modest, politicization can refer to consciousness-raising and the recognition of previously unseen norms and practices; at its most developed, politicization refers to the process of becoming active in organized political demand making. While politicization is a process, it is not necessarily a uniform one: politicization can occur unevenly, with some aspects developing independently of others. Thus, it is possible, for example, for someone to participate in political action without first establishing a sense of collective identity. But the likelihood of such action is generally viewed as greater among populations with a relatively more developed sense of political consciousness.

This understanding of politicization incorporates two important dimensions in the development of oppositional consciousness: it involves an ideological shift in the subjective meanings one attaches to one's circumstances, and a behavioral shift in the extent to which one is willing to personally participate in political demand making (Frease 1975). The ideological dimension emphasizes the social and psychological aspects of interpretation and attribution: do we see our problems as caused by our own personal failings, or by uncontrollable forces such as fate, God, nature, or bad luck? Or do we attribute blame for our problems to controllable forces external to ourselves—such as the government, an employer, or an insurance company (Felstiner et al. 1980–81; Ferree and Miller 1985; Gamson 1992b; Hay 2007)?[9] The conceptual shift away from thinking about one's situation as an individual problem or as a problem caused by fate or nature, to thinking about it as a social or public problem, is widely understood to be a necessary, if insufficient, condition for political action (Gamson 1992b). As Mills ([1959] 2000:8) famously observed:

> Perhaps the most fruitful distinction with which the sociological imagination works is between the "personal troubles of milieu" and the "public issues of social structure." . . . *Troubles* occur within the character of the individual and within the range of his immediate relations with others. . . . *Issues* have to do with matters that transcend these local environments of the individual and the range of his inner life. . . . An *issue* is a public matter.

9. A voluminous literature on framing has sought to understand the ways in which social movement organizations influence these processes of attribution through the production and dissemination of collective action frames (see, e.g., Ferree, Gamson, Gerhards, and Rucht 2002; Snow, Rochford, Worden, and Benford 1986; Snow and Benford 1988; Steinberg 1999). The framing literature has been criticized for disproportionately emphasizing the strategic efforts of movement organizations rather than those individuals who are presumably the targets of framing efforts (Benford 1997; Futrell 2003; Hull 2001). As a result, little is known about how individuals interpret their circumstances in the absence of contact with social movement organizations. It is these individuals who are the focus of inquiry in this case.

The behavioral dimension of politicization emphasizes how individuals convert their attributions into action (Frease 1975; McAdam 1988). If we understand our unmet needs as the basis for public debate and decision making, how, if at all, do we choose to make our voices heard in the public arena? A substantial literature on political activism has identified a wide range of resources necessary for the mobilization of political grievances, including organization and money (McCarthy and Zald 1977; McCarthy and Zald 1973), time and availability (Jasper 1997; Snow et al. 1980), a sense of collective identity (Hunt and Benford 2004; Polletta and Jasper 2001; Taylor and Whittier 1992), and a perception of political opportunity and efficacy (Gamson 1992b; Klandermans 1984; McAdam 1982; Piven and Cloward 1979).

This conception of politicization as involving processes of both grievance construction and mobilization permits the examination of a wide range of potential obstacles to the development of political demand—from the unwillingness or inability to view personal troubles as political issues, to ideological influences on the construction of grievances, to perceptions of political inefficacy, to the organizational and political constraints that prevent grievances from being mobilized in political arenas. It's important to emphasize, however, that politicization does not necessarily lead to policy reform. I am not arguing, in other words, that if only the American public were more politicized, we would necessarily see substantive policy reform. Even in a population of fully politicized individuals, there are a host of other obstacles that reform proposals confront in the legislative process itself. My concern here is not with the likelihood of policy reform, but with the formation of political demand: under what conditions do people challenge norms about state nonintervention in social welfare provision?

DISCURSIVE INTEGRATION

The concept of discursive integration is used here to help understand at a cognitive level exactly how people create understandings of their circumstances that either reinforce or challenge traditional norms. Discursive integration is the process of synthesizing new solutions to unmet needs—new models or political logics—with more familiar ways of thinking and talking about social welfare provision (Polletta 2000; Primus 1999). It involves "starting where people are at"—what people know and believe and value—and reworking those elements which are constitutive of the dominant ideology in ways that people believe will solve the problems they confront in everyday life (Hunt 1990).[10]

10. Some scholars have referred to this process as *creativity* (Csikszentmihalyi 1996; Perrin 2006).

In most cases, this refashioning simply reinforces the status quo: imagined policy solutions rarely challenge underlying beliefs about responsibility for social welfare. But in some cases, discursive integration creates understandings of social welfare provision that ultimately transcend the dominant ideology. Key to understanding the fine line between reinforcing and reimagining the social organization of care is the concept of cultural categories.

It is axiomatic in sociology that people rely on social categories and distinctions for making sense of their place in the world. We draw these distinctions in all areas of social life: between "normal" and "deviant" sexuality, "masculine" and "feminine" genders, "deserving" and "undeserving" citizens, and so on. Such classifications not only serve as a way of learning the rules of any social group (e.g., what do I have to wear, how should I carry myself, how should I talk if I want to be appropriately feminine?), but also a reminder of what happens to people when they deviate from those rules. These distinctions play an important role in shaping how we see the world and the people who populate it.

Policymaking also involves the use of social categories. Policies define who is officially poor and not poor; who is a minority, disabled, married, unemployed, an honorable veteran, and so on (Steensland 2006). These official legal categories have both material and symbolic consequences. At the material level, they are the basis for the distribution of state benefits, services, rights, and entitlements. There are, in other words, measurable consequences associated with how one is classified by the state, and therefore these definitions are the subject of considerable political contestation.

But policies also have symbolic or interpretative effects. Policies provide the public with information and sources of meaning (Pierson 1993). They define membership and assign status or standing in the political community, and they communicate to beneficiaries cues about their worth as citizens and their privileges and rights as members of the polity (Mettler and Soss 2004; Soss 2005). Social policies can also send messages to the broader public about group characteristics, making some groups appear trustworthy or devious, morally virtuous or repugnant, and this can affect the public's ideas about which groups are deserving or undeserving of government assistance (Schneider and Ingram 1993; Schneider and Ingram 1997).

This influence goes both ways: not only do political categories have material and symbolic consequences, but cultural categories can also shape social policies (Skrentny 2002; Fraser 1989; Orloff 1999).[11] Brian Steensland (2007) elegantly shows the influence of cultural categories on

---

11. For excellent review articles on the influence of culture on state processes, see Padamsee (2009) and Steensland and Smith (2012).

policymaking in his account of the failed guaranteed annual income plans of the late 1960s and 1970s. One of the primary obstacles to guaranteed income legislation, Steensland argues, was the cultural distinction that Americans drew between different categories of poor people. Americans have long considered some groups to be more worthy of government assistance than others: the "deserving poor," for example, have historically included people who, because of their age, gender, family status, or physical limitations are not expected to work and therefore "deserve" state assistance. The "undeserving poor," by contrast, are people who are perceived as having the capacity to work and therefore deserve only minimal assistance from the state. The guaranteed annual income proposals would have done away with these distinctions; instead of providing benefits based on the capacity to work, they would have determined eligibility based on economic need alone. In other words, all categories of poor people—the undeserving poor, the deserving poor, and the working poor—would have been collapsed into the same government program and treated the same way. It is in these cases of *symbolic pollution* (Douglas 1966)—where the "impure" status of one group threatens to contaminate the "pure" status of another—where we can most clearly see how invested people are in these cultural categories. In the case of the guaranteed income proposals, neither the public nor stakeholders viewed these categories of poor as moral equivalents, and in the absence of a boundary formally separating the groups, the stigma associated with the undeserving poor threatened to contaminate the social status of other, more deserving beneficiaries. Steensland argues that this symbolic pollution killed not only specific legislative proposals, but the very idea of guaranteed income as a policy solution to poverty.

The fear of, or aversion to symbolic pollution is key to understanding why discursive integration can in some cases produce understandings of one's circumstances that legitimate the dominant ideology and in other cases challenge that ideology. People are invested in these cultural distinctions because they reflect things like self-worth, status, and morality. They derive a sense of identity from these categories. Being a "dutiful" family member by taking care of one's parents or spouse—no matter what the cost to one's health or economic security—reflects positively on who you are and what you stand for. But the contemporary reality is that many people can no longer satisfy the care needs of family on their own and this threatens their status as "dutiful" family members. In searching for ways to reestablish their identity as "dutiful" children or partners,[12] they look for solutions to unmet needs that are consistent with that status and/or that reinforce the boundary between

---

12. For a related "caregiver identity theory," see Montgomery and Kosloski (2013).

"dutiful" and "not dutiful." As the analysis in the following chapters will show, the policy solutions in the United States that accomplish this are residualist[13] public assistance programs: safety nets such as Medicaid and Temporary Assistance to Needy Families that retain the primacy of family responsibility for social welfare by offering only minimal assistance to families in need. Medicaid resonates with family caregivers as a policy solution to unmet care needs by providing state assistance in ways that do not compromise caregivers' status as "dutiful" family members. The state, in other words, does not threaten to take over caregiving responsibilities from family, but seeks to reinforce them. The consequences of this are significant, for in maintaining their status as "dutiful" family members caregivers who are drawn to the Medicaid model not only reproduce the ideology of family responsibility, but they minimize public demand for more interventionist social policies.

Under what conditions, then, can discursive integration synthesize new models of social welfare provision with longstanding beliefs and practices in ways that could transcend the dominant ideology? Here we have to remember that at any given time people are navigating the boundaries of not just one cultural category but many. And we can expect that there are times when resolving symbolic pollution in one arena creates symbolic pollution in another. The counterhegemonic potential of discursive integration lies in reworking the multiple elements of distinct cultural categories in ways that maintain positive social standing across categories.

In the case of family care provision, for example, seeking assistance from residualist social welfare programs reinforces the primacy of family responsibility and the status of care providers as dutiful family members, but it contradicts what it means to be a "deserving citizen" in this country. Deserving citizens are understood as hardworking, tax-paying democratic participants who are rewarded by the state with entitlements to certain forms of social welfare provision. By contrast, residualist welfare programs are reserved for the undeserving poor. For people seeking to maintain a positive perception of self-worth across cultural categories (i.e., to be both a "dutiful" family member and a "deserving" citizen) they must integrate beliefs about deservingness with norms about family responsibility for care. This has the potential to create a fundamentally new understanding of the social responsibility for care, for it combines elements of family responsibility with notions of entitlement and state obligation, concepts that lie at the heart of a more interventionist model of social policy.

13. In contrast to residualist policies, *social insurance* policies are designed to redistribute risks: by universalizing financial security through mandatory contributions from workers, they are intended to prevent the collapse of a family's living standards.

Thus, if symbolic pollution involves the contamination of the "pure" status of one group by the "impure" status of another, here we find that people can preserve the "pure" status of one group by redefining the boundaries of another cultural category. It is this process of re-drawing boundaries that produces understandings of long-term care provision that fundamentally challenge American beliefs about the state's responsibility for maintaining social welfare.

POLITICAL SOCIOLOGISTS AND THE ABSENCE OF POLITICAL DEMAND MAKING

The strategy of this book—studying the absence of political action as a way of illuminating obstacles to politicization—is unusual in the study of political sociology. In general, political sociologists are trained to study observable forms of political demand making: activity which they can measure, or at the very least, see, such as voting, lobbying, litigating, social protest, and armed conflict (but see Auyero and Swistun 2009; Crenson 1971; Goss 2006; Steensland 2007). There have been important exceptions. Most notably, scholars have long tried to unravel the mystery of why the labor and socialist movements have historically been so weak in the United States relative to other countries. Research on American exceptionalism, however, has in many ways remained distinct from scholarship on social movements, which continues to be dominated by a focus on mobilization, rather than nonmobilization.

The persistent focus on positive cases of mobilization in social movement theory has had at least two troubling consequences for the development of theories of political mobilization. First, it has perpetuated the impression that the successful mobilization of grievances involves no more than assembling a list of necessary ingredients—such as resources, collective action frames, and a sense of collective identity and political efficacy among potential participants. The emphasis on emergent collective action makes it difficult to distinguish between those elements that are actually conducive to political mobilization in a given case and those factors that are detrimental or irrelevant to mobilization (Emigh 1997). In a negative case, by contrast, where theoretical predictions appear to be contradicted in some fundamental way, what needs to be explained is not the emergence of collective action, but the persistence of nonaction (Gaventa 1982). Obstacles to mobilization become the focus of the researcher's analysis.

Second, the focus on positive cases has produced a kind of distortion in the development of theories of mobilization. Many of the tools and concepts we have today for understanding political mobilization are based on studies of social movements that took place during eras of heightened activism—most notably during the 1960s and 1970s, a period we now recognize as atypical in American history for the extent of social unrest (Tarrow 1994). The emphasis in the literature on emergent collective action makes it difficult to assess how changes in American political and social life over time may affect the utility of theories forged from data from an earlier era—every positive case seems, after all, to confirm the validity of existing theory. A negative case, by contrast, presents a theoretical anomaly, a contradiction that forces researchers to rethink and potentially reconstruct existing theory to account for changing historical conditions (Burawoy 1992; Emigh 1997).

The bias toward studying positive cases of political mobilization can be traced in part to assumptions in theories of democratic pluralism about the political (in)significance of non-mobilization (Crenson 1971). Pluralists assume that in a political system open to any group of citizens with the interest and energy to make demands on the state, any "important" problem will necessarily be converted into a political issue.[14] As Robert Dahl (1963:93) observed: "The independence, penetrability, and heterogeneity of the various segments of the political stratum all but guarantee that any dissatisfied group will find spokesmen in the political stratum." From this perspective, the failure to translate private grievances into political demands must signal either a lack of true discontent regarding the issue, or a lack of interest in communicating complaints to elected representatives. In either case, the issue would be considered, according to the logic of democratic pluralism, politically insignificant (Crenson 1971).

But as Matthew Crenson (1971) and other critics of pluralist theory (Bachrach and Baratz 1962) long ago observed, there are in fact a great many ways in which citizens in a democracy may be prevented from transforming their private discontents into political demands. Cultural and political norms and values may restrict the range of issues deemed "acceptable" to treat as political grievances (Taylor 1996). Political rules may prevent some individuals from participating as equals in the political process (Clemens 1997; McAdam 1982). Political resources may be unequally distributed among the populace (Haines 1984; McCarthy and Zald 1977; McCarthy and Zald 1973). Movement leaders seeking a positive political reception for their demands may pursue some of their

---

14. While pluralist theory has been widely discredited since its heyday in the 1950s, the underlying assumptions about the accessibility of the democratic system to organized, concerned citizens arguably lives on in the conventional wisdom about democratic politics.

constituents' grievances but omit others (Ferree 2003). The point is that there are any number of barriers to political demand making, and to equate lack of voice in the political arena with lack of political discontent potentially mischaracterizes the nature and degree of politicization among affected citizens.

It is possible, of course, that the pluralists are partly correct: the absence of political demand for new social policies could be due not to political, organizational, or material constraints on demand making but to insufficient interest. It may be the case, in other words, that Americans simply do not view new social welfare needs as important enough or serious enough to treat as political issues. As Crenson (1971:27) observed in his foundational study of the "unpolitics" of air pollution:

> Though the issue may seem terribly important to an outsider, we cannot assert that there is something "unnatural" in the citizens' neglect of it, nor can we argue that they must have been deceived concerning their true interests or that some entrenched powerholders have frustrated the desires of the people by enforcing silence.... *The public may be genuinely uninterested ...*

Lack of interest could also be attributed to ideological beliefs about responsibility for social welfare: citizens may view unmet social welfare needs as personal or family problems rather than public problems appropriate for state intervention, or they may be wary of an expanded state role in social welfare provision. Alternatively, to paraphrase William Gamson (1995:89), some citizens may be completely convinced of the desirability of expanded state entitlements for unmet social welfare needs, but gravely doubt the possibility of obtaining them in the current economic and political environment.

All of these are plausible explanations for the lack of significant demand for social policies to ameliorate strains on contemporary families. But rather than conceptualizing these explanations as competing hypotheses, this book seeks to situate them within a single framework for understanding processes of politicization and social change in contexts involving deeply institutionalized social practices, values, and beliefs. The objective is to observe processes of politicization in families as they struggle with one of the most rapidly growing sources of unmet social welfare needs in the United States: long-term care. By analyzing how individuals seek solutions to the everyday dilemmas of contemporary long-term care provision, this book seeks to identify the factors that impede—and facilitate—the development of oppositional understandings of the ideology of family responsibility.

THE CASE OF LONG-TERM CARE

Nearly one in three households in the United States today is in the position of taking care of an adult with a chronic disease or disability (National Alliance for Caregiving and AARP 2009). Over the course of the last century, aging populations and dramatic changes in health care provision, household structure, and women's labor force participation have created what many observers have dubbed a "crisis in care": the demand for care of the old and infirm is growing at precisely the same time as the supply of private care within the family is substantially contracting (Garey et al. 2002; Glenn 2000; Harrington 2000).

Demand for long-term care is driven in large part by dramatic changes in life expectancy: today, one in every eight Americans is aged sixty-five or older, and that proportion is predicted to increase to nearly one in five by 2030 (Gonyea 2005). The Census Bureau predicts that by 2050, more than 40% of adults aged sixty-five or older can expect to live to at least age ninety. The prevalence of chronic health conditions and disabilities increases markedly for this age group. Nearly half of the "oldest old," for example, suffer from Alzheimer's disease or a related form of dementia—an exceptionally expensive and emotionally and physically exhausting condition for families.

If changing demographics have increased the care responsibilities of families in recent decades, the deinstitutionalization of a wide array of acute care services has made that care substantially more difficult for families (Abel 1991). Patients today are generally discharged from hospitals "quicker and sicker": they are released from formal care much earlier than ever before (Daly 2001b), and as a consequence they tend to be sicker when they arrive home. Family members are frequently called upon to manage medical technologies, drugs, and decisions about pain or bleeding that were once considered the exclusive domain of trained medical specialists (Glazer 1988; Koren 1986).[15]

As care for the sick and disabled has shifted increasingly to private households, the ratio of adult caregivers to dependents in the home has declined. Women's large-scale entry into the paid labor force, increasing numbers of single-parent families, a decline in the average household size, and the increasing tendency among young people and the elderly to live on their own, have all resulted in fewer available adults in the home to care for the elderly and the ill (Garey et al. 2002; Harrington 2000; Pierson 2001b).

15. See Chapter 2.

The United States is not alone in witnessing these dramatic social transformations: virtually all advanced welfare states have confronted similar demographic and social changes. As families increasingly need help with social tasks that have historically been carried out "for free" within the household, these states are now being called upon to increase their social expenditures for care. In Europe, Canada, Australia, and Japan, governments have responded to that call. Government support for care is in fact one of the few areas of social provision in recent decades that has witnessed growth among countries in the Organization for Economic Cooperation and Development (OECD) in the form of new or expanded social welfare initiatives (Daly 1997). Whether caring services are provided through public means—as is the case in the countries of Scandinavia where households have ready access to public child care and elder care[16]—or through private but marketized means—as in the case of most OECD countries which provide a wide variety of transfer payments to subsidize the costs of market-based care (Daly 2001a; Ungerson and Yeandle 2007)—the contemporary problems of care provision are increasingly recognized by welfare states as requiring adaptations in existing social policy arrangements (Daly 2005; Pierson 2001b).

In the United States, which has long been known for its anemic social welfare system, families have largely been left on their own to forge solutions to contemporary care dilemmas (Gornick and Meyers 2003). As the pool for unpaid family caregivers has contracted, many families have sought to purchase caregiving services—such as in-home supportive services, adult day care, or nursing home care—to supplement or replace the family provision of care. The costs of such services are significant and have escalated sharply. In 2009, the average cost of a private room in a U.S. nursing home was just under $80,000, up 43% from 2000. The hourly cost of home health care in 2009 was on average $21 per hour, up 31% from 2000. The cost of companion or personal care was marginally less, at $19 per hour.[17] Conventional health insurance policies generally do not cover long-term care support services at all, and long-term care insurance has proven to be an expensive, unreliable, and hence substantially underutilized market (Harrington Meyer and Herd 2007).[18] Medicare provides acute care coverage for most

16. Since 1989, every elderly resident in Denmark is entitled—as a right of citizenship—to public elder care services, including free home help (Meyer 1994).

17. Statistics are from the Metlife Institute's *2009 MetLife Market Survey of Nursing Home, Assisted Living, Adult Day Services, and Home Care Costs.*

18. By some estimates, approximately 40% of older Americans could reasonably afford a long-term care insurance policy, but only 7% have actually purchased one (Holtz-Eakin 2005; Moon and Herd 2002).

of the nation's elderly, but very little assistance for patients with chronic illnesses,[19] and Medicaid, a means-tested health care program, provides long-term care assistance only for the very poor.

Unlike most of the industrialized world, the United States also lacks social policies that would permit workers to take paid time off to care for sick family members. The Family Medical Leave Act (FMLA) allows qualified employees to take twelve weeks of unpaid leave to care for family members with "serious health conditions." This affords some degree of job security for covered employees, but the law has several significant limitations. Most notably, more than 40% of American workers are not covered by the FMLA, either because they work for smaller employers, who are exempt from FMLA mandates, or because they do not have enough tenure to qualify for FMLA protections. The fact that the FMLA leave is unpaid also discourages many workers from taking time off or forces them to cut their leaves short. Finally, many companies will not allow workers to take FMLA leave for the kinds of routine medical needs that accompany long-term illnesses (see generally Pitt-Catsouphes et al. 2006) and a significant percentage of covered employers are simply not compliant with FMLA regulations (Kelly 2010).

By most measures, then, both private and public support systems for long-term care are proving increasingly inadequate for meeting the needs of contemporary American families. One response to this new reality is to ask: *If Americans aren't complaining about these conditions, why should policymakers care?* First, we don't know why Americans aren't complaining—to repeat my point from above: lack of voice in the political arena should not be confused with lack of political discontent. Second, and perhaps more critically, the inadequacies of existing systems of care provision have enormous social costs, affecting not only the health and economic security of affected families, but also economic productivity and the viability of existing welfare state programs.

Among the most well documented social risks associated with long-term care provision are those affecting the health of family caregivers. Studies have consistently found higher levels of depression and anxiety disorders among caregivers compared to their non-caregiving peers (Marks et al. 2002; Pinquart and Sorensen 2003; Poulshock and Deimling 1984).

---

19. Medicare covers one-hundred days of care in a nursing facility for those recently discharged from a hospital and who need skilled nursing care or rehabilitative therapy, and provides some home health benefits for those beneficiaries with chronic or disabling conditions who require skilled nursing care following hospitalization. Unlike Medicaid, however, Medicare provides no assistance for those who need help with personal care, such as bathing, dressing, feeding, adult day care, or respite care.

Between 40% and 70% of caregivers have clinically significant symptoms of depression, and one-quarter to one-half of these meet the diagnostic criteria for major depression (Zarit 2006). Caregivers are also at greater risk of cardiovascular disease (King et al. 1994), and have diminished immune systems which put them at greater risk of infection and chronic diseases such as cancer relative to their non-caregiving peers (Kiecolt-Glaser et al. 1991; Schulz and Beach 1999; Shaw et al. 1997). Finally, researchers have linked caregiving stress to greater alcohol and psychotropic drug use (Alzheimer's Association & National Alliance for Caregiving 1999; George and Gwyther 1986), and a lower likelihood of engaging in preventive health behaviors (Schulz et al. 1997).

Because more than two-thirds of all family caregivers are women, not only do the emotional and physical costs of care provision fall disproportionately on female caregivers, but so too do the economic costs (Harrington Meyer and Herd 2007). Women in general are more likely than men to reduce work hours, take a leave, or give up work entirely to accommodate caregiving responsibilities (National Alliance for Caregiving and AARP 2009). Time out of the workforce to care for family members not only has short-term financial consequences in terms of lost wages and missed opportunities for job promotion and training (England and Folbre 1999; Health & Human Services 1998), but it poses a long-term threat to retirement security, as women end up making fewer contributions to Social Security, pensions, and other retirement savings vehicles. Men also report difficulties in balancing the demands of work with caregiving responsibilities.[20] Nearly 82% of male caregivers work at least part time, and like their female counterparts, these caregivers report needing to take time off from work, reduce work hours, turn down a promotion or take a less demanding job due to the demands of family care responsibilities (National Alliance for Caregiving and AARP 2009).

The economic consequences of these work conflicts are significant not only for American families but also for U.S. businesses. Replacement costs for employees who leave the workforce, as well as the costs associated with absenteeism, increased health care costs, workday interruptions, unpaid leave, and reductions in hours from full to part time, all take a toll on the bottom line of American businesses. One study has calculated the cost to employers for all full-time employed caregivers to be just under $34 billion a year (MetLife Mature Market Institute and National Alliance for Caregiving 2006).

---

20. For a history of men's caring, see Coltrane and Galt (2000).

Finally, there is growing evidence that inadequate support for contemporary care provision is straining existing U.S. welfare state programs by diverting them from their initial purposes. The United States Medicaid program, for example, was originally established in 1965 to ensure that low-income families had access to acute medical care and that poor elderly Americans had access to care for chronic illnesses. But over the past several decades, Medicaid has become one of this country's most important public sources of long-term care assistance for middle-class families. Specific Medicaid benefits vary from state to state, but all states must provide nursing home care to residents who meet strict means-testing requirements. Given the average annual cost of nursing home care, the financial consequences of an extended stay can be devastating for families, and as a result, the means-tested program has been used more and more in recent decades by middle-class elderly who "spend down" their resources until they are effectively impoverished, at which point they qualify for Medicaid. Today, critics have expressed concern that the growing ranks of (formerly) middle-income elderly who seek Medicaid assistance are siphoning finite resources away from other Medicaid beneficiaries, mainly poor children and their families, and that states will eventually be unable to meet their Medicaid obligations due to the rising costs of long-term care. France, Germany, and other governments have responded to similar "misuses" of state programs by addressing the underlying long-term care needs of their citizens (Morel 2006), but the U.S. government has so far remained unmoved by the growing strains on Medicaid caused by the contemporary problems of long-term care provision.

Rising levels of unmet long-term care needs thus pose real, well-documented threats not only to the health and economic security of American families, but also to the efficiency of American businesses and the integrity of the existing welfare state. The issue of long-term care is arguably an extreme case of the growing gap between unmet needs and social policy. But if existing social arrangements for care provision are proving so inadequate, why does the ideology of family responsibility maintain such a firm grasp on Americans' consciousness? Why so little demand for new social policies? This book seeks to understand how deeply institutionalized social arrangements persist in the face of unmet need and under what conditions they might be challenged.

STUDY DESIGN AND METHODOLOGY

The emphasis on processes of politicization in this book represents a significant departure from most studies of the politics of social provision.

Theorists of the welfare state have thus far focused on macro-level dynamics: the ways in which the political economy, institutional structures, party alignments, interest groups, and cultural categories shape policymaking (e.g., Esping-Anderson 1990; Huber et al. 1993; Pierson 2001a; Steensland 2006; Steinmo and Watts 1995), or conversely, the ways in which policy structures shape subsequent debates about policy alternatives (e.g., Hacker 2002; Pierson 1993; Pierson 1994; Skocpol 1992; Soss and Schram 2007). Micro-level, or "bottom-up" analyses in the welfare state literature have been limited to attitudinal research about specific social problems, public policies, and program beneficiaries (Brooks and Manza 2007; Cook and Barrett 1992; Jacobs 1993; Manza and Cook 2002)[21] or to research about political participation (Campbell 2003; Verba et al. 1995). This study of politicization, by contrast, moves away from analyzing attitudes and beliefs as fixed attributes, and instead examines the development of attitudes and beliefs, emphasizing the contexts in which individuals form and use such understandings to guide their actions (Ewick and Silbey 1998; Mansbridge and Morris 2001; Morris 1992). Thus, where opinion research emphasizes what people think about a given social problem, research on politicization focuses on those conditions and experiences that give rise to the belief that there is a social problem at all.

The research design in this study also departs from traditional social movement analyses. While social movement researchers have long been interested in questions about the construction of social protest, the focus of their analyses has largely been on social movement elites—the messages that movement organizations and leaders deploy to mobilize constituents and acquire new resources, as well as how they negotiate the competing messages of other movement organizations, opponents, and the mass media (Gamson and Modigliani 1989; Klandermans 1988; Snow et al. 1986). Few social movement researchers have studied the processes involved in the construction of political consciousness among individuals who are not involved or affiliated with a reform movement or its organizations (but see Hull 2001).

William Gamson, more than any other, has made this question central to his work. In *Talking Politics* (1992b), Gamson analyzed the construction of political consciousness in conversations with small groups of working-class Americans. Using the conversation in each "peer group"[22] as the unit of analysis, Gamson analyzed how participants constructed opinions about

---

21. But see Soss (2002).

22. Traditional focus groups are typically composed of seven to ten participants who are unfamiliar with each other and who will likely never see each other again. The interaction often resembles a group interview more than a discussion, with the researcher playing an active role. In his study of the construction of political consciousness, Gamson relied on an alternative "peer group" design that involved small groups of familiar acquaintances rather than strangers, and played down the facilitator's role in keeping the conversation going (see also Perrin 2006).

four controversial issues posed by the researcher and what their discourse revealed about the political consciousness of the participants. Gamson's design provides a useful model for researching groups who have not successfully organized as a political constituency, but the artificiality of the group conversation—four unrelated issues selected by the researcher—tells us little about how political consciousness is shaped within the context of citizens' everyday experiences. Studying the development of political consciousness in everyday life is made more difficult by the fact that it is a subjective process, requiring techniques for observing how individuals evaluate their experiences or conditions while minimizing reactivity to researcher suggestion (see Felstiner et al. 1980–1981).

To address these methodological concerns, this study employed a three-stage observational design: nonparticipant observation of support group meetings for family caregivers, peer group discussions involving the same support groups, and one-on-one interviews with group participants. To assess the influence of other actors in politicizing the respondents in this study, I also interviewed the social workers who facilitated the support groups under observation, as well as staff and leaders from advocacy organizations seeking long-term care policy reform.

Family Caregivers

Over a four-month period in the fall of 2004, I observed sixty-eight meetings (1–2 hours in length) of fourteen different support groups for family caregivers in Los Angeles. While support groups did not strictly define "family caregivers" for purposes of participation, their memberships were consistent with caregiver criteria used by the National Family Caregiver Support Program, which defines a caregiver as "an adult family member, or another individual, who is an informal provider of in-home and community care to an older individual" (Title III-E 2000). The City of Los Angeles offered the benefits of a large and strikingly diverse population, as well as a developed social service sector supporting a network of support groups for caregivers dealing with a wide range of diseases and disabilities. I compiled a list of support groups from state, county, and city social service websites, the Alzheimer's Association, and the Los Angeles Caregiver Resource Center. Because race, ethnic, and class stratification in Los Angeles occur largely along geographic lines, I selected support groups located in most of the key "neighborhoods" of the greater metropolitan area.[23] This ensured

---

23. These included: Santa Monica, West Los Angeles, Fairfax/West Hollywood, North Hollywood, downtown Los Angeles, East Los Angeles, Sherman Oaks, Pasadena, and some surrounding suburbs.

a relatively diverse sample with respect to a variety of socioeconomic indicators.[24]

To control for variability in caregiving experiences across diseases or disabilities, support groups were limited to two specific classes of diseases: dementia and cancer. The burden of caregiving is well known to be greatest among those caring for patients with dementia (Ory et al. 1999), and it is these ten caregiving support groups that were the primary focus of the study. The burden of caring for family members with dementia is exacerbated by the fact that the costs of supportive services for patients with dementia are rarely covered by Medicare or private health insurance policies. Because the costs of caring for patients with cancer are more frequently covered by health insurance plans, the smaller group of cancer caregivers provided a useful comparative group for examining the extent to which coverage for supportive services influenced the process of politicization. In total, 158 caregivers participated in the first phase of the study.

In the second phase of the study, I led nine support groups in a peer group discussion about specific legislative initiatives involving long-term care. Eighty support group members participated in this phase of the study.[25] The purpose of the peer group meetings was to observe how participants related their personal caregiving experiences to larger sociopolitical issues of long-term care provision, and how they envisioned "solutions" to the dilemmas raised in providing long-term care. During the peer group sessions I introduced four general policy proposals pertaining to funding for respite care, caregiver allowances, tax credits for caregiving expenses, and paid family leave, and asked participants to discuss how the proposals would affect their personal situations and to consider the benefits and drawbacks of each proposal. At the end of the discussion, participants were asked to raise any areas of care provision that had not been addressed by the proposed policies.

Finally, I conducted one-on-one in-depth interviews with sixty-six support group participants to elicit more intensive discussions about their caregiving experiences. The semi-structured interviews, which ranged in length from thirty minutes to two hours, were designed to elicit more intensive discussions about their caregiving experiences, including their (non)utilization of supportive services and benefits, their political backgrounds, and their views of state, market, and family responsibility for long-term care.[26] For the fifty respondents who had participated in the first and second

---

24. Descriptive statistics for the sample can be found in Appendix A.

25. All support group members were invited to participate in the focus groups. Focus group participants received $50 for their time.

26. To identify any possible sequencing effects in this design, I reversed the order of the interviews and peer group session for one support group. No significant effects were observed.

phases of the study, the interviews also provided an opportunity to explore the assumptions and reasoning behind comments made at other points during the observation period.

This multi-method approach was designed to compensate for the limitations of each individual method with respect to the issues of researcher reactivity and control. Nonparticipant observation provided a window into processes of grievance and meaning construction with minimal researcher reactivity. I played a passive role in observing the conversation of meetings, neither asking questions nor controlling the subject matter of the discussion. But to the extent that nonparticipant observation minimized the effects of reactivity, it also minimized my control over the substance of participant conversations. One-on-one interviews provided a way to elicit more specific and focused information from respondents. Yet even the most carefully crafted questions run the risk of influencing respondent perceptions and responses. Peer groups are something of a middle-ground, permitting observation of the interaction of participants and the interplay and modification of ideas (Albrecht et al. 1993), while also serving as a useful tool for observing the natural vocabulary with which participants construct meaning about specific issues posed to them.

One could reasonably argue that in recruiting participants from support groups, the project runs the risk of sampling on the dependent variable, as family caregivers who join support groups—a semi-public forum—are likely to be relatively more politicized than caregivers who have not joined support groups. To assess the effects of selecting participants based on support group participation, I also interviewed a smaller sample of thirteen unpaid family caregivers who had not joined support groups. These caregivers were recruited by support group facilitators, who were often social workers with a client base outside of the support group, as well as the Los Angeles Caregiver Resource Center, to ensure that participants had approximately the same level of contact with supportive services as support group participants.

A number of other limitations regarding the representativeness of the sample should be noted. Not only did I recruit caregivers who had already made contact with social services (an important step, as this study demonstrates, toward politicization), but they were living in Los Angeles, a notoriously liberal metropolitan area in a famously Democratic state, and they were primarily caring for patients with dementia, one of the most challenging and expensive health conditions for family caregivers. In this regard, I would expect the degree of politicization among participants in this sample to be higher than it is among caregivers who have not made contact with social services, who are living in rural and/or socially conservative parts of the country, and who are caring for patients with shorter-term or less costly forms of chronic disease.

However, it's important to emphasize that the sample for this study was not intended to be representative of all "family caregivers." Nor was the purpose of the study to determine how many caregivers hold oppositional understandings of care provision. Rather, the study was designed to identify those conditions and experiences that give rise to politicized interpretations of long-term care, and to identify what types of obstacles prevent those interpretations from developing into political demand for new social policies.

Finally, researchers have long documented the ways in which the caregiving experience differs for people of different racial and ethnic groups, genders, and socioeconomic status. These differences range from who becomes a caregiver, to the amount and type of care provided, to the willingness and ability to pay for supportive services. In this study, these distinctions among groups played a surprisingly minor role with regard to processes of politicization. That is, while the analyses in the chapters that follow highlight some differences between social groups, by and large the process of politicization was strikingly similar across social groups.

Organizational Actors

The study also sought to understand the perspective of those organizational actors involved in long-term care policy reform who might influence the politicization of family caregivers. At the end of the observation period, I compiled a list of all the organizations which advocate for long-term care policy reform that had been mentioned by participants and social workers, and sought interviews with twenty-nine staff members and leaders from twenty of these organizations. Because there is no comprehensive long-term care public policy at either the federal level or in the state of California, the administration and delivery of services and benefits for patients with chronic diseases or disabilities takes place within a patchwork "system" of administrative agencies, nonprofit organizations, and for-profit care facilities. To solicit impressions of reform opportunities from advocates who interact with these different dimensions of long-term care provision, I defined "advocacy organization" broadly to include any organization seeking to influence public policy and resource allocation decisions within political, economic, and social institutions (cf. McConnell 2004). This definition includes not only organizations that seek to influence local, state or federal elected officials through legislative advocacy, but also organizations that specialize in administrative advocacy, or efforts directed at government agencies such as the Center for Medicare and Medicaid Services or the California Department of Social Services; program advocacy, or efforts directed at changing organizational practices within service organizations such as nursing homes, or at improving the quality of and access to supportive services; and legal advocacy, or efforts to enforce and expand the rights of caregivers through the courts. Appendix B lists each participating organization and the primary form of advocacy in which they specialized. Interviews with advocates (30–60 minutes in length) sought information on the primary goals and strategies of their organizations; their perceptions of family caregivers as a political constituency, including characteristics of caregivers that make them more or less likely to mobilize; and their perceptions of political opportunities for long-term care policy reform.

Finally, I conducted in-depth interviews (30–45 minutes in length) with twelve of the licensed social workers that facilitated the support groups for family caregivers in this study. Most of these social workers were associated with adult day care centers, hospitals, or other social service agencies in Los Angeles. Interviews sought information on the availability of social services for caregivers in LA, the challenges service providers confront in trying to provide support to family care providers, the effects of support group participation and utilization of supportive services on caregivers, and social workers' own perceptions of their role as support group facilitators.

Fieldnotes from observations and taped focus group conversations and interviews were coded and analyzed using ATLAS.ti, a qualitative analysis software program, to identify the factors that influenced processes of politicization in this study.

OUTLINE OF BOOK

The aim of this book is not to provide a definitive answer to the question of why there is so little political demand for social policies that would address unmet social welfare needs. There are any number of factors beyond the scope of this book that surely play a part in answering that question. What this book does seek to do is to use the gap between unmet social welfare needs and existing social welfare arrangements to explore the durability of the ideology of family responsibility for care. By tracing the politicization of family caregivers as they seek to resolve the caregiving dilemmas they face in everyday life, this book will illuminate both the conditions that impede the development of political demand making—and thereby reinforce the ideology of family responsibility—and the conditions that encourage caregivers to reimagine taken-for-granted assumptions about family responsibility for long-term care.

Chapter 2 provides the political context for understanding the contemporary long-term care crisis, outlining the demographic and sociopolitical changes that have contributed to the crisis in care, including the important role of the state. Chapter 2 also describes how these demographic and sociopolitical changes have transformed the experience of providing care for family members with chronic diseases like Parkinson's or Alzheimer's.

Chapter 3 explores the first essential dimension of politicization: the process of reinterpreting longstanding "private" needs as matters of legitimate public deliberation and decision making. How do individuals who are deeply committed to the ideology of family responsibility for care come to view a personal issue like caring for ailing parents or partners as a subject appropriate for policy intervention? Here the focus is on the role of existing social services in shaping caregivers' political consciousness.

Chapter 4 moves from the question of whether long-term care should be considered a policy issue at all, to the second dimension of politicization: how individuals imagine solutions for the care problems they confront. The process of imagining alternative social arrangements for new or newly perceived social welfare problems involves the evaluation of a range of culturally available models. This chapter considers where caregivers find these models and why some models resonate more with caregivers than others.

Chapters 5 and 6 both consider the third dimension of politicization: the willingness to personally communicate political grievances to an official agency or other perceived responsible party for action. Focusing specifically on those caregivers who articulated political grievances relating to long-term care, these chapters seek to understand their reluctance—or their inability—to engage in political demand making. Chapter 5 considers the role of entitlement or deservingness in politicization: for constituents to participate in political demand making they must first believe they are entitled to something better. Medicaid's key role in politicization raises the question of whether experiences navigating the means-tested public assistance program, with its stigmatizing association with the "undeserving poor," may actually impede political demand making. Chapter 6 examines why caregivers who have been politicized by their experiences, and who are willing and able to participate in political demand making, nevertheless perceive themselves as lacking the opportunity to do so. The chapter examines two long-term trends in the field of political organizations—the decoupling of social welfare organizations from organized politics and the shift in political mobilization technologies toward "targeted activation"—and their role in attenuating the nexus between grievance construction and political mobilization in matters of social welfare.

Finally, Chapter 7 brings together the different dimensions of politicization to elaborate how the ideology of family responsibility persists even in the face of unmet need. Three important sets of obstacles were evident in this study. The first set involves existing social policies as resources in politicization. Existing social policies and services in this case proved to be a powerful source of cultural models for state intervention, and caregivers were adept at transposing or extending them to the contemporary challenges of care provision. But in the context of a notoriously weak American welfare state, such policies and benefits are few and far between for most American families. Second, discursive integration—the process of integrating new conceptions, new models, and new political logics with "old" values, beliefs, and practices—produces understandings of social welfare provision that in most cases reinforce traditional norms about family responsibility. And finally, to effectively communicate grievances as collective demand making, individuals need advocacy organizations to provide information about how and when and where to get involved.

Obstacles to political demand making could be found in every aspect of politicization in this case. But it's important to emphasize that this study also identified considerable evidence of politicization among family caregivers. In the chapters that follow, the stories of politicized caregivers are highlighted alongside the obstacles. The hope of this book is that readers will gain an understanding of why unmet social welfare needs have not produced political demand for new social policy, but also an appreciation of the fact that politicization among this constituency does exist, that it is ongoing, and that any change in the constellation of resources, discourse, and advocates available to these families could catalyze fundamental changes in how this country approaches the issue of social welfare provision.

CHAPTER 2

The Roots and Experience of Contemporary Caregiving

Before we can answer the question of why, despite well-documented unmet needs, Americans don't demand greater state intervention in long-term care, we need to get a sense of what long-term care provision entails today. Why are contemporary families increasingly unable to provide long-term care on their own? What is it like to care for an adult family member with a chronic disease like Alzheimer's? This chapter begins by outlining the demographic and sociopolitical changes that have contributed to the contemporary long-term care crisis—a unique set of challenges confronted by families today that were not present for previous generations of Americans. I then describe in more detail the range of caregiving tasks that families confront in caring for a person with a chronic disease or disability, including the particular problems faced by families dealing with Alzheimer's and other dementia-related illnesses.

THE SOCIOPOLITICAL CONTEXT OF THE CONTEMPORARY LONG-TERM CARE CRISIS
Long-Term Trends Affecting the Caregiving Experience

The individual caregiving experience in the United States, while highly variable, has been shaped by a series of demographic and sociopolitical trends which, taken together, have transformed long-term care provision in this country. As noted in Chapter 1, the conventional view of these changes is that they have served as exogenous shocks to existing systems of public and private care provision: the aging of the population, delayed childbearing, transformations in family size and form, and increased women's labor force participation have all strained families and existing welfare states to the breaking point (Armingeon and Bonoli 2006; Bonoli et al. 2000; Huber and Stephens 2001; Pierson 2001a). Such a characterization suggests, however, that policymakers and families have been caught off guard by these changes, as if these changes appeared out of nowhere to unexpectedly wreak havoc with systems of social welfare provision. On the contrary, to the extent that there is a gap between the long-term care needs of Americans and the capacity of American families today to meet those needs, that gap is in most cases mediated by politics (Hacker 2004). Many of the struggles that are unique to contemporary care provision are not so much the consequence of an aging population or smaller family sizes, but are caused by the failure of existing social practices to change alongside these long-term trends. This inelasticity of social practices relating to long-term care can be attributed to both the failure of policymakers to update social policies in ways that reflect and ameliorate social welfare risks, and the reluctance of families to consider ways of alleviating the burden of chronic care provision that extend beyond the exclusive domain of family.

Observers often identify the aging of the population as one of the primary engines of the contemporary care crisis: people are living longer and therefore require greater levels of care than ever before. At the turn of the 20th century, most people did not survive until old age, and until the advent of antibiotics, they died from acute rather than chronic conditions. Over the last century, the population aged sixty-five or older increased eleven fold (Administration on Aging 2012). In 2011, more than 13% of the population (41.4 million people), was sixty-five or older.[1] The U.S. Census Bureau estimates that by 2040, approximately 21% of the population will be aged sixty-five or older, and the population aged eighty-five and older will triple from 5.7 million in 2011 to 14.1 million (Administration on Aging 2012). Americans are not only living longer today, but they are living longer with chronic health conditions: the U.S. Department of Health and Human Services estimates that nearly 70% of Americans who reach the age of sixty-five will need some form of long-term care in their lives.[2]

But the "graying" of the population has not only increased the need for care provision; it has also affected the experience of contemporary caregivers in at least two ways. First, just as care receivers are living longer, so, too, are caregivers. The strength and stamina required to care for somebody

1. Census 2000 Brief, C2KBR/01-12, U.S. Census Bureau (2011).
2. U.S. Department of Health & Human Services. National Clearinghouse for Long-Term Care Information. http://longtermcare.gov/the-basics/how-much-care-will-you-need/, accessed July 27, 2013.

with Alzheimer's often exceeds the abilities of even younger adults; for people who are older, frailer, and often in poor health themselves, caring for a partner with a chronic disease is almost impossible without the assistance of others. Many of the participants in this study who sought out paid supportive services, did so because of their own frailties (e.g., bad backs, heart disease, high blood pressure, cancer, and for some, extremely high levels of anxiety and depression).

The second consequence for care provision of longer life expectancy, coupled here with the trend toward delayed childbearing, is that more middle-aged people find themselves simultaneously supporting their dependent children and their dependent parents—a demographic sometimes referred to as the "sandwich generation."[3] Nearly 46% of female caregivers and 40% of male caregivers are also parents of children under the age of eighteen (Aumann et al. 2010). Notably, sandwiched employees spend as much time on their work responsibilities as people without caregiving responsibilities (about forty-two hours a week) (Aumann et al. 2010). As a consequence, working caregivers report feeling starved for time in other areas of their lives: 71% report not having enough time for their children, 63% report not having enough time for their partner, and 63% report not having enough time for themselves (Aumann et al. 2010). Given all these competing pressures, sandwiched caregivers face greater challenges to their health and well-being than non-sandwiched caregivers, and are more likely to report feeling stressed or to report that they have more responsibilities than they can handle (Rubin and White-Means 2009).

In addition to longer life expectancy, social trends in family form in the United States, including smaller family sizes, the geographic dispersion of family members, and increased rates of divorce have also changed the nature of caregiving relative to past generations. Today, more caregivers are confronting long-term care provision on their own, without the help of adult children (in the case of spousal caregivers) or siblings (in the case of caregivers who are adult children) living nearby.

First, the size of American families—the primary pool for unpaid long-term care—has been steadily decreasing over time. According to the U.S. Census Bureau, the average number of people living in U.S. households

---

3. The financial implications for middle-aged people supporting both children and parents have become more striking since the recession. For several decades, sociologists have observed a trend of more parents supporting children well into their twenties, but those numbers spiked sharply in the face of a badly faltering economy. With more students seeking advanced degrees and with decent employment hard to find among young adults, parents have been called upon to continue to support their children well into adulthood. According to the Pew Research Center, nearly 27% of all middle-aged parents were the primary source of financial support for a grown child in 2012, up sharply from a similar survey administered in 2005 (Parker and Patten 2013).

has been dropping as the population has been increasing. When the 300-million milestone was reached in October 2006, the average household size in the United States reached a new low of 2.6 people per home—parents, offspring, and extended squatters included.

Second, geographic dispersion of families in the United States has also contributed to the contemporary care crisis. Older adults today are more likely to live alone than ever before, and the proportion living alone tends to increase with age: today, almost half (46%) of women aged seventy-five and older live alone (Administration on Aging 2012). Nearly three-quarters (72%) of all primary caregivers either live with or within twenty minutes of their care receivers, but nearly 15% live one or more hours away (National Alliance for Caregiving and AARP 2009). Long-distance caregivers are more likely to rely on the assistance of paid supportive services. In some families in this study, siblings rotated care provision between them: one woman with Alzheimer's lived with each of her four children for three months at a time; other adult children took primary responsibility while siblings contributed financially or in other ways.

Third, the high rates of divorce and remarriage today have also complicated the question of how to divide family responsibilities for caregiving. In this study, for example, some caregivers described stepchildren who lived in other parts of the country and who remained largely uninvolved in care provision. Carolyn noted, for example, that her husband's children from a former marriage were not helping at all with the care of their father. She says of her stepdaughter:

> I think she doesn't want to have a relationship because she realizes it'll entail a lot more than she's willing to give. And I'm not asking them to come and take care of him. I'm not trying to send him to them and say okay, he's your dad, you deal. I have never asked that.... But they never make an effort.

Strained relationships between stepparents and adult children or between siblings can make decisions about responsibility for care provision so difficult that in some cases physicians and social workers have to intervene. Bridget, for example, was caring for her husband, who had four adult children from a previous marriage. All of the children were estranged from their father. As her husband's health declined, Bridget's stress level—and blood pressure—escalated sharply. She started having panic attacks. "I had one the other night," she told me in her interview, "because he messed up the bathroom. I just went berserk. Totally berserk. And I had to apologize to him profusely. I said I won't let that happen again, and I'm going to seek some help for this." Bridget saw a doctor who determined that her blood pressure was dangerously high. "[The doctor] wrote a letter stating that his children are to come and get him immediately. I can't do that. I just can't do that." But Bridget did solicit the help of a social worker to help mediate the strained family relations.

Children of divorce, meanwhile, often have their own complicated reasons for being unwilling to fully engage in caregiving. Gwen, for example, was caring for her father long distance—he lived three hours outside of Los Angeles. Her father had left her family when she was just four years old. While he never disappeared from her life entirely, Gwen and her father never maintained anything more than a superficial relationship. When his health began to decline, she was up front about the fact that she didn't want to be his caregiver:

> You know, when the police are calling me, and they're saying you need to do something with him ... I was just like, what would you like me to do about it? ... He's not conservable at this point. He's not a threat. He's so physically strong and healthy that he's not appropriate to move into a skilled nursing facility, which is the only way Medi-Cal is going to cover it. He doesn't have the resources to move into a ... board and care or an assisted living arrangement. And I kind of had to start thinking about where I was going to draw the line. Am I going to pay for all that extra care? And I decided that I was not. Which there's guilt toward, but he pretty much abandoned my family when I was young and pretty much said I don't feel responsibility to take care of you all. So ...

Finally, rising rates of female participation in the paid labor market have also contributed to the contemporary caregiver crisis, as female employment has dramatically reduced the pool of unpaid caregivers in the home. According to the U.S. Census Bureau, women's labor force participation peaked in 1999 at 60%, and has declined modestly since then to approximately 58%.[4] But the work-family conflicts that labor force participation in the United States creates extend to caregivers of both sexes. Nearly six in ten caregivers today are currently employed (57%), with 46% working full time and 11% working part time (National Alliance for Caregiving and AARP 2009). Irma, who worked full time as a school administrator while she was caring for her mother, captures the challenges of managing a full time-job while caring for an ailing parent:

> At one of my schools, I had to report to work from 1 and leave at 10 at night. So I would have to make [my mother's] doctor's appointments in the morning. ... So I would have to go over to her, get her, make sure she's dressed and the food—you're fasting this time,

---

4. U.S. Census. 2012 Statistical Abstract.
http://www.census.gov/compendia/statab/cats/labor_force_employment_earnings/labor_force_status.html (accessed July 27, 2013).

you're not fasting this time, you've got your pills, bring orange juice in the car—take her over to [the hospital], pay twelve bucks to park, wait for the right specialist, get her back to the car, bring her back over there, and then go way across town to the school. And I was doing this for years!

Vincent and his wife each had parents living close by who needed care. Vincent's day began at 5:00 a.m., he worked all day from 7:00 a.m. to 4:00 p.m., and on the way home he typically made a stop to get diapers or prescriptions or miscellaneous groceries for his parents.

That's even before I get in the door, right? Okay, once I'm in the door, then I take a look to see how [my father] is doing. Because sometimes I'm looking at him, and he just looks wasted. Or I can see that the day's routine...has really taken its toll. And if he's fine and dandy we just start taking care of mom. We clean her, change her diaper, put a new diaper back on, and if the bedding is dirty...we have to strip the bed down totally. We bathe her twice a week...

Vincent's wife, Daniella, meanwhile was doing the same thing for her parents and working part time. They saw each other, in the best of circumstances, at the very end of the day. "There's times that it feels like we're miles apart," Vincent observed.

Now I sit home waiting for her [at the end of the day], and she calls me, "Go ahead and take care of yourself, because I don't know when they're going to release me." Because her father will get into a mood...it's like they forget that we're married. But you know, it's hard! And I can see where a lot of people who have done this eventually get divorced. I've heard that divorce is really high amongst caregivers....

A national survey found that nearly seven in ten caregivers make work accommodations due to caregiving responsibilities (National Alliance for Caregiving and AARP 2009). Such accommodations include going to work late, leaving early, or taking time off during the day to deal with caregiving issues. Those caregivers who own their own businesses or work independently often reduce their hours or shut down their businesses entirely. In 2012, nearly one in five (19%) retirees left the workforce earlier than planned because of care responsibilities for a family member (Hellman et al. 2012). Those caregivers who can afford it rely on adult day care or in-home care assistance to help with care provision while they work. In this study several caregivers were upfront about the fact that it barely made economic sense for them to work: paying for supportive services all day is so expensive (as much as $100/day) that it consumed most of their paycheck. At the end of their work days, employed caregivers typically come home to a full round of caregiving: making meals, helping their family member to eat, administering medication, opening the mail, buying supplies, dressing, bathing, and so on. The average working caregiver spends nearly twenty hours per week on these jobs—the equivalent of another part time job (National Alliance for Caregiving and AARP 2009).

One in five caregivers takes a leave of absence while they are caregiving (National Alliance for Caregiving and AARP 2009). In the absence of paid leave laws, employed caregivers in this study described the ways in which they used their own sick leave and vacation time to take care of their family members' needs. "I never had a vacation," one caregiver told me. "All the time that I took off, I spent taking care of my husband. So I haven't had a vacation in years." While California had the first paid family leave law in the country,[5] only a handful of caregivers in this study had used it—either because they didn't know about the law, didn't qualify for the benefits, or because the law doesn't provide the kind of benefits they needed. Most caregivers, for example, frequently needed time off to take their family members to doctor appointments or to handle some breakdown in supportive services, such as a closed adult day care center or an in-home supportive service provider who doesn't show up. While California's paid family leave benefit can technically be used on an hourly, daily, or weekly basis, most caregivers understood the law to be most appropriate for people caring for somebody over an extended period of time—a matter of weeks, not a day or an afternoon. And in fact utilizing the paid family leave benefit requires a seven-day waiting period before payments can begin, as well as written physician authorization. Employers are also permitted to require workers to use two weeks of their paid vacation time before using the paid leave benefit. Some caregivers also avoided using California's paid leave benefit because of the impression it might leave with their supervisors. Irma, for example, was upfront about the fact that she wouldn't use the benefit because she was hoping to be promoted:

> Bosses and supervisors and managers and administrators at the higher levels do not want you to have any personal issues. Get over it, okay? You have to be out six weeks? Get right back here....You just have to keep marching along like a trooper because there could be a backlash if you're trying to get promoted.

5. At the time of this writing three states have enacted family leave laws that would permit paid leave for care of a family member with a serious health condition: California (enacted 2002), New Jersey (enacted 2008), and Rhode Island. Rhode Island's legislature passed legislation creating its family leave program in July 2013 and it is expected to be signed into law by Governor Chafee. All three programs' provisions on family care build off of existing state temporary disability insurance programs and are funded exclusively through employee payroll contributions. California and New Jersey's programs provide partial wage replacement for new parents and family caregivers, but not job protection for workers while they are on family leave. Rhode Island's program is the first to also include job protection.

All of these requirements and norms discourage workers from using paid leave to pay for the typical afternoon they need to drive to doctor appointments.

The lack of institutional support for working caregivers meant that for many caregivers the ability to successfully balance work and family depended on the understanding and compassion of individual supervisors. Notably, most of the caregivers in this study who successfully negotiated the balance between work and caregiving shared one thing in common: they had supervisors who were either caregivers or former caregivers themselves. "I have a very compassionate boss," one such caregiver told me in describing how much time off she'd needed to take to care for her father. "[S]he was a caregiver for her father, who had Parkinson's disease, and I think she has a lot of empathy for what I'm going through." Vincent put it this way:

> I also have a supervisor that is very compassionate due to the fact that he lost his parents. And I told him what the situation was [with my parents] and he told me, he says, "I don't ever want to hear that you're staying here in the office, when your people are trouble. Because I'll kick your buns right out the twenty-third floor." ... And had I had the previous supervisor, I'd've been fired by now. Because he would have said that I was paying more attention to my outer personal life than I was at work.

Note that among caregivers in this study, there was no sense of entitlement to paid time off or flexible work hours. Instead caregivers who found themselves in work environments that accommodated their caregiving responsibilities described themselves as "lucky" and "grateful" to have supervisors that were sensitive to their needs. As one caregiver, Flora, observed:

> I've been really blessed here.... [At the time I was caring for my mother], I reported to the director of the department and the chief deputy ... they were both very good to me, both women. Both had had some caretaking issues in their lives and so were very sensitive to that.... I was very grateful to them for that.[6]

State Responses to Long-Term Trends

All of these long-term trends—an aging population, delayed childbearing, changing family size and forms, and shifting patterns of labor force participation—have converged in ways that have made the experience of long-term

---

6. See Chapter 4 for more on entitlement.

care provision significantly more challenging for families today than ever before. As the chronic care needs of the country are increasing, the burden of care is falling on families with a much smaller pool of available caregivers, many of whom have competing demands for their time and attention from work, children, and other family members. The care crisis, however, does not derive from these long-term trends themselves, but rather from the failure of the state to respond to these changes in ways that would ameliorate the strains on contemporary care provision. Indeed, some state policies—in particular changes in the payment system for hospital reimbursement of costs related to treating Medicare and Medicaid patients—have significantly exacerbated the strains on families providing long-term care.

While trends like the aging of the population are often characterized as apolitical, something beyond the control of any legislature, the failure to update policies to reflect changing social conditions is in most cases a consequence of political struggle (Hacker 2004). The aging of the population, changing family forms, and increasing women's labor force participation have all taken place within a specific political and economic context: the late 1970s and 1980s brought to the fore of American politics a wave of antitax, antigovernment politics that would have profound implications for American social policy (Estes and Swan 1993; Hacker 2006). Ronald Reagan's 1981 inaugural address captured the ascendant political ideology of the time: "In this present crisis," he said, "government is not the solution to our problem; government *is* the problem" (Hacker 2006). Adherents of the ideology of personal responsibility—with its celebration of private markets and disdain for government intervention—transformed the politics of American social policy, using the tax code to systematically shift responsibility for protecting individuals against economic misfortune from the government to individuals and families. In this political context, antigovernment adherents didn't have to orchestrate major policy reforms to achieve their goals of limited state intervention; they simply had to block policy interventions designed to update social policies (Hacker 2004). Every year, the National Center on Caregiving tracks bills introduced in Congress and state legislatures; every year there are dozens of relevant bills introduced at both the federal and state level. But these legislative initiatives rarely survive the lawmaking process. Even the Family and Medical Leave Act, the primary federal protection for approximately 60% of the workforce, was passed in 1993 after more than a decade of legislative debates and two vetoes by President George H.W. Bush (Hacker 2004). The overwhelming absence of successful policy reforms is not, in other words, a reflection of a country caught off guard by the severity or magnitude of the long-term care crisis; it is due to political opposition to expanded state provision.

Even legislative victories have proven to be fleeting. The Medicare Catastrophic Coverage Act of 1988, for example, was the largest expansion of Medicare since the program was enacted in 1965. The new law capped out-of-pocket expenses, expanded skilled nursing facility and hospital benefits, and offered outpatient prescription drug coverage. But an intensely negative public reaction to the Act ultimately forced Congress to repeal the legislation just a year and a half after its enactment. There were several explanations for the negative public reaction (Rice et al. 1990). Unlike the rest of the Medicare program, the additional benefits provided by the Act were to be financed entirely by Medicare beneficiaries, rather than all working adults. People who had already purchased comprehensive health insurance coverage were particularly resentful, as they stood to bear the brunt of the financing, despite the fact that the new legislation added very little to their existing coverage. And perhaps most frustrating of all from the perspective of Medicare beneficiaries, the legislation provided little additional coverage for long-term care, the primary worry among Medicare beneficiaries, and the type of care most likely to impoverish the elderly.

Policy drift also occurred when policymakers enacted policy reforms and then discovered that the reforms had "inadvertently" created new or newly intensified social risks (Hacker 2004). The influence of this type of policy drift on contemporary caregiving was perhaps most striking in the case of health policy changes made in the 1980s that both medicalized caregiving in dramatic ways and created a highly fragmented—and largely unregulated—home health services market.

More and more patients today receive highly sophisticated medical treatments in their homes, treatments that in previous generations would have been administered by trained medical professionals in a hospital setting (Arras 1995). Today, family caregivers serve as "amateur nurses and medical care providers" (Glazer 1990), responsible for managing catheters, oxygen tanks, respirators, IV infusions, feeding tubes, dialysis, blood sugar and blood pressure monitoring, and so on (Arras 1995). One national survey of caregivers found that 43% of family caregivers help with one or more such medical tasks (Donelan et al. 2002).

This dramatic shift in medical service provision from hospital to the home is widely attributed to the Social Security Amendments of 1983, which created a new prospective payment system for hospital reimbursement of costs related to treating Medicare and Medicaid patients (Glazer 1993; Levine 2012). Previously, hospitals, like physicians, had received fees for each service, incentivizing hospitals and doctors to invest in expensive equipment and technologies, order more tests, and administer more services than medical conditions necessarily warranted. Seeking to control skyrocketing health care costs, Congress created diagnosis-related groups

(DRGs) as a cost savings measure (Marmor 2000; Oberlander 2003). DRGs set predetermined payment rates based on diagnosis, not services. This system established limits on the length of time a patient with a particular diagnosis could be hospitalized. Under the prospective payment system, hospitals make a profit if they can discharge a patient before the number of covered days set by the DRG—and, by extension, they can sustain a loss if they fail to discharge a patient within the time period specified by the DRG (Glazer 1993).[7] But the earlier the discharge, the sicker patients tend to be. Indeed many patients simply could not be discharged in the absence of continuing medical treatments. Those treatments are now administered in the patient's home.

As a consequence, caregivers today are often tending to patients with hospital-level needs. Caregivers need to know how to unclog catheters, suction secretions, prepare drug solutions, and troubleshoot equipment when it fails (Arras 1995; Glazer 1990). They must learn how to care for tracheostomies, do "wet and dry" wound treatments, change dressings on still-draining wounds, refill infusion pumps, clean tubes inserted into the chest wall, irrigate catheters inserted in veins to draw blood, and give nutrition, chemotherapy, and antibiotics (Glazer 1990). Notably, these are all treatments that typically fall under detailed state and federal regulations regarding health care training and licensing. Registered nurses (RNs) and licensed practical nurses (LPNs) or aides learn to use sophisticated medical technologies through in-service training workshops and periodic retrainings. But, as Nona Glazer observed, "Under cost containment, customary expectations about training and practice acts have been abandoned. In home care, the most skilled workers...teach persons unskilled in health care—patients and family members—to do technical nursing work" (Glazer 1993:197).

In fact, most family caregivers receive very little instruction on how to use these medical technologies. One national survey found that only one-third of caregivers received the training they needed to perform prescribed medical tasks (Donelan et al. 2002). Ten percent of family caregivers reported seeking informal instruction from a friend or family member who had some medical training (Donelan et al. 2002). Even when family members did receive some training in the hospital, they were expected to learn these techniques in a short amount of time before discharge and during what is often an inordinately stressful time (Glazer 1990). In this study,

---

7. While hospitals and insurance companies calculate the "cost savings" of these reduced hospital stays, the costs to families who take on these additional responsibilities are not taken into account (Glazer 1990).

Irma recalled how her daughter, a registered nurse, had to talk her into taking her mother home from a skilled nursing facility with a feeding tube.

> When [my mother] got the feeding tube, I was kind of freaked out by it because it was
> like okay, I was totally in one of my periods where I was *I can't do any more of this!* ... [My
> daughter] and I were having this discussion one day and she was saying, "Well, why is
> Granny in a nursing home?" And I was saying look, I can't do all this stuff and she has
> a feeding tube and all this, and she's like "And?" ... And I said I mean, how are we going
> to manage that at home? ... So we had every medical equipment you can have in this
> house ... We had a hospital bed, we had the oxygen, we had the feeding tube ...

Many caregivers are unwilling or unable to perform these responsibilities,
either because of age, lack of skills, attitude, or because of traumatic past
experiences in medical care provision (Glazer 1990). Louis, for example,
described how his partner had been repeatedly hospitalized for various
infections. Once stabilized, the doctors would send his partner home, but
his insurance only paid for two weeks of skilled nursing visits. "So I have
to learn how to do all the dressing changing, all the mixing the drugs, give
him [an] injection in certain parts of his body that he cannot do." Three
months prior to his interview, his partner had a severe adverse reaction to
one of the drugs Louis had administered and they had to rush to the hospital. "From that point I refused to do the injection because even though
I know it's the drug reaction ... I feel responsible for what happened." It was
such a bad experience, he said, that he'd rather take his partner to the doctor's office every day for his injection—which he did—than administer the
drugs himself. The shift in high-tech medical services from the hospital into
the hands of unskilled and largely unsupervised family caregivers has added
an additional layer of stress to contemporary caregiving. Many caregivers
are not only confused and intimidated by these technologies, but they often
experience a near constant anxiety about mishandling the medical care of
their family member (Arras and Dubler 1995).

The push to discharge patients from hospitals "sicker and quicker" has
been accompanied by an explosion in home care services that provide per-
sonnel and equipment for administering medical treatments in the home,
often on the patient's tab (Arras and Dubler 1995; Estes and Swan 1993).
These mostly for-profit companies have proliferated—and profited—in
a market that Arras has called "reminiscent of the Wild West" (Arras and
Dubler 1995:23). Because there is little public money involved—services
are paid for either by insurance companies or out of pocket by families—
there has been very little congressional oversight of the home care market.
Largely unnoticed by regulators, home care vendors have amassed enormous profits through price gouging and questionable sales practices, such

as marketing high-tech devices directly to patients at home, selling them expensive equipment that is often not needed or even relevant for their medical condition (Arras and Dubler 1995).

The growth of the home health industry has created a highly specialized market of support services and a fragmented delivery system with no single point of entry for families requiring care assistance. Families must not only navigate a vast array of private home health companies, but also assess whether and to what degree state programs will cover home health services, including those offered under Medicare, Medicaid, the Older Americans Act, the Department of Veterans' Affairs, and state-level programs, each of which covers different kinds of services and is administered under different rules by different authorities at the local, state, and federal levels (Miller et al. 2009). Caregivers as a result confront a wide assortment of badly coordinated service providers that often have separate sources of funding and inconsistent care practices.

In this study, the fragmentation of home health care services was a constant topic of conversation among caregivers. Eddie was still relatively new to caregiving at the time of this study, and his experience captures how overwhelming the home health system can be, particularly for families new to long-term care provision. An artist by trade, Eddie was working at home and caring for his mother-in-law, who had Alzheimer's. When he sat down for an interview, he looked visibly exhausted and stressed. His mother-in-law had taken to wandering off, he told me. He said he was worried about being accused of adult abuse if he helped his mother-in-law change her diaper. Midway through this discussion Eddie posed a question directly to me:

> What I wanted to ask is where do you go to find these out? I mean, there's no agency. It's like you always learn because a mistake has happened, you know, a meltdown or something. And you find out then. Oh you should have done this or that. Or...you could have had this resource or something like that. But it's all after the fact. It takes a toll on us, you know, because we have to clean the mess up.

Many caregivers described how difficult it was to try to learn about a disease and available support services and funding sources, all while trying to provide care for their parent or partner. Barbara articulated this well, as she described her frustration trying to find information while caring for her husband: "Everything is there, there, there [pointing in different directions]. Everything is so disconnected. *And life is moving.* It's like this is a sick person, and I have to keep things going, and it's not like I was able to stop and research everything, because I was so busy just making life happen!" Caregivers talked about needing a "clearinghouse," a one-stop shop where they could get all this information in one place. As Eddie said to me at the close of his interview:

> I would pay almost anything, I mean hundreds, thousands, I don't care...to have some-
> body come into this house and say, "This is what you need to do. This is how to handle
> the situation. And you will be within the law. And you'll be doing the best for your
> mother-in-law in her situation. And you'll be doing the best for your own family."...That
> would be amazingly helpful.

There are, of course, such things as care managers or care coordinators who can help families navigate community services and funding sources for a fee, but most caregivers don't know where to find such help or can't afford it anyway.

The context in which individual Americans find themselves providing chronic care to an adult family member, then, has been heavily shaped by the convergence of macro-level sociopolitical trends which have created a bona fide crisis in care. The aging of the population, the rise in delayed childbearing and smaller families, divorce and remarriage, and the increase in women's labor force participation have all increased the need for chronic care at a time when the supply of care providers in the home has dwindled sharply. Meanwhile, dramatic changes in health care delivery systems have medicalized the home and shifted costs to families that were previously borne by hospitals. This by no means exhausts the list of factors that have shaped the caregiving crisis. The point here is that the combination of family and policy drift—a stubborn refusal to change existing social practices and policies in ways that would ameliorate the strain on families—has created far more challenging conditions for caregiving than any previous generation of Americans has experienced before. The following section describes the contemporary caregiving experience in more detail—physically, emotionally, and financially.

WHAT CAREGIVERS DO

There is, of course, no uniform or generic caregiving experience. Some caregivers are responsible for handling the finances, housework, or transportation needs of a parent or partner, while others are providing much more intensive and personal kinds of care—helping with bathing, toileting, eating, etc. Some people are quite suddenly thrown into caregiving when a partner or parent has a stroke or an accident. Others take on caregiving tasks gradually, as Alzheimer's or Parkinson's disease slowly robs the ability of a parent or partner to function independently.

For some the caregiving role lasts a matter of weeks; for others it lasts years.

The "average" caregiver today is a woman in her late 40s who works outside the home and spends nearly twenty hours per week providing care for a family member for nearly five years (National Alliance for Caregiving and AARP 2009).[8] Family caregivers generally are providing care to people with a wide range of health problems, such as heart disease or high blood pressure, arthritis, lung disease, visual and auditory impairments, diabetes, stroke, and cancer, among many others. This study focused primarily on individuals caring for family members suffering from dementia, with a small comparison group of individuals caring for family members with cancer. The description below tracks these foci, primarily describing the experiences of caring for family members suffering from dementia while highlighting the unique experiences of people caring for cancer patients.

Early Stages of Dementia

Caregivers in this study all had stories about when they first noticed the kind of strange behaviors that led to diagnoses of dementia-related illnesses. The earliest signs that something might be wrong are often so subtle that families dismiss them as symptoms of stress or "typical" aging. Everyone, after all, loses their keys on occasion. But when someone forgets how to use their keys, something is more seriously amiss. In some cases, caregivers noticed that their family member could no longer operate the microwave or the television remote control. There were repeated questions, asking the same thing four, five, six times in a row in a short amount of time. There were smoke alarms that went off when family members would put a roll of paper towels or paper plates on a lit stove and walk away. There were problems driving—repeat accidents and getting lost. Clarice's husband started turning on the heat rather than the air conditioning, or vice versa, and couldn't tell the difference once they were on. He started withdrawing money from their bank account and giving it away, or ordering unnecessary things by mail using their credit card. Serena noticed that her husband always started walking off in the wrong direction. "Always. Never the right way. I'd tell him … when you think you're going right, just go wrong and you'd be right at least sometime. But he was always going the wrong way." She observed

---

8. One-third of all caregivers provide care for five years or more (National Alliance for Caregiving and AARP 2009).

that her husband's strange behaviors were slow to develop, but she noticed one small thing just about every day:

> We'd go to the grocery store and at first he couldn't find things, so I would have to go in with him. Then it was down to he couldn't choose things, so I would let him push the cart. [Then] I couldn't let him push the cart because if we were in the aisle, he wouldn't move over to let people by.

Caregiving at these early stages involves taking over what clinicians refer to as "instrumental activities of daily living" (IADLs), those more complex skills and tasks beyond basic self-care that are needed to successfully live independently (Wiener et al. 1990). They include handling personal finances, meal preparation, shopping, doing housework, yard work and home maintenance, using the telephone, administering medications as prescribed, and driving to appointments. Many people can still live independently even though they need help with one or two of these IADL's. In these early stages of a dependency situation, the stress levels of most caregivers remain relatively low, although the emotional realization that a dependency relationship has begun can be quite difficult, particularly for adult children caring for their parents.

Middle to Late Stages of Dementia

As diseases progress, care receivers increasingly need help with more basic tasks of self-care, or "activities of daily living" (ADLs), such as eating, bathing, dressing, toileting, transferring, and walking. Transferring somebody from chair to bed or into a shower when they are not mobile or actively resisting is physically demanding for anybody, but particularly for older adults, who often have health issues themselves. Caregivers reported in this study that they relied on physical therapy belts to help lift their parents or partners, or in one case a special hydraulic lift. Many people shared stories of having to leave their parents or partners on the floor when they fell out of bed until they could get help in the morning.

Family members who require help with both walking and toileting often require assistance three, four, or even five times a night. Caregivers assisting relatives with these ADLs very quickly became exhausted from the repeated wakeups, the bathroom messes, and the midnight falls. "He'd get up ten times a night!" Sharon recalled of her husband.

> And so I was beginning to look like death warmed over. [Laughs] Because I'm not getting any sleep. And then he would begin to wet himself, so I tried to get him to use a

urinal. Well, that was just so insulting, he said "No you help me." So I would take him in and help him. And then if I left him there, he'd go all over the bathroom. And I was cleaning the bathroom every day.

In addition to the physical exhaustion of providing personal care to a family member with a chronic illness, caregivers often experience a difficult emotional transition with this stage of care provision. For husbands and wives, the need for assistance with ADLs is often the first time they really see or admit that their relationship to their partner has changed in a fundamental way. Taking over instrumental activities of daily living, such as cooking or driving a car, are often such gradual shifts in spousal responsibilities that they don't register with partners as a dramatic change in their relationship. But helping a partner to feed himself or herself or use the bathroom represents a much more unambiguous shift in the relationship.

Adult children caring for their parents often perceive this shift in the relationship earlier, as they are much more aware of the reversal in the dependency relationship between parent and child, but that shift becomes all the more striking when they begin providing personal care (Montgomery and Kosloski 2001; Montgomery and Kosloski 2013). Isabel, for example, was only thirty-three when she began caring for her father, who had Alzheimer's and required assistance with virtually all aspects of personal care. "You need to show him how to eat.... Now I have to change him, bathe him, help him to go to bed. Have to change his shoes. Shave him. Everything. All the personal things that he has to do." One day Isabel shared with her support group how difficult this shift had been for her:

> I was remembering that my dad would always always take care of [me]. If I didn't have any money for anything he'd put some money [right into her hand.] And when things started changing, and I was giving him a dollar so he could smile...I came to realize, wow, I'm taking care of him. But that transition is really hard.

Vincent was caring for both of his parents—providing full personal care to his mother for six years, and assisting his father, who was also in declining health. He said one of the most challenging aspects of caregiving was navigating the transition in their relationship:

> [Y]our heart breaks because you have to even get to the point you have to yell. Or become stern. And you...feel deep down inside you're not brought up to be disrespectful to your parents. But yet...that role has become reversed. And that's the part I couldn't handle for a while. The role switching.... [M]y Dad, even though he's still a little 5'8" man, strong as an ox, has now become almost childlike in some ways....And now Dad'll come to you and say "What do you think of this?" And you say, Dad, you

used to do that all of your life. What do you need me for? "Well, I don't know, I'm confused." And then you start realizing well, yeah, instead of you being one of the cars in the train, now you're the locomotive pulling this whole thing. And that to me is a big task.

Many adult children could point to specific moments where they had to really assert their authority over the wishes of their parents for the first time (e.g., preventing their parents from driving, confiscating their guns, hiring in-home supportive services). All of these moments were accompanied by intense anxiety and guilt. One caregiver, Gwen, confessed that she couldn't get herself to confiscate her father's guns, even after he became more and more psychotic.

People kept saying well take the guns out of his house. And that was something that felt beyond my control. And it was not something I was willing to do. So when my brother came back in the picture, my brother's like 6'6" or 6'7", I mean he's a big guy. And my father really has a lot of respect for him. He's a very wealthy, successful businessman. I told my brother to do it. And somehow he said I just can't do that. It was the one thing he wouldn't do either.

These transitions are emotionally difficult for care receivers as well, and many caregivers bore the brunt of their parents' frustration and resentment about their growing loss of independence. Elizabeth shared with her support group a comment her father had made that had really upset her:

My father said to me one day that I didn't keep my part of the I-love-you bargain. I asked him what he meant, and he said I had taken away his license, I had taken away his gun, I had taken away his money. I said, I didn't take away those things! The DMV took your license, and we had to move the gun for your safety, and I haven't touched your money. In his mind, I was doing all those things. Here I've given up my life, I'm living in your house, I'm caring for you ... what I-love-you bargain didn't I keep?

The emotional aspects of caregiving for a family member are for many people the most difficult part of long-term care provision. In addition to the helplessness and profound sense of loss that comes with watching the physical and mental decline of somebody they love, many caregivers find that relationship issues from the past—including issues they thought had been fully resolved—reemerge in the context of care provision (Abel 1991). Old resentments and past offenses resurface even as new tensions and frustrations emerge. Some caregivers find themselves once again looking to please their parents or win their approval in their efforts to care for them. And in virtually all cases there was a struggle with guilt—a constant theme in support groups. "Guilt," observed one support group facilitator and former caregiver herself, "I think it's tremendous. I don't have dementia, there's nothing wrong with me, what have I got to complain about? You know, why should I be thinking about not wanting to do this anymore? What an awful daughter I am."

As caregivers take on more and more responsibility for personal care, they often experience an increase in social isolation. More than half (53%) of family caregivers say that their care responsibilities keep them from seeing family and friends (National Alliance for Caregiving and AARP 2009). When family members become less mobile or more difficult to take out of the house, caregivers' worlds become smaller: they can no longer reciprocate dinner invitations. They can no longer attend book groups or bridge clubs or church or other social activities that connected them to the social world. As one caregiver, Laurel, put it:

> It's such an insidious thing when you're a caregiver because you don't realize that you're losing contact with your friends—that you're not socializing any more. You're just so tired all the time… and then all of a sudden you wake up one day and it's like you haven't seen anybody for months. You haven't talked to anybody on the telephone, you know?

Another caregiver observed that "people don't want to be around you when there's so much illness…including family." Family and friends often find it awkward and uncomfortable to interact with people with chronic illnesses, particularly when they knew them well as healthy adults, or they get embarrassed at their unpredictable and often inappropriate behavior or their difficulty speaking. The geographic dispersion of family can exacerbate this sense of social isolation. In this study, family care providers often described themselves as "having nobody," even when they had family living in other parts of the city or country. As Susanna, taking care of both her parents, put it, "I'm it. A party of one. That's what I told my son, that's my new motto. Party of one. I don't have anybody…" Caregivers who experience social isolation also experience high levels of caregiver stress (National Alliance for Caregiving and AARP 2009), and therefore greater health problems themselves.[9]

Providing this level of personal care for any dependent adult can be exceptionally difficult, but for families dealing with dementia, the challenges are often much worse. While most people think of Alzheimer's as primarily a memory disease, between 80% and 90% of dementia patients also develop neuropsychiatric symptoms, such as combativeness, paranoia,

---

9. See Chapter 1 for evidence on the link between caregiving stress and mental and physical health impairments.

and wandering—all caused by the slow deterioration of brain cells (Jalbert et al. 2008). As a result, caregivers for people with dementia generally report a greater physical strain compared to other caregivers, and perceive their caregiving situations to be more emotionally stressful (National Alliance for Caregiving and AARP 2009).

The most common symptoms associated with Alzheimer's disease are confusion and memory loss. As memory loss becomes more and more severe, care receivers may not recognize family members, may forget relationships, call family members by other names, or become confused about the location of home or the passage of time. These changes are some of the most painful for caregivers and families. Lonni, who cared for her mother, recalled the first few times her mother came down the stairs with a purse and suitcase and announced, " 'You have to take me home now. My parents are waiting for me.' And…my heart would be pounding. *What!?*"

Karen said of her husband's decline, "It's been called the long goodbye, but it's worse than that because at the time that you're saying goodbye a person's been stripped of everything.…He doesn't even recognize his children. I'm not sure he knows who I am." She recalled returning from an overseas trip and lying in bed when her husband "said very distinctly… 'I'm sorry, but you'll have to leave now.' And I said really, where am I going? He said, 'You have to go home.' Why's that? 'Because my wife is coming home and she will not like finding you here.' "

Flora, who also cared for her mother, recalled how difficult it was to provide so much intensive care for somebody who no longer recognized who she was.

> I was no longer her daughter. And when I would come home every day, she would ask me how my mother was, and how are my sisters. I think I looked like a cousin of hers, and so I think that's who she thought I was. And so she would ask me those questions, which were very painful for me. It was hard for me. It was a hard transition…

The emotional anguish experienced by caregivers whose parents or partners could no longer recognize them could also be seen in the way that caregivers treasured those rare instances in advanced stages of dementia when their parents or partners called them by their name. Isadore, whose wife had advanced Alzheimer's, recounted one day to his support group what a difficult week he'd had with respect to his wife's combative behavior. He paused for a moment and said, "But one good thing in all of this: She called me [Isadore] for the first time in a year." The following week he reported in again: "She's called me by name two or three times now. And she said 'I love you' three to four times." The heart-wrenching way in which caregivers counted, recalled, and savored these moments spoke volumes about how devastating the disease is not only for the patient, but also for the families who care for them.

In addition to memory loss, a significant proportion of dementia patients suffer from periods of aggression.[10] Alzheimer's and other dementia-related diseases can make even mild-mannered people highly combative—refusing to shower or bathe, refusing to get dressed, refusing to eat. Aggressive behaviors can be verbal or physical. They include cursing, hitting, grabbing, kicking, pushing, throwing things, scratching, screaming, biting, and sexual advances. These behaviors can appear out of nowhere, for no apparent reason, or they can be responses to frustrating situations. Many caregivers in this study reported being unable to hire help in the home because their care receiver would assault anybody who tried to enter their house or touch them. Isadore was struggling with his wife's aggression at the time of this study. One day he reported to his support group that he had forgotten to lock his gate, and his wife had walked off. He brought her home and locked the door. Once confined, she became more and more upset, screaming and yelling, and then she went into the next room and started pulling down the drapes and blinds, shredding them, and trying to get out the window. Isadore confided to his support group how worried he was that her increasing combativeness could threaten her ability to attend adult day care—his only respite from 24-hour care provision.

In many cases, the aggression can be quite serious, causing caregivers to fear for their own physical safety. Clarice's husband, for example, was both psychotic and extremely combative. He would not permit Clarice to hire any help in the home, and went into often-violent rages when she tried. He got suspicious whenever she spoke to anybody on the phone or left the house and would call 911 when she was gone for longer than anticipated. Unable to speak privately with his doctor, Clarice would communicate her concerns about his threatening behavior to the doctor by telling her husband she was going to check on the bill. She would then hand the receptionist an envelope to give to his doctor with a note that said "Read before you see the patient." On at least three occasions doctors pulled her aside and told her it wasn't safe for her to go home. She admitted feeling terrorized by her husband until the day she institutionalized him. Even then she felt guilty for doing it.

"Shadowing" is another dementia-related behavior that presents a unique set of challenges for caregivers. Here a person with Alzheimer's closely follows every move made by the caregiver, mimics the caregiver, and/or

10. Estimates of the prevalence of aggression among dementia patients vary widely, from 21%–30% (Lyketsos, Lopez, Jones, Fitzpatrick, Breitner, and DeKosky 2002; Voyer, Verreault, Azizah, Desrosiers, Champoux, and Bedard 2005) to more than 75% (Brodaty et al. 2001).

constantly talks or asks repeat questions. This behavior can be among the most wearying for care providers. One caregiver referred to his wife, who shadowed him constantly, as his "Velcro wife." Caregivers reported feeling smothered by the behavior, unable to do something as simple as walk into the next room or shut the door to use the bathroom.

Shadowing is often accompanied by another behavior clinically known as "sundowning." Beginning at dusk and continuing throughout the night, as many as 20% of Alzheimer's patients experience periods of increased confusion, disorientation, anxiety, agitation, restlessness, insecurity, suspicion, delusions, and hallucinations.[11] At the time of this study, Isadore was struggling with his wife's worsening sundowning behavior. One day he told his support group:

> I've got this night thing where … oh about 9 o'clock … she gets in bed, she suddenly says, "I want to go out.… I've got to see them down the street. They're talking about me, they're out there." And I says there's no one out there. It's cold outside. It's pitch black.[12]

One night his wife became delusional during the night, waking up and seeing people and things, and getting up and walking around. After six or seven wakeups to calm her down and get her back into bed, 72-year-old Isadore was too tired to cope. He tried tying the bedroom door shut with rope, but she escaped. So he tied her up in her room. In the morning he said the room looked like a bomb had gone off. Bedclothes were in one direction, the bed in the other. Lamps were knocked over, stuff everywhere. After this happened two nights in a row, the doctor prescribed anti-anxiety medication for her.

Paranoia is another common behavior associated with Alzheimer's. Like aggression, paranoia simultaneously makes caregiving much more difficult, and yet presents a formidable obstacle to hiring any type of supportive services. The paranoia manifests itself in any number of ways. Patients may hide things and then later believe that somebody took them. They suspect neighbors of coming into their home and stealing. In this study, Doris's husband constantly suspected her of having affairs. She told her support group one week that her husband went to put on a blue blazer, couldn't find it in the closet, and told her he didn't have one. She said to him, "Yes you do," and she pulled it out of the closet for him. He said her boyfriend must have

---

11. Alzheimer's Association. "Sleep Issues and Sundowning." Accessed July 31, 2013. http://www.alz.org/care/alzheimers-dementia-sleep-issues-sundowning.asp.

12. Caregivers in these circumstances are often advised to close curtains and to remove mirrors in the house, as it is often reflections in the glass or mirrors that patients mistakenly believe are other people.

left it and refused to put it on. His paranoia made it impossible for Doris get someone to help with housework or yard work, as he suspected everybody of malfeasance. She described how she tried one time to get someone to do yard work while they were out of the house, but when he returned and realized that someone had been there he "went ballistic," screaming, throwing things, and crying for the rest of the day.

Nearly six out of every ten people with dementia will wander and become lost during the course of the disease, and most will do so repeatedly.[13] Many caregivers in this study shared horror stories of frantic police and neighborhood searches for their family members. One caregiver described to her group what happened when she placed her mother, aged 91, in a temporary skilled nursing facility while she looked into a more permanent home. She said she got a call one day from her mother: "Lena," her mother whispered, "don't worry, I've escaped!" And then her mother hung up. After confirming that her mother was in fact missing from the nursing home, Lena was desperate. Eventually she got a call from a bus driver saying her mother was on a Route 92 bus headed downtown. Lena went to a bus stop downtown and checked every bus, but still couldn't find her. Finally, she got a call from a church downtown, who said they had her. Her mother was sitting watching a parade and had a big smile on her face. She said, "I knew you'd find me!" In addition to the stress and anxiety that wandering behaviors cause, caregivers also expressed concerns about liability, worrying whether they could be held liable should something happen to their family member or to somebody else while they are unsupervised and lost.

When clinicians describe dementia-related diseases as the most physically and emotionally challenging for caregivers, they are focusing on these neuropsychiatric symptoms, which make care provision so exceptionally difficult. For many families struggling with these behaviors, supportive services become critical—in-home care assistance, adult day care, respite care, and eventually, institutionalization. Contrary to the public perception that Americans are quick to abandon their elderly and their sick to nursing homes, only about 3.6% (or 1.5 million) of older Americans live in nursing homes at any given time (Administration on Aging 2012). These residents are typically the oldest old and the frailest old. Close to 93% have mobility impairments and 76% have cognitive impairments (Kaye et al. 2010). The overwhelming majority of people who need long-term care assistance receive that care in the home. About 26% of people receiving care in the

13. Alzheimer's Association. "Wandering and Getting Lost." Accessed July 31, 2013, http://www.alz.org/care/alzheimers-dementia-wandering.asp.

home receive some combination of family and paid help; only 9% receive paid help alone (Doty 2010).

Most family caregivers are still actively involved in care provision even when they rely on supportive services. While they no longer provide as much hands-on personal care, the job of mediating between formal service providers and dependent family members—what Balbo (1982) refers to as "servicing" work—still demands a significant amount of time and attention from caregivers. Abel (1991) observes there are at least three types of "servicing" work that family caregivers do: (1) deciding whether and where to place a relative in a nursing home; (2) locating and arranging for services delivered by community agencies; and (3) recruiting and supervising aides and attendants who are unaffiliated with formal home health agencies.

For families dealing with dementia, the decision to place a family member in an institution is in many cases unavoidable. Many caregivers are deeply committed to personally providing care to their parent or partner, and it's only because they are physically or emotionally unable to provide that care on their own that they consider other options. Some caregivers are forced to institutionalize their family member due to the particular behaviors associated with Alzheimer's, such as wandering or aggression. Some caregivers cannot afford to pay for needed supportive services in the home, and have no choice but to institutionalize their care receiver under Medicaid. Some caregivers institutionalize their family members when they develop serious physical or mental health problems themselves. Barbara, for example, had been caring for her husband, who had advanced Parkinson's, for about seven years. The disease had made him an exceptionally difficult patient—combative, mean, paranoid—and he had repeated visits to the hospital for all kinds of related medical issues.

> A year and a half ago, I started having the feeling that life was too hard. And it was just, life was very, very hard. . . . [I]n April he was hospitalized three times. . . and so the last time it happened, I remember putting my head on the gurney and thinking if I have to do this one more day, I'm going to die. And so I talked to his doctors, all of his doctors, and told that this was where I was am. I cannot take care of him. I don't want to take care of him. I can't even take care of me anymore. And will you support me? I don't want him to go home. And so that's where he's been since then. He's in a home.

Identifying an appropriate facility for family members often takes a considerable amount of research and time, as caregivers have to take into account things like quality, level of care provided,[14] location, and most

---

14. Many facilities do not admit patients with dementia.

importantly, cost. Many discussions in support groups revolved around the issue of cost. One woman who was caring for her father reported to her support group that she had started researching nursing homes just in case her father's condition deteriorated significantly. Unfortunately, she told the group, she started with the private facilities, which meant nothing else was going to compare favorably. The ones she visited cost nearly $6,000 a month, and they were beautiful. "*I* could go there," she said of one of them. "It's like a resort!" She noted there wouldn't be much guilt putting her father in such a nice place. But it wasn't really an option, she sighed, as she couldn't afford it.

The difference in quality between private facilities and some of facilities that accepted Medi-Cal (Medicaid) beneficiaries was in fact quite striking. In another support group, a woman noted that she was going with her husband to look at a place on Sunset Boulevard after the meeting. Karen, a wealthy woman in the group said, "Oh, I looked at that place. That would be depressing. It's more like a hospital than a home." The facilitator interjected, "Keep in mind, [Karen], that your options are different when you're on Medi-Cal." Karen nodded guiltily and said, "Right, I know."

Once a facility has been identified, the "servicing" work shifts to ensuring that the family member is receiving good care. This includes visits, phone calls, and consultations with nurses and doctors. One caregiver in this study reported that after her mother was institutionalized, she talked to her by phone upwards of five times a day. Another was worried that his friend was losing weight and brought him home-cooked food every day. Caregiving for an institutionalized family member also includes buying clothes and other personal items and providing extra care for them when they get sick. And it can include the difficult moments when family members ask to come home. Leonard's family, for example, had a party at his wife's nursing home. He told his support group that during the party his wife leaned over and said softly in his ear, "I want to go home with you." Leonard choked up as he admitted, "That was a heartbreaker." For many, the guilt and anxiety about placing their family members in a formal care institution was relentless. One caregiver, whose husband had become quite violent with advanced Alzheimer's, said she was initially relieved to take him to a nursing home. "But then there was the guilt. Did I make the right decision? Did I do everything I could do?" She visited him twice a day. Sometimes he would be crying like a child, sometimes he was hostile and angry. He had a nursing assistant call her several times a day and he would demand that she get him out of there. "It was awful," she said, reflecting back. "A horrible, horrible experience." While placing a partner or parent was definitely not a horrible experience for most people in this study—most family caregivers reported a dramatic reduction in stress after placement—caregivers observed that they still had significant care responsibilities for their family member.

For caregivers who turn to community supportive services rather than institutional care, the servicing work can be just as demanding (Abel 1991). Identifying adult day care facilities, transportation services, Meals on Wheels, or service agencies who provided in-home assistance all required research into issues of cost and quality, language (in the case of immigrants), and location. Then there are the more intangible issues of "fit" to be considered—is the care receiver comfortable with the new aide or in this day care setting? One caregiver in this study reported that her mother really enjoyed her adult day care center, but she hated the food, so she was looking for another place. "Not because it's not a good facility, it's just not a good match to her. She's coming from southern cooking and you know, [this facility] being so kosher…they're definitely not going to have a lot of the food that she's used to eating."

Finally, many families rely on more informal arrangements for supportive services, hiring home health aides and companions on their own, independent of any formal agency (Abel 1991). Los Angeles is a city with a big pool of immigrant domestic workers, and many caregivers rely on these workers for care provision on a part-time or live-in basis. Here servicing work includes recruitment—asking doctors, nurses, community service agencies, friends and family, gardeners, and housekeepers for referrals. Without the assistance of a home health agency, caregivers who arrange their own home health assistance have to evaluate qualifications, references, and personal characteristics themselves. Family caregivers also have to train and supervise in-home assistants. The high rates of turnover in home health services, together with sudden schedule changes and poor fit with care receivers, mean that caregivers who hire supportive services of any kind frequently find themselves seeking substitutes or replacements—which means more servicing work. Janet had recently retired after a long illness, exacerbated by the stress of working and caring for both her parents. She had the resources to hire 24-hour help but found the servicing work to be an overwhelming job. "It's getting the right person, getting the match, your parents not liking them…you know, just to get the right fit.… That's why I got sick, because I've gone through fifty to one-hundred [caregivers]." The assistance in Janet's case included a five-day caregiver for the work week (and a two-day caregiver on weekends), a bath aide to assist her mother twice a week, someone to deliver groceries, and a driver. She found the process of screening and hiring to be so challenging that she even hired someone to put ads in the newspaper, screen calls, and pre-interview candidates.

Thus while many families require some form of supportive services when caring for patients with advanced dementia-related diseases, the caregiving role itself does not end when someone else takes on the duties of personal care. Instead, the tasks change, the responsibilities shift, and caregivers find themselves engaged in yet another set of challenges.

Caring for Cancer Patients

There are many ways in which the experiences of individuals caring for family members fighting cancer parallel the experiences of people caring for family members suffering from dementia. Caring for patients who have had surgeries, transplants, chemotherapy, and radiation therapy involves assistance with many of the IADLs and ADLs described above. Many of the side effects of steroids and other drugs used by cancer patients include combativeness and stubbornness. And for older patients in particular, treatments for cancer can result in temporary or permanent dementia. Caregivers for cancer patients in this study were more likely than other caregivers to be responsible for using the advanced medical technologies discussed earlier in the chapter—PICC lines, feeding tubes, and the administration of medicines, including chemotherapy treatments—with all of their associated anxieties.

While many of the emotional aspects of caregiving were the same across both dementia and cancer support groups—such as the sense of social isolation, guilt, and so on—there were aspects of the cancer experience that presented their own unique emotional struggles. Unlike dementia-related diseases, for which there is no cure, cancer treatments are typically administered with the hope that the cancer will, at the very least, go into remission. As a result, tests—blood tests, mammograms, cat scans, pet scans—loom large for families dealing with cancer. Caregivers worry that the cancer may have returned or that it has worsened. They worry that treatments won't work, or that they will run out of treatment options. They worry that the side effects of treatment will kill their family members before the cancer does or that their family members will refuse additional treatment. "We worry about when the other brick will hit us, you know?" Todd told his support group, speaking for many. "Cancer robs you of the security of knowing that things will be okay." Todd's wife had successfully battled ovarian cancer after her doctors discovered it while she was in labor with their first child. They eventually had a second child, and when their children were six and two, the cancer returned in metastasized form in her bones and breast. Todd reported to his support group that the new medicine the doctors were giving her was working so far. "You're constantly braced for the bad news," he observed with a touch of weary irony, "so that when you actually get good news, you're afraid to enjoy it."

The financial challenges of caring for a cancer patient were also very different. Whereas the financial dilemmas of caring for family members with dementia revolve primarily around the ability to pay for supportive services to assist with caregiving, cancer patients in this study typically had insurance coverage that paid for a greater range of services. But because most of these patients were in active treatment, caregivers were dealing with the constant influx of large hospital and doctor bills—and insurance policies with significant deductibles. Laurel's partner, for example, was being treated for breast cancer and had insurance that paid only 70%–80% of the costs of her treatment. "The bills keep rolling in for this stuff," Laurel told her support group, visibly overwhelmed. "It's $15,000 a pop for the chemo, and that's not including all the other stuff." Caregivers also described how they had to constantly fight with insurance companies over coverage of treatments and supportive services, and many mentioned a persistent fear that their insurance company could drop their coverage at any time. "You get a notion that they would make any excuses to drop you…" one caregiver observed, "that they [are] going to find some flaw in what you do and then drop you."

The Rewards of Caregiving

In describing the experience of contemporary caregivers in cases involving dementia and other chronic illnesses, I do not mean to suggest that long-term care provision is a uniformly difficult or unpleasant responsibility. At the end of every interview, I asked participants to tell me what had been the most rewarding aspect of care provision in their case. Some people readily admitted that they found nothing rewarding in the experience at all. But most did. They noted the ways in which their relationships with parents or partners had deepened. Like Carolyn, they savored the opportunity to have their family with them and to enjoy them day by day.

> The most rewarding is their sweetness. Sometimes you're frustrated and sometimes you get angry.…But there is…and I can only say like a spiritual quality to doing that, that is just…immeasurable. Immeasurable.

Caregivers also appreciated the opportunity to learn new things about their own character, strengths, and abilities. Louis, for example, noted at the end of his interview that the most challenging thing about his caregiving experience was the fear:

> Fear of the loss, fear of [being] out of control, fear of the unknown, fear of your own security, fear of loneliness, fear of abandonment. So it's a lot of fear…and the rewarding is the opposite of that. Because you learn how to deal with your own fear.

And finally, caregivers enjoyed the feeling of satisfying their obligations to family. Vincent, who was caring for both his parents, captured this well:

> Sometimes just the smile on my mom's face or the hug I get from my father that he knows that I'm doing everything I can possibly do.... And even though sometimes my mom can't talk, or when she does talk she'll put her hand on my face and say "Thank you, thank you." And I say for what mom? "Just thank you." And that kind of rips you in half, you know? That's the rewarding part of it.

While many caregivers derive strong positive benefits from the experience of long-term care provision for family members, the point here is to show that, for more and more American families, the contemporary experience of caregiving often demands more of families than they can actually provide on their own. The chapters that follow seek to understand why Americans don't demand the resources that would allow them to meet their perceived obligations to family. Purchasing assistance with caregiving is well beyond the resources of most American families, and so they make do with what they have, at significant cost to their emotional and physical health, their financial security, the quality of care for their family members, and, when family systems fail, to the long-term stability of American's weak safety net for long-term care: Medicaid.

CHAPTER 3

The Transformation of Private Needs into Public Issues

The first dimension of politicization involves reinterpreting an issue that has historically been characterized as a private or domestic problem as a matter appropriate for public deliberation and decision making. It is not obvious to most people why long-term care should be considered a public policy issue. *Why would we use public dollars to pay for something that family members have always done for free?* Policy reform advocates work hard to emphasize the broad social transformations that have made long-term care such an increasingly intractable problem for contemporary American families. But establishing the connection between one's "personal troubles of milieu" and "public issues of social structure" (Mills 1959:8) often involves more than a cognitive understanding of these long-term social trends. The power of cultural norms lies in their ability to shape deeply held values about things like responsibility for social welfare. We care for our partners "in sickness and health" and we take care of our parents "the way they once took care of us" because it is expected of us. *It's what families do.* These are powerful—and largely taken for granted—cultural norms. For many, to even admit that long-term care provision is "difficult" is to suggest a kind of personal moral failure—an inability to physically, financially, or emotionally live up to one's commitments to family. To conceptualize long-term care responsibility as a policy issue is so far removed from the immediacy of care and the emotional and moral struggles that accompany it that it is easy for many people to either view state intervention as irrelevant, or to conflate state intervention with an abdication of family responsibility.

How then do people come to view such a deeply personal issue as a subject appropriate for policy intervention? Drawing on tools of collective identification long used by social movement scholars for explaining how individuals come to see the personal as political, this chapter seeks to trace similar transformations in long-held assumptions about responsibilities for care. To reinterpret care provision as a matter appropriate for public deliberation and decision making, caregivers in this case needed a way of bridging the ideology of family care with a view of care provision as a community or social responsibility. The integration of new solutions to unmet needs with more familiar ways of thinking and talking about social welfare is referred to here as *discursive integration*.

Social workers and social service providers inadvertently served as a catalyst for this aspect of politicization. Focused not on political consciousness raising, but on persuading family members to utilize supportive services in the community, social workers and service providers worked hard to facilitate the process of group identification as "caregivers." Sustained contact with the discourse of caregiving in social services had an unintentional consciousness-raising effect on caregivers, highlighting similarities in their experiences, reframing their individual problems as collective problems, and emphasizing the underlying structural or sociocultural factors that make long-term care difficult for families in the United States. Group identification with the caregiver identity, in other words, was an important mechanism by which individuals challenged taken-for-granted assumptions about family responsibility for care and began to think about long-term care as a public policy issue.

COLLECTIVE IDENTITY AS A MECHANISM OF POLITICIZATION

Social movement scholars have long observed that in order for individuals to imagine collective solutions to their problems, they must first identify themselves as a member of a group with similar interests and experiences (see also Polletta and Jasper 2001; Taylor and Whittier 1992). Collective identity,[1] in this view, plays a key role in forging a connection between individual problems and collective—or policy—solutions. Social movement researchers have observed that drawing boundaries between an in-group and out-group—or an "us" and a "them"—not only produces a shared

---

1. I use the term *collective identity* in this chapter to refer to group-level symbols, rituals, beliefs, and values through which collective identity is expressed. I use the term *group identification* or *collective identification* (Klandermans and Weerd 2000) to refer to individual-level use of symbols, participation in rituals, and values and beliefs that reflect an individual's appropriation of a collective identity—what it means to an individual to belong to a group and how he or she includes the collective identity as part of his or her definition of self (see also Snow and McAdam 2000).

sense of solidarity, but it produces a common understanding of a group's experiences, one that attributes shared discontents to structural, cultural, or systemic causes rather than to personal failings or individualized circumstances (Gamson 1992a; Taylor and Van Willigen 1996).

Because individuals could have potentially unlimited interpretations of the social world, social movement actors are conventionally viewed as playing an active role in providing interpretive frameworks that orient people toward specific shared understandings of their circumstances—emphasizing particular injustices, attributing responsibility for the injustices to specific actors, and proposing collective solutions. The feminist consciousness-raising groups of the 1970s are perhaps the best known example of a movement strategy for bridging individual "personal" grievances with structural "political" explanations for women's experiences (Evans 1979; Ferree and Hess 2000). In the decades after World War II, women struggled with a growing cognitive dissonance between prevailing social ideals about femininity, marriage, and motherhood, and their actual experiences as women, wives, and mothers (Evans 1979; Rosen 2000). In small, loosely structured "rap groups" or "consciousness-raising groups," women began to discuss the sources of their dissatisfaction: Why did men enjoy more leisure time? Why did employers pay women less than men for the same work? Why did schools steer girls toward teaching and nursing? (Rosen 2000). The consciousness-raising process was a multi-step discussion in which women first spoke about their personal experiences and then brought their individual experiences into a larger discussion, linking them to societal forces rather than to personal factors. Finally, members of these groups attempted to relate their analyses to other theories of oppression.[2]

In social movement analyses, the process of "consciousness-raising" is understood as more than discovering that one's individual grievances are shared by a larger group; the key is developing explanations for collective grievances that attribute blame to specific groups or institutions whose interests are in opposition to one's own. The move from "us and them" to "us against them" is thus understood as an analytically significant step in politicization because it both positions groups in an adversarial relationship

2. Verta Taylor and Marieke Van Willigan (1996) have observed similar processes of collective identification in the self-help groups of the postpartum support and breast cancer movements. In both movements, participants used "survivor narratives," or public testimony, to transform their private experiences into public events and to normalize experiences widely regarded as deviant. Borrowing from the women's health movement of the 1970s, movement actors deliberately placed women's experiences in a larger feminist framework that identified their illnesses as an injustice linked to gender inequality (see also Taylor 1996).

and specifies causal attribution: "we" understand "them" as benefiting from or being responsible for a collectively defined injustice (Gamson 1992a).[3]

Theories of collective identity offer an important framework for thinking about the concrete processes by which people might reimagine their personal struggles with long-term care as political issues. But because our theoretical insights on the relationship between collective identity and politicization have largely been premised on research about social movements, we know very little about how collective identity works to politicize individuals in contexts outside the arena of social movement contestation. In the case of long-term care, there are few obvious targets to blame for the problems faced by contemporary American families. It is difficult, for example, to hold anyone accountable for the increasing ranks of the "oldest-old," those eighty-five and older that require intensive levels of personal care, or for the geographic dispersion of American families that makes care provision more difficult, or for the fact that most women today work outside the home. As Stephen McConnell, Senior Vice President for Public Policy and Advocacy at the Alzheimer's Association, observed in an interview, "We don't have any real obvious enemies in this process."

In the case of long-term care, the "opposition"—or that which is being challenged though collective identification—is not a specific blameworthy opponent, but an ideology that assigns exclusive responsibility for care provision to the family. This raises particular challenges with respect to collective identification. Past research suggests that family care providers are generally reluctant to view themselves as part of a larger group or constituency. In one of the few surveys conducted with a nationally representative sample on the issue of caregiver self-identification, the AARP found that nearly half (45%) of survey respondents who were providing care for a relative or friend with a disability or chronic disease would not identify themselves as caregivers (Kutner 2001).

---

3. This relationship between collective identification and politicization has been observed not only in cases of explicit human domination, but also in challenges to more subtle structures of power. A number of movements, for example, have politicized in-group/out-group dynamics by using experiential knowledge to directly challenge dominant or conventional forms of knowledge. The AIDS movement (Epstein 1996), for example, as well as movements around postpartum depression and breast cancer (Taylor and Van Willigen 1996) have all drawn on shared personal experiences to challenge scientific knowledge systems. Battered women and survivors of rape or incest have similarly relied on shared experiences to challenge legal and medical understandings of sexual violence (see generally Taylor 1996). In all of these cases, politicization is understood as occurring through the same "us against them" dichotomy found in more traditional conflict movements: survivors use their shared status as "lay experts" to challenge "experts" whose scientific or legal interpretations of social problems fail to accurately incorporate the perspectives of those with lived experience.

Part of this reluctance can be attributed to longstanding cultural norms regarding family responsibility for care: the belief in "handling" the issue within the family, and the fear and guilt of being viewed as a "bad" son or daughter or deficient spouse for seeking assistance with caring for a loved one, all reinforce an understanding of caregiving as a private and individual, rather than public or social responsibility (Abel 1991; Brody 2004). In addition, the stigma of dependency in American culture (Fraser and Gordon 1994) adds to family pressure to keep the loss of independence and disability associated with chronic illness within the privacy of the home.

But there is also a more subtle way in which the ideology of family responsibility impedes collective identification. Because the caregiving role often evolves out of a preexisting familial role—husband or wife, daughter or son—caregiving is generally considered a "natural" extension of these family roles (O'Connor 1999). It is only when the demands of caregiving have transitioned well beyond the responsibilities typically associated with being a partner or adult child that family care providers will identify as "caregivers," if at all (Montgomery and Kosloski 2001). The imbrication of the family and caregiving roles means that identification as a caregiver is not simply a matter of identifying with a larger group of similarly situated people, but about acknowledging a significant, and emotionally difficult, transition in the relationship between the caregiver and care receiver.

Spousal caregiving, for example, typically emerges out of a reciprocal relationship where two people have made a personal and legal commitment to care for one another. When a dependency situation emerges in such a relationship, it is often difficult for spousal caregivers to discern changes in the nature of the relationship, as caregiving is almost always part of the spousal role (Montgomery and Kosloski 2001).[4] By contrast, caregiving by adult children often involves a significant change in the very nature of their relationship to their parents. After a lifetime of being "dependent" on parents for support, assisting a parent typically represents a dramatic role shift for adult children. Because this transition is far more noticeable for adult children, they are more likely to identify as "caregivers"—and to identify earlier in the caregiving process—than spousal caregivers (Montgomery

---

4. Notably, while gender norms may make it more likely that care responsibilities will fall on women than men, they do not necessarily make it easier for men to discern the onset of a "caregiving" role. Male and female spouses are quite similar in their tendency to view caring for a sick or disabled partner as a logical extension of the marital relationship; both males and females understand being a "good" husband or wife to involve taking care of one's partner "in sickness and in health" (O'Connor 1999). Caregiving frequently involves a reordering in the gendered household division of labor, regardless of which spouse is sick. But even when caregiving involves new tasks for a spouse, those tasks are still viewed as part of the spousal role.

and Kosloski 2001). But in both cases, the "boundary" in the case of long-term care is less about drawing a distinction between "us" and "them," than it is about recognizing this transition in the relationship between the caregiver and the care receiver.

PROCESSES OF COLLECTIVE IDENTIFICATION
The Cultural Production of the "Caregiver" Identity

The notion of caregivers as a group or constituency did not emerge in public discourse until relatively recently. In the late 1970s, a small group of families who had experienced the struggles of contemporary long-term care provision came together with community leaders in San Francisco to organize the first supportive services for families providing chronic care. While these families were dealing with very different diagnoses, they confronted many of the same frustrations: lack of information, few community resources, isolation, and a lack of "fit" with traditional health systems. In 1977 they organized the first community-based nonprofit organization in the country to address the needs of families providing long-term care. Their efforts eventually led to the creation of the first statewide program of assistance for family caregivers in 1984,[5] and sparked the beginnings of a national movement to recognize the contributions of family members in caring for the elderly and ill.

Beginning in the early 1990s, a spate of newly founded national caregiver advocacy organizations,[6] together with existing social service providers, began a concerted effort to increase public awareness of family caregiving issues in the United States. Virtually all these advocacy organizations were founded by caregivers or former caregivers who had been deeply politicized by their experiences providing care and who shared with service providers frustration with how little attention the issue of long-term care received in American public discourse. As these advocacy organizations and social service providers sought to make visible the challenges of care provision for contemporary American families, they increasingly settled on the vocabulary of caregiving to describe the hands-on physical assistance

---

5. In 1984, California enacted the Comprehensive Act for Family Caregivers of Brain-Impaired Adults, which established the statewide California Caregiver Resource Center (CRC) system under the California Department of Mental Health—the first of its kind in the nation.

6. The National Family Caregivers Association was founded in 1993. The National Alliance for Caregiving was created in 1996. And in 2001, the National Center on Caregiving was formed to advance the development of programs and policies for caregivers in all fifty states.

and emotional and financial support historically performed by spouses and children for their family members.

The terminology caught on quickly. Until 1997, the term "caregiver" could not be found in any English language dictionary (Goldman 2002:3). The occurrence of the term in headlines of U.S. newspapers and magazines in the five-year period from 1996–2001 was more than three times that found in the period from 1990–1995 (Kutner 2001). Today websites, magazines, and mass-marketed self-help books all rely on the discourse of "caregiving" to talk about issues relating to care provision for family members suffering from chronic illnesses, injuries, or consequences of old age. Similarly, local, state, and national advocacy organizations as well as social service providers—including city and county service agencies, adult day care centers, senior centers, in-home care services, and legal services organizations—all promote their programs and services in the discourse of caregiving. In Los Angeles, the site of this study, fliers advertising workshops, classes, support groups, and care consultation for family care providers illustrate the emphasis on caregiving terminology:

Taking Care of You: Powerful Tools for Caregivers

    (Flier advertising 6-week class sponsored by the LA Caregiver Resource Center)

This Day's For You—Caregiver Wellness Day

    (Flier advertising 1-day conference sponsored by Alzheimer's Association)

For You, The Caregiver, We Offer.... Individual counseling, weekly support groups...

    (Advertisement in newsletter put out by Wise Adult Day Service Center)

48 Hour Caregiver Retreats

    (Flier advertising retreat sponsored by LA County Area Agency on Aging and the LA Caregiver Resource Center)

Caregiving: A brief guide to the healthcare benefits, legal options and support services available to caregivers and their loved ones.

    (Educational brochure published by Bet Tzedek Legal Services)

But even as LA social service providers draw on the vocabulary of caregiving to publicize their programs, they widely acknowledge that the caregiver identity is *not* one with which most families resonate. Ann Hammond, president of a coalition of Los Angeles County adult day service centers, put it this way:

A lot of the people are out there giving care to their loved ones who do not identify as caregivers. And so if they see a caregiver support group...they're clueless....And that's something the coalition struggles with, it's something that each [day care] center struggles with. How do we market? We know that there's a body of people out there who need our services. How do we reach them?

Acknowledging the problem of nonidentification among potential beneficiaries, service providers in Los Angeles, including the City's Department
of Aging, have hired marketing and public relations firms to devise strategies for reaching family care providers who have not identified as caregivers.[7] The LA Caregiver Resource Center and Alzheimer's Association have
both produced brochures, for example, that ask whether the reader helps
a family member with any of the tasks in a checklist of activities (e.g., "Do
you do shopping for a family member?"). The brochure indicates that if the
reader has checked "yes" to two or more of the listed tasks, then he or she is
a caregiver. Donna Benton, Director of the LA Caregiver Resource Center:

> [W]hy is it important to understand this word? Why do you use the word *caregiver*?
> Because... if you don't know the magic word, which is called *caregiver*, you may be miss-
> ing out on benefits for you as a caregiver. So while we understand that you just consider
> yourself a spouse or parent or you're just the daughter, you know, doing what you nor-
> mally do, there's this other word called *caregiver*. So it's... very much through education
> and always defining, giving the operational definition.

Both the LA Caregiver Resource Center and the Alzheimer's Association
take pains to distribute their literature in a wide variety of settings: senior
centers, churches, health fairs, doctor's offices, hair salons, laundromats, and
employer assistance programs and other work settings. The LA Department
of Aging arranged with the Department of Water & Power to include a brochure on social services with monthly electric bills for all city residents.
Similarly, the Alzheimer's Association routinely purchases air time on talk
radio stations in Los Angeles to increase public awareness about the disease
and its caregiver support programs.

But resistance to identifying as "caregivers" in many cases has very little to do with definitional confusion about caregiving; it is instead rooted
in deeply held cultural beliefs about family responsibilities for care. The
caregiver identity constructed by social services, caregiver advocates, and
popular magazines and books in many ways challenges these traditional
understandings of family caregiving by characterizing caregivers as making
a public or social contribution. Emphasizing care provision as an essential component of our modern health and long-term care system, with
care responsibilities—and costs—far more significant than families in the
United States have ever faced before, caregiving discourse portrays families
as performing a valuable service that is entitled to public recognition and

7. In 2001, the National Family Caregivers Association and the National Alliance for
Caregiving jointly commissioned a marketing firm to conduct "message testing" of various
materials for a nationwide public education program.

support. Kathleen Kelly, Executive Director of Family Caregiver Alliance, captures this in a 2006 news release (Family Caregiver Alliance 2006):

> Families are the mainstay of our long-term care system, with nearly 80% of long-term care provided in the home, not in institutions. That care includes everything from cooking meals to changing feeding tubes, from dispensing medications to managing incontinence. Were families to cease providing this care, the enormous burden placed on our healthcare system would be crippling. We need to respect and honor not only the staggering dollar value of the care these families provide, but also their dedication to the challenging and sometimes exhausting job of caring for their loved ones.

This understanding of care as a key component of the U.S. health care system differs markedly from longstanding cultural norms about care as exclusively a family problem. The former justifies the need for public support of families providing long-term care while the latter relegates the costs of care provision to the private or domestic sphere. The social service sector plays a key role in bridging these two paradigms for understanding care provision. While the goal of social workers in using caregiver discourse is simply to encourage families to utilize available social services, they rely on strategies of discursive integration that facilitate the process of politicization.

Distinguishing Between Family Roles and Care Work

For individuals with deeply held beliefs in the ideology of family responsibility for care, the first stage of politicization requires a fundamental transformation in how one thinks about one's relationship to the care receiver and the duties of care. Indeed, many family care providers require such a transformation simply to be able to seek help from caregiver supportive services such as in-home health care, adult day care, and respite care. Social workers rely on two themes—the principles of self-care and self-advocacy—to provide family caregivers with a way of consciously distinguishing between one's responsibilities as a family member and one's role as caregiver. By characterizing long-term care provision as work that is above and beyond the "normal" obligations of a partner or child, as something that can be shared or purchased rather than just "what you do" for family, caregiving discourse validates and makes visible the efforts of family care providers, while at the same time recasting caregivers as performing a valuable public service.

Because individuals typically begin caring for a spouse or parent as a natural extension of their familial role, there are strong emotional reasons— love, obligation, grief, fear—for not only assuming care responsibilities, but in many cases prioritizing the needs of the care receiver over their own, even when the burden of care affects their own physical and emotional health. Rachael,[8] a support group facilitator, spoke about this issue from her own personal experience caring for her father.

> My biggest issue as a caregiver for not wanting to hire somebody [to help] was that this is what I needed to do. That I had taken this job on, and if I got help for it, then I was some-how failing and letting my father down....And then when I started to feel like I needed the help, I resisted it because my father didn't want to have anybody else other than me....And there's a part of you that feels wonderful for being needed in that way, and there's that part of you that feels completely strangled.

Bethany Williams and Elizabeth Foster, support group co-facilitators and licensed family counselors, noted that clients often describe themselves as losing their sense of self in the caregiving role. "[A]ll of a sudden their entire focus...is on the person they're taking care of. And they get lost in the midst of it," Williams observed. Foster agreed: "One of my clients gave me...a picture of a woman with a paper bag over her head, because she said that's how I feel. Like she had lost herself, because she had become a caregiver. That's really a recurring theme, I find. That they feel like they don't have a life anymore." Gender norms in the United States—which often socialize women to defer to the needs of others and to derive their sense of self through relations with others—make women more susceptible to this loss of self than men, and it is generally more common to see women struggling with the ability to establish clear and identifiable boundaries in caregiving than men (cf. O'Connor 1999). But it is important to emphasize that men also wrestle with the demands of meeting their perceived obligations as "good" husbands and sons, and in this study most of the male caregivers struggled with being "on call" around the clock in the same way as their female counterparts.

Because so many caregivers feel guilty or selfish for taking time to do things for themselves, a common strategy for convincing caregivers to consider sharing care responsibilities is to frame self care as being good for the care receiver (cf, MacDonald and Merrill 2002). The following excerpt from a chapter on "Taking Care of You" in *The Caregiver Helpbook* (Schmall et al. 2000), a textbook accompanying a six-week caregiving class offered by the LA Caregiver Resource Center, captures this theme well:

> When you board an airplane, the flight attendant gives several safety instructions. One of them is, "If oxygen masks drop down, put on your own oxygen mask first before helping

---

8. The names of support group facilitators are all pseudonyms to protect the identity of caregiver participants.

others." This is because if you don't take care of yourself first, you may not be able to help those who need your help. It's the same thing with caregiving. When you take care of yourself, everyone benefits. Ignoring your own needs is not only potentially detrimental to you, but it can also be harmful to the person who depends on you.

To emphasize the importance of seeking help with care provision, support group facilitators and participants frequently cite statistics about the impact of caregiving stress on the health of family caregivers. One often-referenced study of older spousal caregivers (aged 66–96), for example, found that caregivers who experience caregiving-related stress have a 63% higher mortality rate than non-caregivers of the same age (Schulz and Beach 1999). Diane Roselli, a social worker and facilitator of a caregiver support group at an adult day care center, noted that she often points to such studies as a way of persuading caregivers to seek outside help.

> I give them...a healthy dose of fear [laughs]. I know that sounds terrible, but it's the reality. It's the reality because they're going to burn out and they're going to come down with debilitating illnesses before their loved ones do. And so I tell them that....[T]he effects of stress are going to take you out before the effects of the dementia are going to take out your loved one.... It's really hard. There's a lot resistance there.

Social workers observed that support group participation is a particularly effective way of overcoming the resistance to seeking help with caregiving, as the group provides a space for caregivers to reinforce the principle of self-care through experiential knowledge. As Roselli observed:

> I can tell them...your health is going to go downhill, and this, that, and the other, but that only holds a little bit of weight. But when they hear other people in similar situations...just seeing other people walking through the same experiences and people saying you know, "I was terrified to leave my husband at home, but I did it."...Then they see it's within their grasp.

The following interaction between Nancy, a new participant, and the rest of her cancer support group illustrates how the principle of self-care is often communicated and reinforced by sharing experiential knowledge. Nancy had confided to the group that the stress of caring for her mother had begun to take its toll on her health.

NANCY: I'm Italian and my family comes first, and it just kills me that I can't be there. But yet when I go up there, I want to kill her. And I can't yell at her because she'll say don't yell at me, I've got cancer. And my dad is just overwhelmed.

MIGUEL: I hear that you are trying to fix them all.

NANCY: You just want to help!

MIGUEL: You need to take care of yourself first. We collapse otherwise. We think it's selfish and that we're being bad, but it's one of the many things I learned here. If I'm not balanced, I'm going to say fuck it and walk out.

...

RHODA: You're in the beginning stages. I'm going through it again, just listening! I was exactly like you. I felt all of it—the frustration, the anger, the pain, the crying.

FRANK: The helplessness.

RHODA: It does get better. You learn how to deal with it.... I quit my job to take care of [my husband]. He had his esophagus removed, which is a very, very invasive surgery. He spent five months on a feeding tube. The stress was just unbelievable. You feel like you have to hold up him, me, my kids. You have to take care of yourself.

The principle of self-care—articulated at least once in virtually every support group meeting in this study and always emphasized with new participants—was typically accompanied by a related principle of self-advocacy. Social workers—as well as support group participants—emphasized that reaching out for help was not only a way to preserve one's emotional and physical well-being, but it was a way to increase one's sense of personal efficacy in a context in which one typically has very little control. A brochure entitled "Choosing to Take Charge of Your Life: A Self-Advocacy Message for Family Caregivers," published by the National Family Caregiver Association, captures this message well:

> Obviously you cannot control everything that happens to you or to your loved one. But even though you don't have that power, you do have the power to make active choices about how you are going to deal with the caregiving circumstances of your life.

Social service agencies reinforced this principle by providing a wide range of classes, workshops, and informational brochures on communicating effectively with health care professionals and insurance companies; tips for hiring home help, financial planning, information on applying for public benefits; and legal advice on power of attorney for health care, durable power of attorney, conservatorships, wills and trusts, and nursing home rights. All of these resources were designed to equip caregivers with the skills to be advocates for themselves and their family members and to make educated choices about how, and under what conditions, they provide care.

The following support group interaction illustrates how facilitators and caregiver-identified individuals reinforced the twin principles of self-care and self-advocacy. When Myra first joined her dementia support group at the start of the study, she was quite visibly at a breaking point, describing herself as frustrated, resentful, and angry about her caregiving situation. In this exchange, other support group participants take her to task for not making active decisions to improve her care situation:

CAROLYN: We make decisions about our lives. You know how to. You have the skills…but you're not using those skills to change your situation. You've forgotten how to do for yourself. So how do you get yourself out of that loop?

MYRA: That's such a good question.

CAROLYN: We have this tendency to keep stirring the same pot of shit. The past is over, it's dead. You need to come up with something to do right now!

MYRA: Being in charge suited me fine. I consider myself a strong person. I'm used to making the decisions.

REBA: But you don't know how to take care of yourself.

FACILITATOR: Did anyone come here knowing that?

(Everyone shakes their head "no.")

FACILITATOR: It's a process.

The implicit message in encouraging new caregivers to get themselves "out of that loop" was the importance of seeking help from supportive services in the community and/or health care professionals. As Carolyn later advised Myra, "These are things that make us grow up! You don't know what you can do! Unless you want to crawl into the grave after your husband, *take care of yourself.*"

Over the four-month observation period, every support group in the study witnessed at least one example of a new participant who sought assistance from formal supportive services and returned to the group newly converted to the philosophy of self-care. Clarice's experience is typical in this regard. Having previously cared for her parents, she was now caring for her husband, who was 86 and suffering from dementia. At her first support group meeting, she shared her frustrations about taking care of her husband and her reservations about seeking help:

I'm very angry. By the time this ends, I'll be an old lady. My years will be have been spent taking care of people. People suggest hiring someone, but I can't. I'm not working. What would I tell my husband?

Other members of the group encouraged her to bring someone in for just a couple days a week. She explained that she didn't want to offend her husband and that she felt guilty leaving him: "I know I only have so many years left with my husband. Why see some mediocre movie? I want to be with *him*." But at the next support group meeting, Clarice admitted that the discussion had really affected her:

> I hated my husband, I hated my life, I hated the disease. I think I realized that I had lost my life. And I was very angry. So I made a big list and I started getting my life back.... I hired somebody I know to come to the house twice a week. I told her I don't know yet what you're going to do, but I feel like I need someone there so I can be removed one step from everything. I need to be out there doing things.

By framing self-care and self-advocacy as strategies for taking better care of their family members, caregiving discourse validates caregivers' need or desire to provide good care for their partners or parents, but it also recasts care provision as something that can be legitimately shared or purchased. In effect, caregiving discourse encourages care providers to see certain aspects of care provision as work, rather than "just something one does" for family. This was a critical transition in the process of politicization not because caregivers imputed market value to their carework,[9] but because in identifying care activities that could be shared or purchased, they consciously distinguished between their responsibilities as family members and their role as caregivers.

This can perhaps best be seen by comparing how non-identified family care providers and caregiver-identified providers described their caregiving roles. Family care providers who did not identify as "caregivers" typically made no distinction between their familial and caregiving roles. Asked directly whether they identified with the term "caregiver," these respondents gave answers such as:

> I think of it as she's my mother.... [T]aking care of her is like taking care of me. And there's no difference. There's not a caregiving situation.
>
> Being married is like caregiver's written in there. So I guess that's about it.
>
> No, I'm just his wife, you know?
>
> I'm more than a caregiver. I'm their only daughter. I'm their everything.

---

9. There is a significant literature on the commodification of carework that addresses issues relating to the market valuation of care. These works include critiques of the tendency to dichotomize the realms of love and money (Folbre and Nelson 2000; Nelson and England 2002; Zelizer 2005); concerns about what happens to care—and workers—when it becomes commodified (Boris and Klein 2012; Glenn 2000; Hochschild 1983; Nelson 1999); the relationships between paid care and racial/ethnic and class inequality (Duffy 2011; Glenn 2010); and more recently, the global consequences of the market for paid care as women from poor countries leave their own families to work as care providers in richer countries (Ehrenreich and Hochschild 2002; Hochschild 2003; Hondagneu-Sotelo 2001).

By contrast, self-identified caregivers explicitly associated their identification as caregivers with a disassociation from their familial role. Gabriela, who at the time of this study was caring for her husband, was typical in this regard:

> I took care of my mom. My mom had cancer. Okay, I took care of her 'til the end. My dad had Lou Gherig's disease, and I just figured it was part of my duty. And there again, when my husband started...I thought oh, I'm home, I'll stop working...that's my duty. So I just figured it was a duty. And not until the [support group] did it make me aware. Now, it's not my [duty], you know...I'm a caregiver! Yeah!

Similarly, Doris was asked when she began associating with the term "caregiver." She replied:

> Probably when I started the [support] group. Prior to that he was my husband. These were things you did. These were things you put up with.

The transition to thinking of oneself as a caregiver was difficult for many people to make, and new support group participants often struggled with the process openly. Kathrina, for example, a caregiver to her stepfather who had Alzheimer's, was a new member of one of the support groups in the study. Asked in an interview if she associated with the term *caregiver*, she replied:

> I'm still struggling with the term "caregiver." I mean, is a parent with a three-year-old and a five-year-old a caregiver?...Or if you have a five-year-old and say he's got cancer. Do you become then a caregiver instead of a mother? I don't know.

By characterizing long-term care provision as work that is above and beyond the "normal" obligations of a partner or adult child, caregiving discourse validates the efforts of family care providers: it makes visible those tasks that are often discounted by family care providers as "just something one does" for a family member. But it also demarcates a distinction between one's familial role and one's role as a care provider. In this way, caregiving discourse serves as a paradigmatic example of discursive integration: it synthesizes two models for understanding the responsibilities of care by affirming the belief in taking care of one's own, while also introducing a more publicly-oriented understanding of care, one in which caregivers are seen as performing a valuable service that is entitled to both recognition and community support.

To understand and adopt the values and beliefs about care provision embodied in the caregiver group identity, individuals typically required

Table 3.1. RELATIONSHIP BETWEEN GROUP IDENTIFICATION AND SUPPORT GROUP
PARTICIPATION (N=79)

	Group Identified Caregivers	Non-Group Identified Caregivers
Support Group Participation	51	15
No Support Group Participation	1	12

sustained contact with caregiver discourse. Here the design of the study becomes important, as one could argue that by recruiting primarily—but not exclusively—on the basis of support group participation, the study introduces a selection bias: people who join support groups may already be more politicized than people who don't join. But the key variable in this analysis is the extent of contact with supportive services, where caregiver discourse is primarily deployed. Support group participants varied in the degree to which they had made contact with supportive services. Some support group participants, for example, were new to caregiving and had had very little experience with supportive services. In spite of their participation in a support group, these caregivers did not yet identify with the caregiver identity. By tracing the length and form of contact caregivers had with social services, it was evident that care providers who were more familiar with caregiver discourse were correspondingly more likely to collectively identify as family caregivers. It is thus exposure to caregiving discourse, rather than a preexisting predisposition toward political activity, that explains the importance of support group participation in politicizing caregivers in this case.

As Table 3.1 above illustrates, of the 79 caregivers in the study's interview sample, 52 identified with the caregiver group identity.[10]

All but one of these caregivers were regular attendees of a support group who retrospectively attributed their group identification to support group participation or other regular contact with social services. For example, at the time of her interview, Mary, a relatively new caregiver for both of her parents, had attended a support group for about two months. She attributed her identification with the caregiver identity—and the transformation in how she understood the responsibilities of caregiving—to her recent participation in the support group:

10. This analysis is based on the coding of all references in fieldnotes and focus group and interview transcripts to "identity," including references that indicated solidarity with or membership in a larger group (e.g., "we", "people like us"), and instances of self-identification as caregivers. I also coded exchanges between group members (typically new group members) and/or the facilitators about "who is a caregiver" and what being a caregiver "means."

You know, I used to think we're the kids and that's just the way it is, and now I use that term [caregiver] a lot.... Up until this, I never thought about it. I thought, well, we'll just take care of them the best we can, however that is. And do what we need to do.

Of the 27 interview respondents who did *not* identify with the caregiver identity, more than half (17) had never attended a support group or participated in any significant way in social service programs or classes or they had only recently made contact with supportive services.[11] The remaining 10 respondents were caring for family members who were institutionalized or did not otherwise need a lot of physical care. These so-called "secondary caregivers" often expressed ambivalence about whether they were "really" caregivers at all, and were much less likely to group-identify.[12]

If caregivers' retrospective accounts tell us something about when they began to identify as caregivers, we still need to understand how collective identification actually politicizes family caregivers. How, in other words, do caregiver-identified individuals come to reinterpret deeply held beliefs in family responsibility for care as an issue appropriate for policy intervention?

THE ROLE OF COLLECTIVE IDENTIFICATION IN POLITICIZATION

Because processes of group identification in this case take place primarily in social services— where professional, legal, and organizational norms often proscribe overt "political" activity— there were few, if any, actors in social services to help link individual problems to structural or sociocultural causes. But if political consciousness-raising was not the stated goal of social service providers, processes of group identification occurring in the social service context nevertheless produced many of the same effects as more conventional political consciousness-raising efforts: they (1) emphasized similarities in the experiences of family care providers, (2) reframed individual care dilemmas as problems shared by caregivers as a group, and (3) highlighted the underlying structural or cultural factors which make long-term care provision difficult for many families. These processes ultimately produced strong normative expectations among caregivers for long-term care policy reform.

11. New support group participants had attended three or fewer meetings.

12. Most social workers and service providers do characterize people who have institutionalized their family members as caregivers. See Chapter 2 for a discussion of the caregiving responsibilities that persist even after institutionalization.

First, identification as a caregiver involved recognizing commonalities among family care providers. As Suzanne Mintz of the National Family Caregiver Association observed: "Sure, there are differences if you're a single mom caring for a kid with some congenital thing that you can't even pronounce, or if you're caring for your dad with Alzheimer's disease. The day-to-day things are different, but the emotional issues are the same. The difficulties in dealing with unresponsive systems [are] the same." For many caregivers in this study, one of the most memorable moments of joining a support group was the discovery that other people were experiencing similar problems. Gabriela, who was caring for her husband, recounted the first time she attended a support group meeting:

> When I first went in there I was a basket case. I mean, just hearing everybody share what was going on? I just started to cry. I just thought, my god! I'm not in this alone! We're all in the same boat, one way or another, you know?

Jackie recalled that she did not consider herself a caregiver for her husband, nor did she realize how stressful her care situation had become, until an acquaintance convinced her to attend a support group meeting at the LA Caregiver Resource Center.

> I really wasn't that interested. But I did go to the meeting. And I laughed when I told [my friend], I said I didn't know I had a problem until I went to that meeting! I'm doing the same thing they're doing!

Despite the fact that care providers were often dealing with different diseases[13] and levels of dependency, and despite often dramatic disparities in access to resources and support networks, caregivers repeatedly emphasized the similarities in their experiences: "I'm amazed that even though we might have nine or ten people at a meeting," observed one man, caring for his wife, "all of us have different problems, yet they're all related."

Small-group solidarity, of course, is different from a sense of belonging to a larger collectivity or constituency, and it is here that a second aspect of group identification with the caregiver identity played an important role in shifting participants' consciousness from the individual to the collective level: support group participants' use of caregiving discourse generalized the dilemmas of family care providers. Thus, in addition to emphasizing the commonalities among individual support

---

13. While dementia is most frequently associated with Alzheimer's disease, it is also associated with Parkinson's disease, vascular disorders, strokes, head injuries, infections, drug use, and nutritional deficiencies.

group participants, caregiving discourse portrayed caregiving problems as endemic to all people occupying this structural position. Support group facilitators, for example, typically responded to individual problems raised in the group by recasting them as problems common to all caregivers as a group:

> It's common for you and for all caregivers to stop taking care of yourself.
>
> As caregivers, how do we deal with that?
>
> It's important for caregivers to realize that whatever you're giving is good enough.

The following support group interaction illustrates how participants and the facilitator together recast one individual's situation as a collective problem: Doris was caring for her husband, whose Alzheimer's had made him both paranoid and extremely combative. Two months into the observation period, she was hospitalized with a bleeding ulcer. When she returned to the group and described what had happened, participants around the table cried out: "That's the stress!" and "That's from caregiving!" The facilitator waited for things to quiet down and then said to the group: "See how she puts herself last because she's caring for her husband? *That's what caregivers do.*"

By identifying with caregivers as a group, participants were able to extrapolate from their personal experiences with the health care system, supportive services, or government entitlement programs to see their experiences as common to anyone trying to provide care for a family member with a chronic disease or disability. Carolyn's description of trying to obtain disability benefits for her husband is typical:

> You know, you fill out those forms and you're trying to figure out, I mean they're so difficult! And you think how could a person, for instance, who *doesn't* have a master's degree or *doesn't* speak [English], how do they do these things? How do they? I would think that they just give up. It is so complicated.

Such expressions of solidarity with other caregivers were common among group-identified participants, and reinforced an understanding of caregiving problems as collective grievances.

Finally, by recasting individual problems as problems common to caregivers generally, group identification highlighted the structural or sociocultural factors that made long-term care so difficult. "The point is, it doesn't have to be this hard," observed former caregiver and President of the National Family Caregiver Association Susanne Mintz. "It's hard. It'll always be hard. But it doesn't have to be this bloody hard. And one of the reasons it's so bloody hard is because the systems are just not set up to be friendly to caregiving families.... It's not you, it's *it*."

The relationship between collective identification and recognition of underlying systemic problems was striking in this study. Caregiver-identified participants were much more likely than non-identified care providers to attribute long-term care dilemmas to structural or sociocultural problems rather than individual failings. Of the fifty-two respondents interviewed who expressed a clear identification with caregivers as a group, all but one identified institutional or cultural factors that exacerbated the difficulties of providing long-term care. Some focused on the fragmentation of long-term care services and information or on changing demographics, such as increased longevity, the rising number of single parent families, and the increasing number of adults in the paid labor force, while others emphasized social values—such as lack of respect for the elderly— the high costs of health care in the United States, and misplaced government priorities. By contrast, of the twenty-seven interview subjects who did *not* identify with caregivers as a group, only five attributed their caregiving problems to structural or sociocultural rather than individual conditions. This number drops to three when caregivers who worked in the health professions—and who explicitly attributed their structural understanding of long-term care problems to their work—are removed from the sample of non-identified care providers.

In striking contrast to these institutional and sociocultural explanations for caregiving dilemmas, family care providers who did *not* collectively identify as caregivers largely attributed their caregiving problems to their own personal or family circumstances. As a result, they rarely considered how other families could be similarly affected or how their care provision problems might be redressed through public policy. Linda, for example, was caring for her mother, who had been diagnosed with Alzheimer's. A full-time professional, Linda depended on adult day care to be able to continue working. Her comments on the affordability of adult day care are typical of family care providers who did not identify with caregivers as a group.

> I'll tell you, if my brother weren't paying the bills, I couldn't afford [day care]. I just don't know what I would do. I wouldn't be able to help. I wouldn't be able to help take care of my mother.... You know, I really don't mind paying, but their price is so high, that it's really beyond what I can pay. You know? I would never ask somebody else to pay my bill for me, but this, this has me over a barrel. If my brother were not taking care of this, I would be so out of luck.

The individualized way in which non-identified care providers spoke about caregiving problems contrasts sharply with those identified as caregivers. When family care providers saw their problems as common to caregivers as a group, they were much more likely to articulate expectations for policy intervention. Toni, a caregiver-identified participant caring for both her parents, struggled with many of the same issues regarding the affordability of day care as Linda, but she explicitly framed those issues as matters of public policy:

> My feeling is...that the government knows that the Alzheimer's people can bring down the health services in America. I said that to my husband from the beginning, I said I know they're going to...be pushing for Americans to keep these people at home....But there's no facilities! I mean it's just unconscionable that the government is not running [Alzheimer's day care facilities]....They run [children's] day care, and Alzheimer's care is needed just as much as [children's] day care....There's a very real need for quality day care with Alzheimer's patients.

Similar patterns in the ways caregivers spoke about care dilemmas could be seen in comments about a wide range of long-term care issues, such as respite care:

> *Not Caregiver Identified:* Respite care never was an issue for me because I just felt that it was part of my job, and I never looked upon you know, I need to get away from my mother.

> *Caregiver Identified:* I think [respite] should be incorporated in any MediCal or senior, elderly health care plan. A choice of getting some kind of respite and good care for them while you are getting respite. I think that's so important. I see it so much right now, that the caregiver needs an outlet. And it's not available to you. It's not readily available to you....And if it is, you can't afford it, probably.

Caregivers' observations about eligibility for state Medicaid benefits illustrates a similar pattern:

> *Not Caregiver Identified:* Well it wasn't until my mother was destitute that I was able to tap into any government resources. And I felt that you know, I really needed help prior to that because I just had to wait until she had nothing left to qualify. And I spent a lot of sleepless nights worrying that you know, I'd have to spend everything she had on a nursing home.

> *Caregiver Identified:* I don't think it's fair that the government should expect its citizens to be drained of everything they've acquired until they are reduced to the house they live in, a car to drive, and $19,000 in the bank. Big deal....You're now at a poverty level.

With regard to each caregiving issue, most non-caregiver-identified participants spoke of their caregiving problems in terms that reflected hegemonic
norms about long-term care provision as a private, family responsibility. By
contrast, most caregiver-identified participants not only spoke of each issue
as a group problem, but they expressed a normative expectation that the
problem was appropriate for policy intervention.

Caregiver-identified participants were also more likely than non-
caregiver-identified participants to describe themselves as performing a
vital social contribution, saving the government and health insurance companies money by caring for their family members at home. This was often
articulated in discussions about California's Medicaid program (known
as Medi-Cal), which provides long-term care benefits to the very poor.
"The alternative [to family caregiving] is that they go on Medi-Cal and
then they're paid for," observed one caregiver. "So you're actually doing a
social service by taking care of your own people." By caring for their family members at home rather than institutionalizing them—and, implicitly,
turning to Medicaid for financial assistance—these caregivers saw themselves as deserving some form of public support. As one caregiver, Isadore,
observed:

> I think basically caregiving needs help. If you're really thinking about people placing
> their loved ones in nursing homes and you're talking about [$50,000] on up to $70,000
> a year, and the states are paying for this through one way or another, isn't it far better to
> allocate moneys into the system to compensate caregivers themselves up to a mere frac-
> tion of what [the state would otherwise pay]?[14]

Others inverted this argument: rather than articulating the ways in which
family caregivers saved society money, they emphasized the ways in which
caregivers, when not sufficiently supported, cost society money. Janet, who
retired early on her doctor's advice after the stress of caring for both her
parents made her ill, observed that it would benefit the U.S. population generally if caregivers were to receive some kind of assistance: "[T]he country
really is losing the services of [caregivers] and causing a higher cost because
they're getting ill.... [S]o you're going to have a lot more illness costs because
of the drain on the people that are unable to handle it." These perspectives
shared an understanding of caregivers as making an important contribution—to the health care system, the economy, and society generally—
deserving of public support.

14. For a more detailed discussion of caregivers' reliance on the principle of "deservingness"
in making claims for state intervention, see Chapter 5.

This reconceptualization of caregiving problems as legitimate matters of political contestation was contingent on processes of group identification: in the absence of collective identification, care providers had no frame of reference for evaluating whether their care dilemmas were common to others and hence they had no way of identifying systemic problems in long-term care provision. Focused exclusively on the internal needs of their family, they were unlikely to see care provision as a collective problem that could be remediated through public policy.

Group identification, like politicization more generally, should be understood as a continuum, not an either/or dichotomy. Caregivers in this study could be found at points all along the continuum: some new care providers, for example, self-identified as caregivers but did not yet see the underlying structural dynamics that make contemporary caregiving so difficult or had not fully distinguished between their roles as partners or children and their roles as caregivers. There were also factors external to the process of collective identification that produced rare but noticeable outliers. For example, several individuals did not identify as caregivers, but nevertheless viewed long-term care problems as appropriate for policy intervention. These participants most frequently identified as political leftists who were accustomed to viewing the state as an appropriate target for solving social problems in other contexts. Conversely, there were some individuals who did identify as caregivers but who expressed strong reservations about, or opposition to, policy intervention. Virtually all of these caregivers identified as political conservatives or libertarians, with strong views about a limited role for the state in matters of social welfare. But overall, the data hewed closely to the pattern outlined above: the process of collective identification led to a broader understanding of the structural dynamics at play in contemporary care provision, and to a view of care provision struggles as an appropriate issue for policy intervention.

CONCLUSION

The process of reinterpreting care provision as a matter appropriate for public deliberation and decision making requires much more than an intellectual or cognitive understanding of the ways in which one's family problems may be connected to "public issues of social structure" (Mills 1959:8). The commitment to "caring for our own" is a deeply engrained and largely taken-for-granted cultural norm. To reinterpret care provision as a matter appropriate for public deliberation and decision making, caregivers in this case needed a way of bridging this ideology of family care with a view of care provision as a community or social responsibility. Social workers and social services provided such a mechanism through their construction of a "family caregiver" identity. The discourse of caregiving, as it is used in social services, relies on the principles of self-care and self-advocacy to help family care providers bridge cultural norms about family responsibility with an understanding of long-term care as a community or social responsibility. Characterizing caregiving as work that is above and beyond the "normal" obligations of a partner or adult child, as something that can be shared or purchased, caregiving discourse simultaneously makes visible and validates the efforts of family care providers, even as it challenges longstanding norms about care provision as exclusively a family responsibility.

The bridging of the familiar with the new means that there is always both a legitimizing and an oppositional dimension to discursive integration. On the one hand, by validating certain obligations of partners and adult children as "normal," the discourse of caregiving leaves unchallenged a whole set of norms and practices relating to care that are normatively problematic. The fact that two-thirds of all caregivers are women is not, for example, a "natural" or "normal" social phenomenon, but is the consequence of highly gendered norms and social practices. The characterization of caregiving as work "beyond the call of duty," not only legitimates the call to duty, but it poses significant limitations on the range of care providers who might collectively identify as "caregivers." It is much harder, for example, to make a case that the "ordinary" care of a baby or a sick child is "overtime" work in the same way that caregiving discourse characterizes long-term care. Thus, while the discursive techniques used by social workers may successfully draw some boundaries around what constitutes the "natural" long-term care obligations of a partner or adult child, it's not clear that those techniques could successfully challenge norms about the "natural" obligations of parenting.

On the other hand, there is an important oppositional dimension to discursive integration as well. "Caregiver" is a relatively new policy and cultural category. Resources are distributed—or withheld—on the basis of whether somebody meets the criteria of a family caregiver. And, at least within the world of social services, there are clear cultural expectations about what it means to be a "good" caregiver. Being a good caregiver involves learning the skills and finding the resources to both take care of yourself and to be a strong advocate for your family member. Being a good caregiver involves recognizing that you are not just "doing what family members do," you are making an important social contribution. And being a good caregiver involves recognizing that you are entitled to reach beyond the confines of your own family to take advantage of community services designed to assist families in providing long-term care. Collective identification thus provides a way for people to maintain a positive perception of self-worth across two cultural categories: as both a "dutiful" family member and a "good" caregiver. By integrating new ideas of what it means to be a good caregiver with longstanding beliefs about family obligation, discursive integration forges an alternative, more political understanding of what family care providers do and what they deserve.

The role of existing policies and services in shaping political consciousness in this way cannot be overemphasized. The great paradox in this case is that political demand for new social policies and supportive services depends in critical respect on the availability and utilization of existing supportive services. Participation in support groups, workshops, and caregiving classes in this case played a key role in politicizing caregivers, highlighting similarities in the experiences of family care providers, reframing individual care problems as collective problems, and emphasizing the underlying structural or sociocultural factors that make long-term care difficult for families in the United States. But many caregivers have not or cannot reach out to social service providers. In rural areas of the country, there are few such resources available. Others don't know where to find such services, or face language or transportation barriers in accessing social services (Scharlach et al. 2003). Still others face the formidable opposition of family members to seeking help outside the home (Abel 1991). In the absence of contact with supportive services and the discourse of caregiving, it's not clear how the process of politicization could even begin for these caregivers.

Social policy also played an important role in limiting the degree of "political talk" to which individuals in this case were exposed. Legal, professional, and organizational proscriptions against political organizing in social services (discussed in Chapter 6), meant that, unlike the feminist consciousness-raising groups of the past, support groups in this case were not run by activists or associated with any political movement. While the absence of social movement actors appeared to do very little to impede the process of collective identification, their absence does, as we will see in the chapters that follow, pose very real consequences for other dimensions of politicization. The next chapter examines how individuals imagine policy solutions to their caregiving dilemmas in the absence of social movements or other organizational actors. Why do the political claims articulated by caregivers seem to challenge existing social arrangements for long-term care without substantially altering underlying beliefs about the responsibilities of family, market, and state for the costs and provision of care?

CHAPTER 4

The Construction of Political Solutions to Unmet Long-Term Care Needs

The second dimension of politicization takes us from the general question of whether a given social welfare issue should be considered a policy issue at all, to the more specific question of how individuals imagine alternative social arrangements for the social welfare problems they confront. Put another way: What in particular do they imagine the state could do to assist families with long-term care provision? If in the last chapter we saw that collective identification depended on a discourse that integrated cultural norms about family responsibility for care provision with an understanding of long-term care as a social responsibility, here we find that the construction of political solutions—a process I refer to as *grievance construction*—involves similar processes of discursive integration. But in the case of grievance construction we can see the striking limitations of existing social policies on the political imagination.

Historically, Americans have relied on one of two discourses to make claims on the state to ameliorate social welfare problems: the discourse of rights or entitlements and the discourse of need. Both discourses have historical roots in the male breadwinner/female homemaker ideal that forms the conceptual foundation of the American welfare state, and each has important implications for political demand making. Entitlements to state provision in the United States were originally designed to protect male breadwinners from the economic insecurities associated with market participation (e.g., unemployment, injury, or retirement) that could jeopardize their ability to support themselves and their families (Fraser and Gordon 1992). By contrast, relationships involving care or dependency have historically been treated as the prerogative of families rather than the state; the state initially intervened only when "normal" systems of provision broke down—typically to assist families without a male breadwinner, such as widows, single mothers, and orphans (Fraser 1989; Gordon 1994).

While changing gender norms and patterns of labor force participation have rendered the traditional breadwinner model of social provision obsolete, the cultural assumptions underlying what kinds of social welfare claims rise to the level of "rights" or "entitlements" have nevertheless persisted. Rights-based claims continue to connote (male) independence, autonomy, and self-sufficiency.[1] They are seen as dignified, legitimate, respected claims for state provision (Waldron 1996). By contrast, claims about family "needs"—including care for young children, the sick, the injured, and the elderly—reflect (female) dependency in the modern-day, negative sense (Fraser and Gordon 1994); such claims are viewed as stigmatized and suspect—supplicants' claims for state assistance. Thus, while the discourse of rights remains a powerful means of making claims against the state, it is not a discourse that has historically been used to refer to, or successfully advance, the collective claims of those with needs for state provision that arise from the "private" duties and obligations of care (Gilliom 2001; Gordon 1994).

While these historical legacies do not themselves explain Americans' reluctance to demand social policies to ameliorate the strains on American families, they highlight again the important role of cultural norms and beliefs in mediating between unmet social welfare needs and expectations for new social policy arrangements. Longstanding and deeply-held beliefs about responsibility for social welfare do not easily give way in the face of stresses on family or work life, but instead play an important role in shaping how individuals conceptualize solutions to their social welfare dilemmas.

The analysis of political claims making that follows draws on two literatures that have long examined the shifts in political consciousness that are necessary for individuals to challenge existing social conditions: the social movement framing literature and the socio-legal literature on disputing and legal mobilization. Both literatures are primarily concerned with understanding the conditions in which individuals will pursue—or "claim"—remedies for their perceived problems or injuries. In this chapter, the analytical focus shifts away from the mobilization of existing remedies to instead consider the construction of new remedies as a key transformative stage

---

1. There is a substantial literature in feminist theory that argues that the emphasis on individualism and rationality in rights discourse systematically ignores or underplays the relevance of relationships of care, needs, and interdependency that have been traditionally associated with women (Gilligan 1982; Kittay and Meyers 1987; Noddings 1984; Tronto 1994).

in the development of political consciousness. The process of imagining alternative social arrangements for new or newly perceived social welfare problems involves the evaluation of a range of culturally available models (Sewell 1992; Swidler 1986). In choosing from among these alternatives, individuals turn to those social arrangements that are consistent with more familiar ways of thinking and talking about social welfare (cf., Polletta 2000; Primus 1999). In other words, for individuals to accept an expanded state role in long-term care, they require a model of state intervention that does not substitute the state for family responsibility for long-term care, but that instead integrates the need for state assistance into a belief system that privileges family responsibility for health care. This produces political claims that do challenge existing social arrangements for care provision, but within a welfare state framework that conceives of only a minimal role for the state in safeguarding social welfare.

THEORETICAL FRAMEWORKS FOR ANALYZING GRIEVANCE CONSTRUCTION
Injustice Framing and Naming, Blaming and Claiming

Social movement theorists have relied on the concept of *collective action frames* to understand the subjective work of redefining "as unjust and immoral what was previously seen as unfortunate but perhaps tolerable" (Snow and Benford 1992:173). Collective action frames refer to sets of beliefs and meanings that shape our understandings of our circumstances, including what kinds of action are imaginable, which targets are appropriate for blame, and what political concepts—such as rights—may be employed in a given context (e.g., Ferree et al. 2002; Snow et al. 1986; Snow and Benford 1988; Steinberg 1999). *Legitimating frames* are interpretations that largely reflect and reinforce the status quo; they have a taken-for-granted quality, an inevitability or naturalness that leads to acceptance, rather than critique of one's circumstances (Gamson et al. 1982). By contrast, *injustice frames* are interpretations of experiences or conditions that support the conclusion that some moral principle has been violated and ought to be redressed.[2] Social movement theorists generally view the adoption of injustice frames as a necessary—if insufficient—condition for political

2. William Gamson (1992b, 1995, 1982), who has perhaps most famously elaborated the concept of the injustice frame, observes that people do not necessarily choose between legitimating frames and injustice frames, but may hold both to some degree, using these in different contexts to make sense of their circumstances and justify their actions or those of others.

mobilization (Gamson 1992b; McAdam 1982; Moore 1978; Turner and Killian 1987).

The socio-legal approach to studying grievance construction differs from the social movement approach in its emphasis on individual, rather than collective action. But it shares an understanding of the transformation of perceived injuries into legal claims as an interpretative process, shaped by a host of factors, including one's personal experiences with and knowledge about legal norms and rights, one's social position and ideology, and contact with third parties or other "agents of transformation" (see, e.g., Albiston 2005; Engel and Munger 2003; Felstiner et al. 1980–1981; Greenhouse 1986; Mather and Yngvesson 1981; Nielsen 2000).

The two literatures have developed strikingly similar frameworks— referred to respectively as "injustice framing" (Gamson 1992) and "naming, blaming, and claiming" (Felstiner et al. 1980–1981)—for analyzing the transformations in consciousness that occur in the construction of political and legal grievances. In what follows I elaborate them as a single approach to studying the construction of grievances (cf., Jones 2006; Marshall 2003).

The social movement framing and socio-legal literatures suggest that the first, and arguably the most critical stage in grievance construction is the process of redefining—or "naming" (Felstiner et al. 1980–1981)—as unjust or unfair those conditions or practices previously seen as acceptable or tolerable. In their seminal article on the emergence of disputes, William Felstiner et al. (1980–1981:635) observe that "naming" a problem—saying to oneself that a particular experience is in some way injurious—is perhaps the critical transformation: "Though hard to study empirically...the level and kind of disputing in a society may turn more on what is initially perceived as an injury than on any other decision." William Gamson (1995:91) argues that to inspire mobilization for change, the evaluation of harm must be something more than a cognitive or intellectual judgment about what is equitable; rather it must be a hot cognition, "the kind of righteous anger that puts fire in the belly and iron in the soul." "Naming" an injury, then, requires attention to the emotional valence attached to an individual's perception that some standard or principle has been violated. Social movement scholars generally understand anger and indignation to be high activation emotions, motivating people to challenge the conditions that they perceive as injurious (Britt and Heise 2000; Jasper 1998). By contrast, emotions such as shame or guilt or embarrassment are considered low activation emotions, tending to paralyze rather than mobilize individuals to act (Taylor 2000). The quality or degree of emotions individuals attach to social conditions depends in part on what or who they perceive to be responsible for the injury (Ferree and Miller 1985).

Thus, the second shift in political consciousness requires a target against which these emotions can be usefully vented—what Felstiner et al. (1980–1981) refer to in their framework for grievance construction as "blaming." Gamson (1992b) observes that while these targets can be anything from corporations or government agencies to individuals or groups, an injustice frame requires some degree of concreteness in the target. To the extent that individuals see only impersonal or abstract forces as responsible for suffering—nature, society, God, "the system"—they are more likely to accept the status quo and make the best of it.[3] If reification and excessive abstraction act as impediments to grievance construction, so too can internalization of blame: people who blame themselves for a situation are less likely to see it as injurious (Britt and Heise 2000; Felstiner et al. 1980–1981). Thus individuals must have a way of seeing the cause of their injury as the result of specific, identifiable forces external to themselves (Ferree and Miller 1985).

Finally, individuals must specify a remedy—or "claim"—some course of action to ameliorate the perceived harm (Felstiner et al. 1980–1981; Gamson 1992b). It is in the specification of "claims" that social movement and socio-legal researchers noticeably depart from their emphasis on political consciousness. Both literatures characterize "claims" as constructed separately from the interpretative processes of grievance construction; they focus on the conditions under which grievants will pursue externally defined remedies for their injuries, rather than how individuals themselves conceptualize remedies as part of the grievance construction process. In the social movement framing literature, the analytical focus is on how social movements persuade potential participants to collectively mobilize for movement-defined solutions to social problems (see, e.g., Ferree 2003; Snow et al. 1986; Snow and Benford 1988). Similarly, in the socio-legal literature on disputing and legal mobilization, researchers typically assume the presence of legal remedies and focus their inquiries on the conditions that shape the willingness and capacity of people to pursue those remedies when they have experienced actionable injuries (see, e.g., Albiston 2005; Engel 1980; Engel and Munger 2003; Gilliom 2001; Macaulay 1963; Marshall 2003; Nielsen 2004). In both literatures, "claiming" is characterized as what individuals do as a result of the grievance construction process, rather than as part of the grievance construction process itself.

By contrast, here the conceptualization of "claims" itself is seen as an important transformation in processes of politicization. Grievance construction occurs in concrete social action, as individuals evaluate and

---

3. Gamson (1995) also warns of the opposite problem: by overly concretizing targets, there is a danger that people will miss the underlying structural conditions that produced the social condition at issue.

select from the ideational and institutional resources available to them for seeking potential solutions to problems in their everyday lives (see also Ewick and Silbey 1998; Mansbridge 2001). These resources include, but are not limited to, social movement collective action frames and existing legal remedies. But they may also include market-, or family-based models, models rooted in religious ideology, international models, and public policies designed for other purposes or for constituencies other than potential grievants. Understanding how individuals select from among these available models to formulate solutions to their problems is critical to explaining why grievance construction so often seems to reinforce the ideology of family responsibility even as it seeks to challenge it.

Discursive Integration and the Construction of Claims

The concept of discursive integration has its roots in scholarship on the construction of rights, most notably Francesca Polletta's (2000) work on "novel" rights-claiming. Polletta sought to identify how civil rights activists developed "radical yet resonant" claims—rights claims that were not yet recognized in formal law, but which were effective in mobilizing people. She found that one of the primary ways in which activists developed resonant rights claims was by integrating rights discourse with more familiar ways of talking about and understanding the world. Civil rights activists, for example, often merged legal and religious idioms, combining arguments about citizenship and constitutional rights with principles of Christianity and spirituality. Polletta's findings are consistent with research conducted by Richard Primus (1999), who argues that throughout American history, political elites seeking to offset the effects of war, poverty, or other adverse social conditions established and legitimated new rights by articulating principles that synthesized the new rights with previously existing understandings of rights (see also Sewell 1992).

Research on novel rights-claiming offers an important insight into how resonant understandings of new rights claims are established: new claims must be discursively integrated with previously existing ways of thinking and talking about the world. Notably, however, this research suffers from the same limitations as the broader social movement framing and socio-legal literatures: Polletta emphasizes the construction of claims by social movement elites in their attempts to mobilize participation in the civil rights movement, and Primus emphasizes the efforts of legislatures, courts, and political elites in legitimizing new understandings of rights. In both cases, grievants remain on the periphery of the analysis, depicted merely as an audience rather than as agents in the construction of new rights claims.

Claiming, I suggest here, involves shifts in political consciousness similar to those observed in the naming and blaming stages of grievance construction. Whether, for example, one chooses to call on the state to ameliorate unmet needs depends critically on how one also understands the responsibilities of the family and market for safeguarding social welfare. Similarly, how one conceptualizes the form of state intervention (e.g., as state entitlements or state regulation of the market) depends on beliefs about the efficacy of market solutions and about what kinds of needs are substantively deserving of the privileged status that the "entitlements" label bestows. In other words, the process by which individuals imagine solutions to newly perceived injuries—the process of evaluating and selecting from a range of available models—is deeply imbricated with the assessments of family, market, and state responsibility that occur at earlier stages in grievance construction.

The following analysis examines processes of grievance construction among family caregivers, seeking to identify under what conditions the strains of long-term care provision form the basis for political claims for state intervention and why these claims so often fail to challenge the ideology of family responsibility.

INJUSTICE FRAMING AMONG FAMILY CAREGIVERS

This section more closely interrogates the conditions that mediate between contemporary long-term care needs and claims for state long-term care entitlements. It begins by elaborating the widely held view of long-term care provision as a family responsibility—what this book refers to, following social movement framing theory, as a legitimating frame. It then compares the experiences of caregivers who relied exclusively on legitimating frames in talking about their care circumstances with those who relied on injustice frames, seeking to identify (1) how individuals come to name longstanding care practices as harms or injustices requiring remediation, (2) under what conditions they assign responsibility for remediation to institutions other than the family, and (3) how they construct solutions to the long-term care problems they encountered.

Legitimating Frames

As previous chapters have illustrated, caregivers in this study uniformly demonstrated a tenacious commitment to the idea that it was their duty as family members to bear the primary burden of long-term care provision.

The belief in family obligation is an archetypical example of a legitimating frame: the provision of care for a family member—no matter what the cost—was understood by most caregivers as the natural and normal thing to do. Indeed for many, the idea that anyone else—and in particular the government—should bear responsibility for either the costs or provision of care was simply inconceivable.

At the time of this study, Vincent was caring for his mother, who had been bedridden for five years following a stroke. Vincent worked full time and cared for his mother before and after work. A Vietnam vet, he joked that caregiving was the most difficult tour of duty he had ever experienced, but he did it, he insisted, out of a sense of obligation:

> Because they brought me into the world, and my mom would do the same thing for me if I came back from overseas shot up or no legs or you know, something God forbid that woulda happened. But I felt I owed it to her. . . . That's what we were brought up with. From the time we were hatched, so to speak, that we were to take care of our older folks.

Asked why he has not hired any assistance with the caregiving, Vincent acknowledged it was partly finances, but also a sense of obligation: "I think family would rather do it themselves. It's a matter of pride."

By conceptualizing their work as fulfilling a duty to their families, caregivers understood their situations as both natural and inevitable. Alex was caring for his wife, who was diagnosed at fifty-eight with Alzheimer's disease. In a discussion with his support group about the challenges of caring for his wife, Alex observed: "We've been married thirty-five years. And I do it because if it was me, I'd know she'd do the same for me." Alex was typical in his matter-of-fact acceptance of his responsibilities: "[T]o me, you just do what you have to do." Similarly, Larry had given up his home to care for his parents, both of whom had been diagnosed with dementia. Complaining to his support group that his niece and nephew didn't seem to share his values about caring for family, he opines, "Because it's an obligation that they have to do! So you sacrificed your life to move back with mom and dad? So you do it. You just do it. You just make the best of it."

When caregivers experienced frustration or exhaustion or resentment about their circumstances, the family responsibility frame served to mediate those emotions, often transforming them into feelings of guilt or embarrassment. Caregivers felt guilty for not doing enough or for wanting a break, and they felt embarrassed when they admitted they needed help. As one new participant, Myra, confided to her dementia support group:

> I'm not a good caretaker, because of my resentment and anger. I lose my patience. "Is today Tuesday?" "Yes, today is Tuesday." Then a minute later: "Is today Tuesday?" "Yes,

today is Tuesday." And after a while I'm *screaming*! And you feel terrible. And you feel guilty. And you feel like you're not a good person.

By transforming high-activation emotions such as anger and resentment into low-activation emotions such as resignation, shame, or guilt, the family responsibility frame simultaneously legitimates and reinforces norms about family obligation for care provision.

It's important to emphasize that the family responsibility frame was resonant to some extent for all of the family caregivers in this study, including those who also adopted more oppositional perspectives. But what is remarkable here is not the strength of the normative commitment to family responsibility, but the absence of a widely-resonant oppositional frame. Caregivers whose feelings about their circumstances challenged or contradicted the expectations of family obligation struggled to find a language with which to articulate another view. Barbara's experience in this regard is typical. Caring for her husband had grave consequences for Barbara's emotional and physical health—she was suicidal at one point—her employment status—she was demoted—and her financial well-being—she spent all her savings and obtained a home equity line of credit on her house to pay for supportive services. She says of all of this:

> I think we're somehow brainwashed. There's something [about] the way we're brought up in this country. There's no empathy....When my husband was first sick, and my family came up...my mother said are you having any fun yet? And it's like, do you think cleaning up poop and pee and taking care of a baby who's fifty years old is fun?...And I think somehow in this country, we're raised that it's your responsibility, you've got to do it. Don't complain and whimper...and then you're rewarded verbally. You know, if you do the job. Oh you're such a good person. Well, no I'm not! I don't like it!

The lack of a widely available discourse with which to challenge norms about family caregiving in the United States provides a useful opportunity to explore how individuals come to imagine alternative social arrangements for care.

Injustice Framing: Naming the Harm or Injury

Most researchers agree that to (re)evaluate deeply entrenched beliefs, individuals require some trigger—an unexpected event or piece of information that causes them to think about their basic values and how the world diverges from them in some important way (Jasper 1998; Snow et al. 1998). In this study, beliefs about family responsibility for care provision were not questioned—or even considered—by participants in this study unless or until they confronted some disparity between the care they felt obligated to provide their family members and their capacity to satisfy that obligation. In other words, the "harm" or "injury" in the case of long-term care is the belief that care provision is in some key respect falling short; that there are financial, physical, or emotional obstacles that caregivers on their own simply cannot overcome.

In many cases involving chronic care, particularly for dementia, caregivers reached a point where they could not personally provide all of the care they perceived to be required by the care receiver. Many worked outside the home on a full- or part-time basis; some had child care responsibilities; some maintained separate households in other parts of the city, state or country; some had health problems themselves; and most simply needed to attend to other parts of their lives. In theory, there are a wide variety of market-based supportive services available to help caregivers in these circumstances, including in-home skilled nursing or companion care, adult day care, respite care, and nursing home care. But in practice, caregivers confronted a wide range of obstacles to utilizing these services.

A 2003 survey of California caregivers found that the most significant reason for unmet care needs in California is lack of information about supportive services: most caregivers don't know where to turn for help when they need it.[4] Because there is no comprehensive long-term care public policy at either the federal level or in the state of California, the administration and delivery of services and benefits for patients with chronic diseases and their families takes place within a byzantine "system" of state and local agencies, nonprofit organizations, and for-profit businesses. Without a formal gateway to services, the primary challenge for many caregivers is simply finding help to address their unmet care needs. A second frequent reason for unmet care needs is cost: supportive services are expensive and are rarely covered by Medicare or private health insurance plans.[5] Medi-Cal, California's health program for low-income families, is the only public

4. A 2003 survey of randomly selected California state residents who provide care to someone aged fifty or over found that two-thirds of all caregivers who wanted education, training or information about services did not know where to go to get those services (Scharlach, Giunta, Dal Santo, and Fox 2003). Similarly, three-quarters of caregivers needing financial or legal assistance on care-related issues did not know where to obtain it.

5. Private health insurance generally accounts for 7.2% of long-term care expenditures (Georgetown University Long-Term Care Financing Project 2007).

program in the state to offer substantial coverage for long-term care services, but because income and asset eligibility standards are typically very stringent, few families actually qualify for benefits. In addition to concerns about where to find and how to pay for supportive services, caregivers also struggled with the availability of services, service quality of supportive services, the availability of transportation, and language constraints among service providers. All of these common obstacles to utilizing supportive services were reported by caregivers in this study, and in virtually all cases, the perception of unmet care needs served as a potential "trigger" for a shift in perspective about care responsibilities.

There were important racial differences in this perception of unmet need: more than three-quarters (14 of 17) of Black and Latino (7 of 9) interview subjects in this study reported unmet care needs, compared to only a fifth of Caucasian interview subjects (10 of 48). Social workers and service providers in this study observed that in Los Angeles, where neighborhoods are highly segregated by race and ethnicity, issues of availability and accessibility were particularly a problem in minority neighborhoods. Caregivers of color as a result were disproportionately more likely than white caregivers in this study to experience conditions that politicized them.[6]

Of the seventy-nine caregivers in the interview sample, forty-seven (or 60%) described themselves as successfully meeting the perceived care needs of their family members. These caregivers included those whose family members needed relatively little assistance, typically because their conditions had not yet significantly deteriorated, those who had ample resources with which to find and/or purchase supportive services,[7] those who had significant assistance in care provision from other family members, and those caregivers who obtained supportive services at low or no cost through California's means-tested Medicaid program. In all of these

6. Due to the nonrandom sample, these statistics were not tested for significance.

7. The capacity of caregivers to meet their perceived care needs was partly, but not exclusively, tied to income. Participants with reported incomes over $50,000 were more than two-and-a-half times more likely to say they could meet their care obligations. Because the sample is non-random, it is not possible to determine whether these differences are statistically significant, but the findings are consistent with the fact that market-based supportive services are expensive and available only to those with ample resources. Note, however, that perceptions of unmet need are highly subjective and tied to the consumption patterns to which people of different classes were accustomed. Caregivers in this study with several million dollars in assets worried about the costs of paying for a nursing home that cost over $150,000 a year, while caregivers with much more modest assets worried about the costs of nursing homes costing closer to $40,000-$50,000 a year. Regardless of how close participants actually were to "needing" economic assistance for care provision, the subjective stress and worry about being able to satisfy the perceived care needs of their family members was, in effect, a great equalizer: the fear of falling into destitution or failing to provide adequate care for family was a powerful motive for supporting an expanded role for the state.

cases caregivers still faced the emotional and physical challenges of providing care to a family member with a chronic disease or disability, but they experienced no disparity between the care they felt was their duty to provide, and their capacity to fill that obligation.

It is important to emphasize that there are strong cultural and psychological reasons for individuals to describe even the most challenging care situations as satisfactory. The perceived social stigma associated with being "bad" spouses or adult children if unable to provide all the necessary care for one's partner or parent, as well as the need to psychologically justify the often extraordinary sacrifices made for the sake of family, arguably encourage many people to either describe themselves—or to genuinely see themselves—as successfully meeting the care obligations of their family members even in those instances where assistance may well be necessary. In addition, the analysis of unmet need here focuses only on unmet care needs that could be redressed through public policy. There are also well-documented (see, e.g., Abel 1991; Brody 2004) emotional obstacles to obtaining formal care for a family member that are arguably more difficult to remedy through public policy, and these were not coded for analysis. As such, it is likely that the incidence of unmet care needs among participants is actually higher than that reported by participants in this study.

Not surprisingly, caregivers who described themselves as successfully meeting the care needs of their family members were substantially less likely to characterize their care obligations as unfair or unjust. Of these forty-seven caregivers, thirty-two (or nearly 70%) relied exclusively on the family responsibility frame when talking about their care circumstances, reflecting the belief that families should bear the full cost and burden of care provision, without the state's intervention. By contrast, caregivers who struggled to satisfy their perceived care obligations were far more likely to reevaluate taken-for-granted assumptions about family responsibility. As the following section elaborates, these perceptions of injury did not always lead to grievances, but without the perception of a divergence between expectations and reality—without the admission or realization of unmet care needs—grievance construction simply did not take place. Of the seventy-nine caregivers in the interview sample, thirty-two (or 40%) mentioned unmet care needs. Of these, twenty-six (or more than 80%) relied on an injustice framing in describing their caregiving dilemmas.

Trenton's experience caring for his eighty-year-old wife, who had Alzheimer's disease, illustrates how the struggle to provide adequate care can trigger this process of grievance construction. At the start of this study, Trenton was responsible for cooking, cleaning and maintaining his home, as well as bathing, dressing, and assisting his wife with most aspects of daily living. Like most caregivers in the study, the ethic of family responsibility was the primary frame through which he understood his circumstances. "Because I care so much for my wife, I do a pretty good job....I took fifty-five years...and I owe her something." But midway through the observation period, Trenton began developing chest pains, which he attributed to the stress of caring for his wife by himself twenty-four hours a day. His support group urged him to hire some help in the home, and he looked into it, but he was concerned that if his wife remained ill for a number of years, he might simply run out of money: "[E]ventually if she lives long enough...then I would probably have to sell my house. And if I should live five, ten years after she's gone, I don't know where I'm going to be." Trenton eventually did hire someone to help him in the home on a limited basis, and his relief was palpable when he reported this news back to his support group. But he continued to worry about the cost, and those concerns triggered his first assessment of the taken-for-granted norms about family care provision. Normally, he told his support group, families can take care of themselves. "But then all of a sudden this [disease] comes about and then when it does, it drains [us] so financially...." When I interviewed Trenton several weeks later, he revisited this theme, articulating for the first time the expectation that the state had a role in helping families with care provision: "[S]omebody within the government in some day in time, they're going to have to realize that this is almost an impossible situation! There's no way that you could maintain a comfortable lifestyle without some federal aid."

Injustice Framing: Blaming

If unmet needs created an opportunity to reevaluate deeply entrenched beliefs about family responsibility for care, how caregivers evaluated the discrepancy between their beliefs about family care provision and their capacity to provide that care depended critically on who they blamed for the divergence. To the extent that caregivers in this study internalized the blame for their predicaments, they were likely to feel shame, guilt, or embarrassment—low activation emotions that are unlikely to lead to injustice framing (cf., Britt and Heise 2000; Taylor 2000). In these cases, beliefs about family responsibility again strongly influenced perceptions of personal responsibility for care problems. Some caregivers blamed themselves for not purchasing long-term care insurance when they had the opportunity. Others blamed themselves for not arranging their finances in ways that would legally qualify their care receiver for state Medicaid long-term care benefits. Most were just embarrassed that lack of income or poor health would stand in the way of meeting their care obligations to family. In all of

these cases, self-blame played a prominent role in defusing potential grievances. Belle, for example, had virtually no income at the time her husband
was diagnosed with Parkinson's-related dementia, and for a time, she and
her husband lived out of a warehouse they owned. She could not afford
in-home care for her husband, and yet could not qualify for Medicaid as
long as she owned property.

> Before we sold the building, our income was $580 a month. And so that was not much.
> So our taxes went unpaid and all these things happened.... We had collateral, so we were
> not able to get support [from Medicaid]. We didn't have enough money for postage
> stamps, but they told us we could sell our properties and take care of it. But I guess that's
> true. We can't expect everybody else to pay our bill.

Similarly, caregivers who blamed impersonal or abstract targets for their
frustrations—bad luck or "life"—were more likely to be resigned to the
conditions in which they found themselves, with little sense of agency
about or awareness of the structural conditions underlying their predicaments (cf., Gamson 1992b). Heidi, who gave up her job and home to care
for her mother, spoke of caregiving as a calling:

> I gave up my life, you know?...And yes, I would like to go out there and do what I want
> to do, but you know...when that thing inside you says you have to do something, you
> cannot serve two masters.... [E]ither I put her someplace not so nice and say okay, me
> first. Or I do what my heart tells me to do regardless of what I missed out on. That's my
> choice. That's what I want to do. And sometimes...this is not what I *want* to do, but this
> is what I'm *called* to do.

Caregivers with strong religious beliefs, such as Laverne and Tom, typically
expressed a similar resignation to their circumstances, often observing that
God puts people in such difficult situations for a reason:

> You ask God for patience, he'll put you in a situation where you got to develop it.

> We are grateful for the chance to let go and make changes in our lives. How lucky we are
> to have God give us this gift.... It's not a curse, it's a gift.

In each of these cases, religion played a role in defusing potential grievances
by promoting acceptance of even the most difficult conditions.

High activation emotions like anger or moral indignation require an
attribution of blame to specific, identifiable forces external to the potential
grievants (cf., Ferree and Miller 1985). Because care provision is so widely
understood to be a family responsibility in the United States, the state was

not a natural target for blame when most participants began caregiving. Indeed, many had never considered the role of the state (in any capacity) with regard to long-term care provision. When asked if participants thought their caregiving experiences had changed their attitude about the government's responsibilities for long-term care provision, responses such as Susan and Louis's were common:

> I've never really thought of the government as being part of, you know, my world in that sense.

> I haven't much thought into that. I just feel like I'm responsible for my home life.

That most caregivers wrestle with serious long-term care dilemmas without ever questioning the assumption that family should bear exclusive responsibility for care provision highlights again the degree to which the ideology of family responsibility is hegemonic in the United States—so naturalized, so taken for granted, that people can't even imagine the social alternatives. But it also points to the importance of expectations in injustice framing: we experience moral indignation only when our expectations for how we should be treated have been violated. Joan, who for eighteen years had been caring for her husband, participated in a peer group discussion about long-term care public policy. Silent for much of the discussion, she finally confided to the group that the idea of government responsibility for the costs of long-term care was new to her:

> I think...that as a caregiver, we don't feel any entitlement. We never stamp our feet and say this is ridiculous, someone should be paying for this....I mean, I just thought hey, it's the luck of the draw, isn't it? You know?...But if someone said, you know what? The government...I mean this whole discussion is like hey wow, that's another way to look at it, isn't it? Someone should be paying for this!

Joan's revelation to the group illustrates how the introduction of an alternative frame can create new expectations, or in Joan's words, a sense of entitlement. But where did caregivers derive these alternative views of long-term care responsibilities?

The social movement framing literature assumes that social movement organizations play a crucial role in shaping public conceptions about which targets are appropriate for blame for harmful or unjust social conditions. In the case of chronic care provision, however, most caregivers are unaware of advocacy organizations seeking long-term care public policy reform (see Chapter 6). Participants in this study rarely mentioned advocacy organizations in support group meetings or interviews, and when provided with a list of state and national advocacy organizations seeking policies to assist families in long-term care provision, respondents demonstrated extremely low levels of name recognition. While many knew of larger organizations like the AARP or the Alzheimer's Association, few caregivers in this study demonstrated any awareness of the specific collective action frames these organizations were promoting with regard to long-term care policy reform.

If the social movement literature suggests that advocacy organizations would play a key role in providing individuals with blameworthy targets, the socio-legal literature on legal mobilization assumes that knowledge of and access to legal remedies or benefits shapes individual conceptions of blame. In this case, public policies did play a key role in shaping attributions of blame for caregiving problems, but not in the way socio-legal scholars would predict. There are few, if any, existing legal remedies or state entitlements available in the United States for families to "mobilize" in the conventional sense of enforcing rights or claiming benefits. But public policies designed for other purposes or to assist other beneficiaries constituted at least some of the ideational resources available to individuals constructing solutions to long-term care problems.

Caregivers were exposed to a wide range of alternative models of care provision during the course of caregiving, all of which served as potential paradigms for assigning responsibility for care struggles to institutions other than the family. In evaluating these alternatives, caregivers were primarily drawn to those models that integrated their need for assistance with previously existing beliefs about the respective responsibilities of family, market, and state for care provision.

As Table 4.1 shows, for a clear majority of grievants in this study, the most resonant model for assigning responsibility for care dilemmas to an

Table 4.1. SOURCE AND DISTRIBUTION OF INJUSTICE FRAMES (N=41)

Source of Injustice Framing[a]	Number (%) of Grievants Drawing on Source as Primary Injustice Framing
Means-Tested Medicaid Program	22 (54%)
Social Insurance Programs	0 (0%)
International Comparisons	4 (10%)
Insurance Companies	5 (12%)
Politica l or Moral Principles Regarding Care as a Government or Social Responsibility	10 (24%)
Other[b]	1 (2%)

[a]The categories were nonexclusive, meaning that it was conceivable that an individual could cite more than one source of injustice framing. In fact, only one individual, a British citizen who was caring for her mother in Los Angeles, drew extensively on more than one source for her injustice framing: both Medicaid and the comparative case of long-term care in England.

[b]One caregiver articulated a sense of moral indignation about state civil liberty laws, which make it very difficult to institutionalize elders living in unsafe environments.

institution other than the family was California's means-tested Medicaid program (Medi-Cal). California's Medi-Cal program offers relatively generous long-term care benefit packages for those who qualify for the program, including full prescription drug benefits and coverage for adult day care, in-home supportive services, and nursing home care. Because the income and asset eligibility levels for the program are so stringent, very few caregivers in this study actually qualified for state assistance. But, importantly, many participants knew of somebody who did qualify for Medi-Cal. Stories about Medi-Cal benefits circulated within support groups and friendship and neighbor networks, providing not only concrete examples of what the state could provide in the way of long-term care assistance, but also creating an expectation that certain types of services *ought* to be subsidized by the government and available to a wider segment of the American population. It is typically in conversations about Medi-Cal that caregivers most clearly articulated an injustice framing.

Susanna, for example, was caring for her parents, both of whom suffer from some dementia, her mother quite seriously. Her parents were unable to qualify for Medi-Cal benefits, as their pensions placed them just above the eligibility cut-off line. Susanna observed, angrily, in her interview:

> I have girlfriends at work say oh, just call up so-and-so, they can help you. [They'll say] my mother has 24-hour care.... [But] they don't pay a penny because they get on welfare.... you have to be poor all your life or whatever, not work. And then when you're older, you get all the benefits, and that's just not fair! I think that's very unfair. My parents both have worked all their lives, and daddy had two jobs for sixteen years. And now he can't qualify because supposedly they make too much money.

For many caregivers, Medi-Cal simultaneously provided caregivers with a concrete model for thinking about care provision as a shared responsibility with the state and a blameworthy target: because the state was distributing Medi-Cal benefits only to the state's poorest residents, it became the mark for many of the frustrations of those struggling to meet the care needs of their family members.

Again, without the experience of needing assistance with care provision, the transformation in how caregivers viewed the responsibilities of family and state for the costs of care provision rarely occurred. Kathrina captures this close relationship between unmet need and new views of state responsibility in a story about her friend's mother, who suffered from severe diabetes and received benefits through Medi-Cal. In her friend's family, the youngest son lived at home, and due to their low income, he qualified for payments from the state under California's In-Home Supportive Service program as his mother's caregiver. "[T]he son was getting paid by the state to take care of the mom. And I thought, you know, why are they paying you to take care of your parent? It's ridiculous! The kids should chip in and you should pull together and all this rah rah stuff." But Kathrina notes that once her stepfather was diagnosed with Alzheimer's, her perception changed dramatically. "When it hit *me*, I thought, oh my God! *Where's the help?* [laughs] I don't know, and I'm thinking you know I pay so much damn taxes!...I know I pay for the roads and all this stuff that I use, but where's the help back? Yes, [this experience has] changed my thinking a lot."

If the need for assistance with the costs or provision of long-term care changed the way many participants viewed the responsibility of the state, it was notable that Medicaid proved to be a more resonant model for state provision than Medicare. In many ways, Medicare would seem to be the more likely model for assigning responsibility for chronic care dilemmas to the state: not only are social insurance programs far more respected than means-tested, "welfare" programs such as Medicaid (Cook and Barrett 1992), but most participants or their family members actually qualified for and received Medicare benefits for acute health care. While Medicare does not cover most costs associated with chronic conditions, it does cover one-hundred days of skilled nursing care and rehabilitative therapy, as well as some home health benefits for those recently discharged from a hospital. Caregivers were aware of these benefits just as they were aware of Medicaid benefits. It seems plausible, then, that caregivers would make the argument that if Medicare pays for the costs associated with a heart attack, then it should also do so for costs associated with chronic diseases like Alzheimer's or Parkinson's. Or if Medicare pays for the costs of home health for 100 days, it should subsidize the costs of home health for individuals who require in-home assistance over longer periods of time. But remarkably, no caregivers in this sample referenced Medicare as a source for their injustice frames.

This study suggests that one reason the Medicaid model of social provision resonated more with caregivers than the Medicare model is that Medicaid more closely accords with American cultural beliefs about family responsibility for care provision. In the United States, Medicaid and Medicare represent two distinct approaches to social welfare provision. Medicare is based on a social insurance model in which the state takes primary responsibility for meeting certain social welfare needs (retirement income for example, or acute health care for senior citizens); Medicaid is based on a residualist or need-based model, in which families or individuals take primary responsibility for meeting social welfare needs, and the state steps in only when their most basic needs are not being met. Of these two forms of state provision, the underlying logic of Medicaid benefits arguably resonated with caregivers because it provided them with a way of bridging their normative commitments to family with their need for government assistance. Participants who assigned responsibility for long-term care dilemmas to the state believed, in other words, that the state had a role in helping families with care responsibilities, *but only when traditional systems of family provision break down.*

The importance of finding a model for state assistance that modified but closely accorded with participants' preexisting beliefs about long-term care provision can also be seen in the failure of international systems of public provision to serve as resonant models for assigning responsibility for unmet care needs. Most European countries, as well as Australia, Japan, and Canada, offer a wide range of government benefits for family care providers, ranging from free or subsidized home care, adult day care, and institutionalized care to tax credits and direct payment allowances for caregivers (Carrerra et al. 2013; Daly 2001a; Daly and Rake 2003). Several caregivers who relied on an injustice frame invoked the social norms, values, and policies of these other countries as a yardstick for measuring how the United States fell short. Reba captures this use of international comparisons in this comment to her support group:

> Everything is paid for in other countries with things like [day care]. But we don't do that here.... That's what ticks me off... [W]e're supposed to be forward- thinking? All the other countries in Europe and everywhere else have made ways to do things for their people in the country. But we don't.... I don't mean that I want everyone to hope the government will pay for everything. I'm saying that there has to be a different attitude about the people in this country. That we need to have some thought given to us.

But if examples from other countries introduced another model for state intervention in long-term care, they failed to resonate with caregivers in this study. Because so few caregivers knew details about what other countries provided in the way of long-term care benefits, their comparisons were mostly limited to broad generalizations about social values or policies. More importantly, as in these comments from Doris and Tony, their comparative examples were frequently countered by equally general observations about the limitations of the health care systems in other countries and the problems faced by citizens who lived there:

> Well we know that those socialized countries or some of them, they have a very very high tax rate, much higher than we have. So that's something to look at too, paying for it.

> I had a coach down at the University of Arizona, his wife had a heart attack over in Hungary.... [He] said those hospitals over there in some of those countries, you wouldn't go in there if you were dying.

In general, participants understood the health care systems of other countries to be so different from health care provision in the United States that
international comparisons ultimately failed to resonate as a meaningful
source of oppositional understandings of long-term care. Of the forty-one
interview participants who articulated an injustice frame in this study, only
three relied on international comparisons to do so.[8]

Those participants who relied on sources of injustice frames other than
Medi-Cal similarly emphasized models that closely tracked their preexisting beliefs about care responsibilities. As Table 4.1 illustrates, five interview participants, for example, drew on their experiences with insurance
companies in articulating an injustice frame. These caregivers—most typically caregivers for cancer patients—reported constant struggles to obtain
coverage for various treatments and services and an ongoing fear that their
insurance companies would "drop" their care receiver at their slightest mis-
step. In these cases, caregivers argued that if the insurance market bears
the risk of acute health care provision, it should also bear responsibility for
long-term care provision. Daniella, for example, was caring for her mother,
who had advanced Alzheimer's disease. Neither she nor her mother could
afford to pay for assistance, but her mother's insurance company did not
cover supportive services, and her mother didn't qualify for Medi-Cal. "I
feel [her insurance company] should give us a lot of help because that's
where her insurance is with," Daniella observed. "It's a *disease*, it's *medical*,
so why shouldn't they offer more?"

Given the pervasiveness of the insurance market in acute health care
provision, it was notable that no participants assigned responsibility for
unmet care needs to long-term care insurance companies. Participants in
this study widely disparaged the long-term care insurance market for being
unaffordable, inaccessible to people with diagnosed chronic diseases, and
unreliable in delivering benefits to those who had actually obtained policies. Few caregivers knew anyone who was significantly assisted by any
form of insurance coverage. (Of the nearly 180 caregivers in this study, only
six reported using long-term care insurance to cover the costs of supportive services.) In most cases, grievants in this study viewed long-term care
insurance as an ineffective tool for addressing the kinds of care crises that
participants routinely confronted.

Finally, some caregivers based their injustice frames on political or moral
beliefs about the government's (or society's) responsibility to ensure the
health and economic security of its citizens. Ten caregivers who identified
themselves as "political liberals" emphasized that these were beliefs they

8. One of these caregivers was a British citizen.

held prior to their caregiving experience, and they experienced little dissonance between their need for state assistance and their expectations of the state in protecting the social welfare of its citizens. "I think that's an important function of government," one such participant observed. "I think ancient cultures, ancient civilizations always took care of their old.... The way [the government doesn't] want to pay for this or pay for that, I think is appalling."

In assigning responsibility for unmet long-term care needs, then, caregivers were exposed to a variety of state- and market-based models of care provision, but they were primarily drawn to those models that closely accorded with preexisting beliefs about family, market, and state responsibility for care provision. As the next section elaborates, participants relied on a similar discursive logic in constructing solutions for their long-term care dilemmas.

Injustice Framing: Claiming

The final shift in political consciousness necessary for grievance construction is the prescription of a remedy, some course of action to redress the perceived injustice (cf., Snow and Benford 1988). It is in the specification of a remedy that we most clearly see how new claims for public provision are forged within, rather than independently of, processes of grievance construction. It is also in the specification of solutions to care dilemmas that we see why these claims seem to call for a substantially expanded state role, without really altering the underlying assumptions individuals hold about family responsibility for care.

Caregivers' claims for public provision in this study closely tracked the specific care needs giving rise to their grievances. Those caregivers who struggled to afford day care for their care receivers argued for subsidized day care (or, less commonly, state-run day care centers). Those who needed help inside the home argued for subsidized home health care. Those who complained about the fragmentation of health services insisted that the state should create centralized, accessible "caregiver centers," or that it should fund more social workers to assist caregivers. While the form of state intervention varied significantly, virtually all of the claims that emerged from processes of grievance construction reflected a substantially expanded view of the state's responsibility for long-term care provision. But how did grievants view the claims for state intervention they imagined? Did they see their claims for state intervention as claims for new rights or entitlements—seeking a permanent commitment by the state to ensure that all citizens (or workers) have access to adequate long-term care? Or did they view their claims in ways more consistent with past policies involving care and dependency—as a temporary intervention necessary only in cases where "normal" systems of care provision break down?

To answer these questions, I analyzed the interpretative frameworks used by respondents to talk about their care circumstances together with evidence of rights consciousness among the same participants. The data suggest a striking correspondence: participants who relied exclusively on legitimating frames for understanding their care dilemmas rarely understood their care needs as the basis for claims to rights or entitlements. By contrast, most caregivers who relied on injustice frames for understanding their caregiving dilemmas understood the concept of "rights" more broadly to include aspects of long-term care provision.

Caregivers in this study generally articulated four understandings of "rights" in the context of long-term care. First, some understood "rights" to be limited only to certain kinds of civil and political rights. These caregivers could not understand how to extend the rights frame in a meaningful way to the context of care provision. This was most clearly seen in responses to a targeted rights question: "If someone from another country were to ask you what rights family caregivers like yourself have in the United States, how would you answer that question?" The most common response to this question was one of befuddled incomprehension. Unlike those caregivers who requested some clarification of the question (e.g., "Do you mean paid caregivers or unpaid caregivers?"), these respondents fundamentally did not understand how to apply the concept of rights to their circumstances. The following responses from Bridget and Alex are typical in this regard:

> My goodness! [laughs] What rights do family caregivers have? My god. You got me. What *rights*?

> What rights? [long pause] I don't know about rights. To me, you just do what you have to do.

For these caregivers, the presumption that families should bear the primary burden of care provision was so taken for granted, that the possibility of state obligations for care as a matter of right had never occurred to them. Their discomfort with the appropriation of the term in the context of care provision was evident in the following response from Belle:

> I never thought of a right for a caregiver. And yet I hear it all the time. Rights for this and rights for that. I wasn't in that generation. I'm way back where you fended for yourself, I think.... Never thought of it that way.... Oh shoot. What right do you have to want a right? [laughs] What kind of answer is that? I can't answer it!

A second interpretation of "rights" referred to established legal rights associated with elder abuse, power of attorney, conservatorships, and decision making in the end stages of the care receiver's life. "[O]nce you get the legal controls," observed one typical respondent, "like the durable power of attorney for financial and medical affairs, I would think that you have a lot of rights." In a similar vein, some caregivers talked about their "rights" in cases of elder abuse. Concerns about liability for the actions of patients with Alzheimer's was a recurrent theme among participants, many of whom sought legal advice to ensure that they knew their rights in the event they had problems with Adult Protective Services or the police.

A third interpretation of "rights" included the "right to give care." Unlike those respondents who made reference to specific legal rights available to them through, for example, power of attorney, these caregivers, like Gabriela and Consuelo, referenced a moral right to advocate on behalf of their care receivers:

> I can decide what I want to happen to [my husband].... They can't come and tell me what to do with him! I can decide. My family and I can decide. So I think I have every right to do whatever I want.... I don't think no one can come and tell us anything. I think we have that right here.

> I would say that you have the right to get optimum help for the person that you're caring for. You have that right. It's a right.

Caregivers also referenced the "right to give care" to themselves, echoing a common theme among social workers and social service providers about the importance of maintaining one's own emotional and physical health while providing long-term care.[9] Betty's response in this regard is typical: "What rights I have as a caregiver?...Just for myself, that is for me to take better care of myself and to lead a balanced life.... That's so important because if [I] go down the tubes so does my husband."

A final interpretation of "rights" emphasized social rights or entitlements, state-funded benefits and services such as financial support for caregivers, subsidized day care, respite care, etc. Whereas caregivers who understood rights to refer to formal or informal decision making powers in care provision tended to understand themselves as having as many rights as any other person has rights, caregivers who understood rights to include social provision observed that caregivers in the United States have no rights.[10] "I don't

---

9. The emphasis on "self-care" in social services is elaborated in Chapter 3.

10. Remarkably, only two caregivers in this study referenced entitlements under the new California paid family leave policy, which had gone into effect just months before the observation period for this study began.

know that [caregivers] have any rights," observed a typical caregiver in this regard. "I don't think caregivers are really addressed in our system." The frustration with the absence of rights for families providing long-term care could be observed in Gwen's sarcastic response to the targeted rights question:

> We have the right to care for our family. [laughs] We have the right to be burdened by it....We have the right to take our own private dollars, usually about five grand, and attempt to get conservatorship and then hopefully get that money back some time in the future....We have the right to be fired from our jobs if we have to take off too much time.

When given a follow-up probe— "What rights do you think caregivers ought to have in the United States?"—these participants gave answers consistent with the "claims" they had articulated for their caregiving dilemmas: financial support, subsidized day care, respite care, and home care.

The distribution of these four understandings of rights corresponded to participants' use of legitimating versus injustice frames. Three-quarters of those caregivers interviewed who relied exclusively on a legitimating frame in talking about their care situations interpreted "rights" narrowly, as legal or moral rights to give care—or they didn't understand how to connect rights to care provision at all. By contrast, more than three-quarters of the caregivers who relied on an injustice frame during the course of the study described "rights" more expansively to include rights to government entitlements.

The gender composition of these groups is worth noting. A nonstatistical comparison finds that while men and women were equally likely to articulate an injustice framing in this study, they had somewhat gendered understandings of what rights "mean" in the context of long-term care. For example, all of the caregivers who interpreted rights to mean a right to care or advocate on behalf of their care receiver were women. Women were twice as likely to be so confused by the targeted rights question that they could not provide a coherent answer. While there were only modest differences in the proportion of male and female caregivers who understood rights to include social rights, the deviant cases are noticeable: all of the caregivers who articulated an injustice framing but who held more limited understandings of rights were women, whereas roughly half of the caregivers who relied on a legitimating frame, but who understood rights to include rights to social provision, were men. Again the sample sizes here are both small and nonrandom—hence a test of statistical significance is impossible—but these findings would be consistent with longstanding cultural understandings of men as independent, rights-bearing citizens, and women as dependent, and non-rights-bearing caregivers (Fraser 1997).

For caregivers who relied on an injustice frame for understanding their circumstances, the processes of "naming" and assigning responsibility for unmet care needs produced solutions to long-term care dilemmas that challenged traditional demarcations between family and state responsibility for care provision. With the exception of those who identified themselves as political liberals and who held strong views of the state's responsibility for health care prior to caregiving, most of the grievants in this study had given little thought to the state when they first began caregiving. That they now envisioned their care needs as the basis of claims to new rights or entitlements—despite a strong cultural bias against extending the concept of rights to contexts involving care and dependency (Fraser 1989; Gordon 1994)—suggests a significant transformation in how they evaluated the importance of public provision in solving problems regarding long-term care.

And yet, importantly, grievants' claims for public long-term care provision bore the imprint of the grievance construction process in which they were forged: rather than conceptualizing these rights as entitlements based on market participation or citizenship—as the popular Social Security and Medicare programs are typically justified—grievants in this case justified these entitlements on the basis of need. Where grievants like Gladys and Dori were drawn to need-based models of public provision as a way of assigning responsibility to the state for unmet care needs, they also relied on the discourse of need in articulating claims for public provision (cf., Gilliom 2001):

> [I]f you need the help, the financial help...you should be able to get it....I think just like with children, the government will give you a subsidy for low-income families. And I don't know how you would determine who would [be eligible]. I don't think that's your question, just there is a need.

> The homemaker service they have now is only for low income. It should be extended to anyone and everyone who needs that money.

This understanding of public long-term care provision as being based on need rather than citizenship or market participation accords closely with the discursive logic participants used in the attribution of blame: to conceptualize long-term care needs as justifying new state entitlements, participants required a way of integrating their need for state assistance with deeply held beliefs about family responsibility for care provision. The social insurance model of public provision in most cases failed to provide such a framework, instead symbolically suggesting to many caregivers that the state would be "taking over" long-term care obligations that more properly belonged to the family. Ruth, a caregiver for both her parents, captures this concern that relying on the state for more than need-based benefits might be perceived as abandoning one's responsibilities to family:

> I have mixed feelings about it.... I'm definitely believing in home support services, defi-
> nitely believe people need to have assistance with respite care and caregiving.... So I'm
> much more for the government helping people out with these things. But I also can't say
> that I totally believe that I don't have any responsibility in this. So ... I think what I would
> like for people to do, for government to do, is to help people when they need help.

A need-based model of state provision, characterizing care provision as primarily a family responsibility and providing government "help" or "assistance" only when families need it, presented caregivers with a way of accepting state intervention, without in any way diminishing their commitments to family.

Two caveats are worth mentioning here. First, in arguing that a need-based model of social provision was more resonant than a social insurance model, I do not mean to suggest that caregivers were opposed to the idea of extending Medicare benefits to include long-term care provision. Few caregivers in this study ever demonstrated outright opposition to any form of government assistance. Rather, I seek to explain why participants' claims for public long-term care provision seemed to call for an expanded state role without challenging the ideology of family responsibility. In this case, even those caregivers who challenged norms about family responsibility for care nevertheless retained the cultural assumption that care provision is a responsibility of families first, insisting that the government should assist families only when all "private" systems fail.

Second, in arguing that a need-based model of social provision was more resonant than a social insurance model, I am also not suggesting that caregivers were in any way content with the current system of Medicaid-administered long-term care benefits. On the contrary, participants' perceptions of injustice were due largely to their inability to obtain Medicaid benefits under the current system: most participants in this study were middle- or working-class caregivers whose family members were not eligible for Medicaid benefits under the program's strict means test. Thus, while participants believed that the government should assist families with care provision only when they could not meet their basic needs, they nevertheless held an expansive definition of "need," one that envisioned not just the poor, but the middle class, as appropriate beneficiaries of public provision.

CONCLUSION

How do people imagine alternative social arrangements for the social welfare problems they confront? While social movement and socio-legal scholars have long studied the ways in which collective action frames and existing rights and benefits shape political action, many people today are seeking solutions to new social welfare dilemmas without the benefit of social movements, legislatures, or judges. As individuals in these circumstances evaluate and select from a range of available institutional and ideational resources, we can observe how traditional conceptions of family responsibility persist in the political imagination even as social conditions rapidly change.

Virtually all of the caregivers in this study maintained strong normative commitments to the idea that families should bear primary responsibility for long-term care on their own. So widespread was this presumption of care as a family responsibility that the possibility of any alternative interpretation did not occur to most caregivers until or unless they faced some crisis in care. How participants evaluated their care crises—whether they saw unmet care needs as a source of guilt or embarrassment or anger and moral indignation—depended largely on whom they blamed for their unmet care obligations. For most caregivers, the government was not a natural target for blame; few had any specific ideas when they began caregiving about what the government could or ought to do to assist in long-term care provision. The experience of caregiving, however, exposed caregivers to a variety of alternative policy models for care provision, ranging from Medicare to systems of social welfare provision found in other countries. The most resonant model for assigning responsibility for the costs or provision of long-term care to an institution other than the family was California's Medicaid program, which provides long-term care benefits and services to the state's poorest residents. California's Medicaid program was a resonant model for so many participants—despite the fact that most did not actually qualify for benefits—because it retains the primacy of family, reinforcing rather than challenging underlying beliefs about family responsibility for care.

The political claims or proposed solutions that caregivers imagined for their care dilemmas were similarly forged in this process of discursive integration. Repeatedly, these calls for state intervention in long-term care conceived of only a minimal role for the state in safeguarding social welfare. What was notable in this process was the way existing policies served as such salient models for the political imagination. Alternative models of social provision found in other countries proved to be "too foreign" for most Americans in this study, and social insurance entitlements seemed too "anti-family." Without other policy alternatives to serve as cognitive resources, discursive integration consistently seemed to produce claims for state intervention that reinforced that status quo. How then, do people ever come to imagine claims for state intervention that fundamentally challenge the dominant ideology?

Here we return to the oppositional potential of discursive integration. As individuals build on "old" or familiar political concepts, it is possible for their claims to transcend the dominant ideology (Hunt 1990; Steinberg 1999). Even by integrating elements of residualist social policies with the ideology of family responsibility for care, grievants constructed new ways of thinking about the state's responsibility for social welfare provision and what kinds of needs ought to be protected as "rights" or "entitlements" by the American welfare state. By calling on the state to ameliorate care dilemmas long considered private family affairs, grievants demonstrated a substantive shift in their beliefs about the role of the state in matters involving care or dependency. The counterhegemonic potential of this should not be discounted. But how is that potential realized? Under what conditions do people construct political claims that call for an interventionist state policy that truly addresses the unmet social long-term care needs of contemporary American families?

CHAPTER 5

Communicating Grievances— Policy Feedback and the Deserving Citizen

The previous chapters examined two dimensions of politicization: the process of reinterpreting private needs as matters of legitimate public deliberation and decision making, and the formulation of political claims for policy intervention. For many caregivers, their experiences as care providers produced strong, normative expectations that unmet long-term care needs ought to be ameliorated through policy intervention. A fully politicized individual, according to our definition, would take those expectations one step farther and communicate their political grievances to an official agency or other perceived responsible party for action. The next two chapters consider the reluctance of caregivers—or their inability—to engage in political demand making.

There are, of course, many explanations for why caregivers might not participate in organized reform efforts. Most obviously, many caregivers are too overwhelmed by the demands of long-term care provision to devote time or energy to reform efforts. Others view themselves as "not political enough" to participate in organized demand making. If these caregivers represented the full spectrum of individuals affected by long-term care provision, our inquiry would end here. But in fact, many people are deeply politicized by their experiences providing chronic care. The aim of this chapter and the next is to focus on a specific group of family care providers—grievants who are willing and able to make demands on the state for policy reform and who are embedded in organizational fields that theoretically should facilitate participation in organized demand making—to identify what obstacles prevent them from making political demands to an official agency or perceived responsible party for action.

Chapter 6 will argue that the primary obstacles to political demand making in this case are largely structural—that dramatic changes in the field of political organizations have made it difficult for individuals who experience unmet needs to express their grievances as political demands. But before elaborating this argument, this chapter examines another potential obstacle to political demand making raised by the literature on social policy regarding the demobilizing effects of existing social policy. It has become virtually axiomatic in studies of political mobilization that for constituents to participate in political demand making they must first believe that they are entitled to something better (Gamson 1992a; McAdam 1982; Piven and Cloward 1979). One can imagine solutions to all the problems in the world, but without a sense of political entitlement, without the perception that one deserves that which one is claiming, actual participation in political demand making is unlikely.

In Chapter 4, we saw that Medicaid plays a key role in shaping political grievances by providing a model for how the state might assist families in long-term care without detracting from the primacy of family responsibility. But Medicaid is more than an ideational resource; it is also the only source of public benefits for long-term care in the United States. While most Americans do not qualify for Medicaid under its strict means test, many of the caregivers in this study nevertheless applied, sometimes multiple times, for benefits to assist with care provision. That these mostly non-poor caregivers sought access to a public benefits program normally stigmatized as "welfare" would seem to contradict longstanding distinctions between contributory social insurance programs for the "deserving" middle class and public assistance programs for the "undeserving" poor. As research on "policy feedback" has shown, all social policies communicate messages to individuals about citizenship, self-worth, and the effectiveness of political voice. While clients of "top tier" social welfare programs such as Social Security and Medicare receive mostly positive lessons about themselves and their relationship to the state, evidence suggests that "welfare" policies like Medicaid or Temporary Assistance to Needy Families (TANF) signal to clients that they are not only inferior to other more deserving citizens, but that speaking out is both ineffective and potentially risky (Mettler and Soss 2004). Theories of policy feedback and the welfare state thus predict that the experience of seeking assistance for long-term care from Medicaid may actually diminish caregivers' sense of themselves as deserving citizens and thus impede organized demand making.

This chapter's analysis of the experiences of non-poor caregivers with Medicaid and other sources of long-term care assistance suggests, however, another possibility. Rather than viewing themselves as inferior or stigmatized for seeking assistance from a "welfare" program, most nonpoor Medicaid applicants extended the lessons learned from "top tier" social insurance to the context of contemporary long-term care provision. In other words, rather than being diminished by their experiences with Medicaid, non-poor caregivers in this study recast Medicaid as a middle-class entitlement owed by the state to "deserving" citizens like themselves.

This recasting of Medicaid offers the clearest illustration of how discursive integration can potentially produce understandings of caregiving conditions that transcend the dominant ideology. We've seen in previous chapters that because so many partners and adult children increasingly cannot meet the care needs of their family, the line between "dutiful" family members who take care of their own no matter what the cost and family members who abandon or fail to meet their obligations to care has become blurred. Caregivers seeking solutions for unmet needs are drawn to policies that not only address unmet need, but also reinforce their status as responsible family members—in this case, Medicaid. But the turn to Medicaid violates another important cultural distinction in this country between "deserving" and "undeserving" citizens. By seeking to maintain a positive perception of self-worth across cultural categories, as both dutiful family members and deserving citizens, some caregivers in this study integrated powerful notions of citizenship, entitlement, and state obligation with their traditional beliefs about family responsibility for care. In many cases, this produced a fundamental rethinking of the state's role in long-term care provision, one that matched neither the social insurance nor public assistance models of state provision that have historically constituted the American welfare state.

POLICY FEEDBACK

The idea that existing policies can shape future politics is not a recent discovery in the study of political systems. Political scientists and sociologists have long examined the ways in which policies shape political interactions between interest groups and policymakers (Lowi 1964; Lowi 1972; Wilson 1973); the beliefs and actions of the mass public (Piven and Cloward 1979); and the degree of social solidarity among citizens (Marshall [1950]1992).[1] But it wasn't until historical institutionalists coined the term

---

1. See Mettler and Soss (2004) for a historical overview of the empirical antecedents to the literature on policy feedback.

"policy feedback" in the last decade or so, that scholars began to tie together these diverse lines of inquiry in a more comprehensive effort to understand the ways that "policies, once enacted, restructure subsequent political processes" (Skocpol 1992:58).[2] While some policy feedback research has examined policy's effects on state capacities and the ways in which new policies create, build upon, or undercut administrative arrangements (see, e.g., Pierson 1993; Pierson 1994; Skocpol 1992), more recent research has explored policy's effects on the capabilities of social groups, such as the effects of policies on identities or political goals (see, e.g., Campbell 2003; Mettler 2005; Schneider and Ingram 1997; Soss 2005).

This more recent research has identified two kinds of effects that policies can have on the capabilities of social groups. First, policies can affect citizens materially by providing resources and incentives that shape political strategy and behavior and give beneficiaries a self-interested stake in defending program benefits (Pierson 1993). Andrea Campbell (2003), for example, found in her historical analysis of Social Security that retirement benefits provided the once-marginalized senior population with politically relevant resources like income and free time (see also Verba et al. 1995). The program also increased political participation over the years by tangibly connecting beneficiaries' fortunes to government action (Campbell 2003).

Second, policies can have interpretive effects on the mass public by providing information and sources of meaning (Pierson 1993; Steensland 2007). Public policies not only define membership and assign status or standing in the political community, but they also communicate to beneficiaries cues about their worth as citizens and their privileges and rights as members of the polity (Mettler and Soss 2004; Soss 2005). Social policies can also send messages to the broader public about group characteristics, making some groups appear trustworthy or devious, morally virtuous or repugnant—and this can affect citizens' ideas about which groups are deserving or undeserving of government assistance (Schneider and Ingram 1993; Schneider and Ingram 1997).

Finally, there is considerable evidence that the "cognitive cues" citizens receive from social policies affect both their attitudes toward government and their political participation (Mettler 2005; Soss 2002). These feedback effects largely (but not exclusively (Bruch et al. 2011)) track the "two tiers" of the American welfare state (Fraser 1989; Skocpol 1988). The upper tier consists of universal social insurance programs such as Social Security and Medicare. Policymakers and the American public generally view social insurance benefits as "earned entitlements" for "deserving" citizens who

---

2. See also Pierson (1993; 1994); Steinmo et al. (1992), and Hall (1986).

have "paid into the system" over the course of their working lives. When policies treat beneficiaries with dignity and respect, they convey to citizens that they are entitled to certain goods, services, or procedures from the state, and this, in turn, shapes their psychological predisposition to participate in public life (Campbell 2003). Suzanne Mettler (2005) finds, for example, that after World War II, veterans from less- advantaged backgrounds were treated under the G.I. Bill as esteemed members of the polity and as a consequence they became far more active political participants than theory would have expected. Similarly, Joe Soss's (2002) study of citizen experiences with Social Security Disability Insurance (SSDI), a social insurance program, found that client experiences with the program produced perceptions of themselves as secure citizens, safe enough to assert themselves by contesting agency decisions and, importantly, confident that they could be effective in influencing decision-making processes.

The "bottom tier" of the American welfare state consists of "welfare" programs such as Temporary Assistance to Needy Families (TANF) (formerly Aid to Families with Dependent Children (AFDC)), food stamps, Medicaid, and public housing assistance. Heavily stigmatized, beneficiaries of these programs are widely perceived by policymakers and the public to be undeserving poor people trying to get government "handouts" for free (Fraser 1989; Skocpol 1988). Evidence suggests that means-tested policies that mark individuals as inferior and that subject beneficiaries to surveillance and threats of disciplinary action sharply diminish beneficiaries' perceptions of political efficacy (Soss 2005). Soss found, for example, that in their encounters with welfare agencies, AFDC recipients reported feeling humiliated and vulnerable to retribution. Recipients inferred from their experiences with the program that speaking out is both ineffective and potentially risky.[3]

Not only do policy designs shape clients' beliefs about the effectiveness of asserting themselves to program officials, but they can also influence broader beliefs about political participation. Soss finds that many individuals tend to view government as "one big system"—without distinguishing, for example, between administrative agencies and political institutions. As a consequence, they often interpret their experiences exercising their voice in one particular social welfare program as evidence of what they can expect from petitioning the government more generally (Soss 2005). When individuals were asked whether government officials listen to people like them,

---

3. The mobilization of welfare beneficiaries during the height of the welfare rights movement in the United States attests to the fact that these policy lessons can be "relearned" or transformed through exposure to alternative perspectives or collective action frames (Bussiere 1997; Kornbluh 2007).

60% of SSDI clients reported that they believed they do; only 8% of AFDC clients agreed. Soss finds that even after controlling for a variety of background characteristics, AFDC clients were significantly less likely to be politically active than other individuals with the same demographic profiles.

As the following section elaborates, the surging number of middle-class families who seek long-term care assistance from the means-tested Medicaid program are exposed to two very different types of policy lessons: On the one hand, they are familiar with the positive civic lessons communicated by American social insurance programs, encouraging a sense of entitlement and political efficacy, but on the other hand, they find themselves seeking assistance from a public welfare program that marks beneficiaries as inferior and undeserving. In striking contrast to conventional understandings of the effects of stigmatized social policies, this study finds that the lessons learned from social insurance programs are durable, flexible, and capable of being extended to the new context of long-term care.

MEDICAID AND THE MIDDLE CLASS

Because private health insurance and Medicare offer few, if any, benefits for long-term care services, Medicaid has evolved into this country's most important public source of long-term care assistance. Originally established to ensure that low-income families had access to acute medical care, most state Medicaid programs now provide coverage not only for acute care, but also prescription drug benefits and, perhaps most critically, nursing home care. Some state Medicaid programs, including California's, also provide coverage for adult day care and in-home supportive services. Unlike Social Security and Medicare, Medicaid is not a contributory program. Beneficiaries do not have a legal right to long-term care benefits on the basis of tax payments or a lifetime of work. By most accounts Medicaid is considered a paradigmatic case of a stigmatized "welfare" program.[4]

---

4. It should be noted that studies in recent years have found that stigma associated with TANF is more pronounced than stigma associated with Medicaid (Stuber and Kronebusch 2004). This may be because the public today recognizes that many people do not have access to health insurance and therefore sees Medicaid beneficiaries as more deserving of state assistance than undeserving "welfare" recipients (Stuber and Kronebusch 2004). Despite the relative difference, however, there is still strong evidence of stigma associated with Medicaid. Some of this can be traced to the act of "applying for assistance," which may be perceived as welfare related (Stuber and Kronebusch 2004). In other words, the social meaning attached to the act of acknowledging need may itself be stigmatizing for many potential applicants. Recent studies seeking to better understand low take-up rates with respect to means-tested programs (between 40% and 70% of families do not participate in government programs for which they are eligible), have found significant effects of stigma (Stuber and Kronebusch 2004; Stuber and

But because Medicaid is the only public program to offer any form of assistance with the costs of long-term care, the means-tested program has been used more and more in recent decades by middle-class families, and it is this fact that has turned the program into a flashpoint for political contention. Although less than 10% of Medicaid beneficiaries use long-term care services, long-term care accounts for approximately one-third of total Medicaid spending (O'Brien and Elias 2004). Concerns among fiscal conservatives that Medicaid is evolving into a "middle-class entitlement" have provoked a storm of criticism from the political right. Commentators charge that not only are the middle- and upper-income elderly who seek Medicaid drawing finite resources away from other Medicaid beneficiaries, mainly poor children and their families, but they are fostering a middle-class "sense of entitlement" that creates a significant barrier to the expansion of long-term care insurance or other more rational financing systems for long-term care (Moses 1993; Moses 1996). "[W]hy should someone buy private long-term care insurance," observes a report on Medicaid estate planning paid for by the Health Insurance Association of America, "if, for less money, they can hire an attorney, shelter their assets, and get 'nursing home insurance' through Medicaid?" (Burwell 1991:5). Such criticism has been accompanied by legislative initiatives designed to make it more difficult for the non-poor to use Medicaid as a safety net, including restrictions on asset transfers, penalties for attempts to illegally shift assets for the purpose of gaining Medicaid eligibility, and controversial estate recovery programs to recoup assets after the death of middle-class homeowners who receive Medicaid benefits (Grogan and Patashnik 2003b; Harrington Meyer and Storbakken 2000). Concerns about the effects of Medicaid trends on the long-term care insurance industry have also sparked a wave of proposals to offer more liberal tax incentives to make long-term care insurance more affordable for the middle class.

If conservative Republicans have been concerned about the development of a "middle-class entitlement" to Medicaid, Democrats in the 1990s were eager to promote this characterization. Grogan and Patashnik (2003a; 2003b) have documented how, during the clash with Gingrich-Dole Republicans over the 1995–1996 budget, President Clinton went to great lengths to define Medicaid as a core social welfare entitlement, as valuable to middle-class families as Medicare and educational and environmental programs (Grogan and Patashnik 2003b:60). No president in the history of

---

Schlesinger 2006). Research has consistently found that recipients describe their experiences of applying for public assistance as negative and unpleasant (Auletta 1982; Piven and Cloward 1993; Saunders 2006; Soss 2002), and these experiences could affect their willingness to enroll in means-tested programs.

the program had ever referred to Medicaid in such terms. The Democratic Party also adopted similar characterizations of Medicaid in its political platform (Grogan and Patashnik 2003a; Grogan and Patashnik 2003b).

In 2005, Congress held a series of hearings on escalating Medicaid costs which introduced a new theme into the long-term care debate: personal responsibility for long-term care planning (Grogan and Andrews 2010). For the first time, conservative policymakers suggested that the root of the long-term care crisis is a lack of personal responsibility among Americans to prepare for their own long-term care needs. This view of personal responsibility drew on longstanding cultural tropes about "welfare" programs: Medicaid was promoting government dependency by enabling middle-class Americans in their prime working years to avoid planning for their care in old age, leading to economic dependency in later life (Grogan and Andrews 2010). In the face of a sharp economic downturn and increasing pressure from state governments to rein in the costs of Medicaid, even Democrats in recent years have backed off their characterizations of Medicaid as a core middle-class entitlement, returning to the more traditional rhetoric of Medicaid as an important safety net for our most vulnerable populations (Grogan and Andrews 2010).

As the following analysis shows, however, most grievants in this study conceptualized Medicaid in terms that matched neither the discourse of academics—distinguishing between social insurance and means-tested programs—nor the talking points of Republicans and Democrats. For working- and middle-class families, the journey from the top tier of the welfare state to a public assistance program historically relegated to the "undeserving poor" is one fraught with frustration, indignation, and resignation. But during that journey, caregivers demonstrated the power of lessons learned from policy and the creativity of the political imagination. The following analysis traces the arc of this journey, beginning with the challenge of seeking solutions to care needs within the family and eventually finding one's way to Medicaid.

THE MIDDLE-CLASS JOURNEY TO MEDICAID

Consistent with the ideology of family responsibility, most families struggling to provide long-term care believed it was their responsibility to care for their own and that they should do so with their own resources. As a result, when most families needed economic assistance in order to pay for long-term care supportive services, their search typically began in the private sector; only when they had exhausted all possibilities did they seriously contemplate state assistance. The following narrative traces the most common trajectory for the working- and middle-class families in this study as they moved through private sector solutions and then confronted eligibility requirements for public assistance.

Private Sector Solutions to Purchasing Supportive Services

At the time of this study, Henry was caring for his wife, who was diagnosed with Alzheimer's disease in 2002. At seventy-nine and in poor health, Henry conceded that he could not adequately care for his wife by himself, but he refused to place her in a skilled nursing facility, wanting her instead to live at home. He looked into hiring a live-in caregiver. Upon learning the cost of in-home care, Henry's reaction was typical of the working- and middle-class caregivers in this study:

> When I found out what the cost was going to be, I'm telling you…I did a lot of praying. Because [my wife] and I, we're just average Americans I guess. We're not rich. We live on Social Security and a small pension. But I mean, we were getting by all right. But we didn't have no $45,000 surplus dollars! Most people don't!

Caregivers who confronted the high costs of market-based services relied on three strategies for resolving their caregiving dilemmas: (1) foregoing supportive services and relying exclusively on unpaid family care; (2) paying for supportive services out of pocket and/or pooling family resources; and (3) relying on nonprofit grantmaking institutions, reverse mortgages or long-term care insurance. All of these strategies reflected a normative commitment to keep the costs of care provision within the family.

Faced with the prospect of paying significant out-of-pocket costs for supportive services, many caregivers in this study chose to forego outside assistance altogether or to delay assistance until their situations had worsened considerably. Indeed, many had been reluctant to ask for help even before they became aware of the economic costs, and once confronted with the costs, it was not difficult for them to reconsider their need for outside assistance. Sharon represents this dynamic quite well. Exhausted from the responsibility of caring for her husband all day and repeatedly waking up during the night to assist him to the bathroom, Sharon felt she had reached a physical and emotional breaking point: "You get used to doing it all yourself," she recounted. "You go inward. This is what I have to do. It's twenty-four hours a day, but I can do it." Sharon paused. "Then you realize you can't." She described the sense of duty she felt at the time: "I felt, you know, I was his wife. And I wasn't working so I should take care of him.... I felt that was what I should do. But I remember as it began to sink in how much care he was needing, that maybe I should get some kind of help." Not knowing where to turn, she asked her husband's physician for information. "[H]e said there are places that you could call ... like nurses' aides and things like that, but they're pretty expensive. And I thought well, I could still do it myself.... I don't know if we can afford all that."

Many of these caregivers worried that the condition of their care receiver could deteriorate significantly in the future, and thus chose to forego paying for supportive services in order to preserve their resources in the event they might later need more advanced—and therefore expensive—help (cf. Brody 2004). Still others struck a middle ground by purchasing some assistance, but far less than they would have preferred—fewer hours of in-home assistance, for example, or fewer days at adult day care. But for many caregivers, forgoing supportive services was not an option, regardless of the cost. Caregivers who worked in the paid labor force, for example, often needed supportive services so that they could leave the house to work. Other caregivers were simply unable—physically or emotionally—to provide an adequate level of care without the assistance of supportive services.

Of those caregivers who did hire care assistance, virtually all of them paid for the assistance out of pocket, tapping into their lifetime savings and retirement accounts. Retirees in these circumstances often lamented the fact that the money they had saved for retirement or to pass on to their children was now being spent almost exclusively on caregiving. "[T]here isn't much life," observed one retiree, caring for his wife, "because everything you've saved for was going to be used for your old age and happiness and travel and so forth and enjoying your life. And then your life took a quick turn in the other direction." Adult children like Lonnie worried about the future consequences of the financial outlays they made to provide care for their parents.

> [Y]ou find yourself in the position of having to take care of a loved one, you use up all of their resources and a lot of your own resources, and who's going to take care of you, you know, when you reach that age when you need assistance? Your resources are gone, caring for someone a generation older than you.

When the costs of purchasing supportive services were beyond the individual caregivers' capacity to pay, it was common for other family members to make financial contributions to alleviate the burden. Many of the elderly caregivers in this study expressed discomfort in burdening their adult children with care responsibilities, yet most had few alternatives but to accept the financial assistance.

By relying largely on unpaid family caregiving labor and by paying for supportive services out of pocket or with the assistance of other family members, caregivers in this study reinforced the normative commitment to keep the costs of long-term care within the family. But for many working- and middle-class caregivers, the cost of purchasing supportive services, particularly for patients who needed intensive, twenty-four-hour care, eventually exceeded their family's ability to pay. Three other non-state sources of assistance—nonprofit social services, reverse mortgages, and long-term care insurance—were available to assist families, but each presented significant obstacles to utilization.

In Los Angeles, there is a variety of nonprofit supportive services available at low or no cost to low-income families, ranging from in-home supportive care and adult day care, to legal assistance and Meals on Wheels. The eligibility requirements for these discounted services are often not as stringent as Medi-Cal, but most middle-class families in this study nevertheless found that they could not qualify for help. Bet Tzedek Legal Services, for example, provides legal assistance on issues specifically related to long-term care, but for middle-income families these services are not subsidized. "I can't afford them," one caregiver observed. "I went to them, to ask them about elder care, and it was maybe $2,000 and we didn't have it." Religious organizations also offered limited forms of assistance in Los Angeles, but when they were offered, many caregivers were reluctant to use them. At one support group meeting, for example, the facilitator mentioned a new in-home care service called Faith in Action run through a local religious organization. But participants in the group—most of them very religious themselves—expressed concerns about using such a service, noting that the volunteers were not bonded and that there were no real protections against fraud or abuse other than trusting that the volunteers were very religious.

Working- and middle-class caregivers spoke in support groups, focus groups, and interviews about the experience of calling one nonprofit organization after another seeking grants or discounted services. "I've gone down every avenue and every route," observed a frustrated Susanna, who was caring for both of her dementia stricken parents, "but no, according to them, [my parents] earn too much money....Well they've *worked* all their lives. Excuse me!" Another participant, caring for her mother, similarly observed: "You don't really...know how bad it is until you're put in the situation where...every door keeps being slammed in your face." All of these working- and middle-class caregivers described a nonprofit sector that offered few options for helping them with supportive services outside of small and infrequent grants. Irma's attempt to pay for in-home assistance for her mother, who has Alzheimer's, captures the average

middle-class experience of patching together scarce funds to pay for supportive services:

> We were able to find a grant for her, but it was only for a couple of months, and now
> we don't have that. So it's essentially coming out of [my income]. And then if I need it,
> someone can send me $50 or my brother can send me $70 occasionally, and we put it
> together. But if push really comes to shove, it's on me. It's really on me. But we're looking
> around for other grants for her. We tried the arthritis angle, we tried the stroke…

The one source of nonprofit assistance available to some working- or
middle-class caregivers in Los Angeles is the LA Caregiver Resource
Center[5] (LACRC). Indeed the LACRC was created in part as a response
to the need for assistance for middle-class families: In striking contrast
to other nonprofit organizations, caregivers who receive funding from
Medi-Cal are not eligible for LACRC grant assistance. The LACRC maintains a respite fund from which it distributes grants to families providing
care for adults with brain-impairing conditions, such as Alzheimer's disease, stroke, Parkinson's, and traumatic brain injury. Several caregivers in
this study reported receiving one-time grants ranging from $400 to $3,600,
which they used for the purchase of adult day care, respite care, or in-home
care assistance. Depending on funding availability and demand for grants,
the waitlists for a single grant from the LACRC range from one to three
years. At the time of this study, there were 8,900 people on the wait list.
While caregivers were uniformly appreciative of the assistance, most of
them noted that the grants were just a fraction of what they needed to meet
the care needs of their family members.

In the absence of significant assistance from the nonprofit sector, a second potential non-state source of funding for long-term care services is the
reverse mortgage. A reverse mortgage is a type of home loan that allows
families to convert a portion of the equity in their home into cash. Instead
of paying the lender a monthly mortgage payment, the lender pays the borrower according to the payment plan selected.[6] Unlike traditional home
equity loans, however, no repayment is required until the borrower dies or
sells his or her home.[7] Once the home is sold, the estate must repay the

---

5. At the time of this study, the LACRC was funded partly by the State of California though
the California Department of Mental Health and the LA County Area Agency on Aging, but
it also received a significant portion of its budget from the USC Davis School of Gerontology,
where it is based, and from foundations, grants, and private donations.

6. Borrowers are still required to pay real estate taxes, insurance, and other payments such as
utilities.

7. The loan can also become due if the borrower no longer uses the home as a principal residence or fails to meet the obligations of his or her mortgage.

cash received from the reverse mortgage, plus interest and other fees. The remaining equity in the home, if any, can then be passed onto the borrower's heirs. Only two caregivers in this study had pursued such a loan for themselves. One of them was Henry, introduced earlier in this chapter, who was looking for a way to keep his wife at home, even as her dementia worsened. Unable to afford the $45,000 needed to pay for a full-time caregiver—and unable to provide physical care himself, due to his own age and physical health—he signed the paperwork for a reverse mortgage. Even after receiving $2,500 a month from the loan, Henry was still paying $15,000 a year out of pocket. He nevertheless referred to the reverse mortgage as a "godsend."

Most caregivers, however, refused to pursue a reverse mortgage because they were reluctant to give up their homes. Their house, they insisted, was the principal asset they owned, and the asset they intended to pass onto their children. Several adult children in this study pleaded with their parents to use the equity in their houses for long-term care support. "If the money takes care of you, then that's a load off my back," recounted Vincent as he described this argument with his father. "And that to me, is worth more than all the inheritance…" But this was a battle no adult children in this study won.

Long-term care insurance provided one last private-sector financing option. Here issues of availability, affordability, and coverage limitations all remained significant obstacles to utilization. Many older caregivers hadn't known long-term care insurance existed when it would have been affordable to purchase a policy and when medical exclusions would not have been an issue.[8] For others, the insurance premiums were simply too expensive. For people in their forties and fifties, other financial pressures—raising kids, paying for college, and saving for retirement—competed for scarce resources, and few were thinking about long-term care then at all.

While these caregivers reflected on long-term care insurance as a missed opportunity, some caregivers had purchased insurance policies but were reluctant to actually use them. Many of these caregivers discovered, long after the policies were purchased, that the policies contained coverage limitations they had not anticipated—restricting coverage to two or three years, for example, or to nursing home care only. Families faced with illnesses of indefinite duration were reluctant to start the clock on these policies for fear that their caregiving needs might be far more significant in the future. Reba, for example, had just started taking her husband to adult day care

---

8. Private insurers typically offer coverage only to individuals in good health at the time of enrollment. People with a history of heart disease, diabetes, arthritis, hypertension, dementia, or recent hospitalization are routinely screened out. Thus, it was obviously too late for most caregivers to obtain long-term care insurance for their chronically ill family members.

at the start of this study's observational period. She called her insurance company to find out whether it would cover the cost (nearly $100/day) and reported back to her support group: "I've been paying a lot of money for long-term care, and then I called the person that sold me the care, and they said it's only good for two years." The insurance representative told Reba that the company would pay for the day care, but the costs would be subtracted from the total coverage provided under her policy.

> And I says well that's terrible!... So he says but [use the policy anyway]. I says no, I'm not. He said what if you never use it? I says I'll use it, but I want to use it when I can.... [T]he more I use it up, it's like a big amount they give you and once it's over, it's over.

Such stories cropped up regularly in support group meetings, creating the impression among caregivers in the study that the long-term care insurance market is unreliable, and in some cases untrustworthy. Few caregivers knew anyone who was significantly assisted by any form of insurance coverage. Of the nearly 180 caregivers in this study, only six reported using long-term care insurance to cover the costs of supportive services.

If the operating assumption for most working- and middle-class caregivers in this study, then, was that they should do their best to cover the costs of supportive services through private-sector solutions, that assumption was sorely tested once they confronted the costs of purchasing care. Whether they turned to adult day care, in-home assistance, or skilled nursing facilities, the cost of purchasing care in most cases substantially drained savings the caregivers had hoped would last their lifetimes or exceeded their capacity to pay altogether. With few, if any, satisfactory financing options available to them in the private-sector, these caregivers looked to the state for assistance.

Public Sector Solutions to Financing Supportive Services

Because care receivers often obtain their acute care coverage from Medicare, many families typically assume—incorrectly—that Medicare will also cover the costs associated with nursing home care and other forms of supportive services. The process of understanding Medicare's coverage limitations involved a steep learning curve for these caregivers. Carolyn, for example, was fifty-seven when her husband began suffering from the beginning stages of a rare degenerative brain disorder.

> I think most people think that you put somebody in an institution and the government's going to pay for it. Well that's not true. And we don't know that until the issue comes up....And all the help that you think you could get? You don't. You have to pay for

it.…I don't think people understand this.…I can't tell you how many times [people] say well you can always put him into an institution. Well no you can't. No you can't. And that's the fact of life. And people don't know that.

Once confronted with Medicare's coverage limitations, virtually all of the caregivers who sought financial assistance for supportive services next looked into Medi-Cal, California's Medicaid program. As in most means-tested state assistance programs in this country, the income and asset eligibility requirements for Medi-Cal are very stringent.[9] While those who qualify for CalWORKs (previously AFDC) or Supplemental Security Income (SSI) are automatically eligible for Medi-Cal, most of the care receivers in this sample had incomes well above the eligibility requirements for either program. Reaction from middle-class caregivers to the standards for Medi-Cal eligibility was frequently one of open dismay. "I looked into…Medi-Cal," Trenton, a middle-class retiree, told me. "[I]t's practically *impossible* for a person with adequate means to get into Medicaid. You have to be penniless almost!" For the non-poor caregivers in this sample, the means test was set so far below their standard of living, they could not comprehend living on what Medi-Cal permitted. Elliott, whose annual retirement income was over $70,000, was one of many who reacted to the Medi-Cal eligibility standards in this way: "But Medi-Cal is almost like you're a homeless person!…How can you exist on that little money?" The fact that Medi-Cal was a program designed to assist the *poor* was lost on many of the caregivers who looked into Medi-Cal financing. As one middle-class caregiver noted, incredulously: "You have to be almost poverty-stricken, don't you? Yeah. I was amazed."

The stories of family caregivers with significant care needs who could neither afford to pay for supportive services nor qualify for Medi-Cal painted a vivid portrait of the dilemmas faced by those caught between the failures of the private and public sectors. Just prior to this study, Serena's husband, diagnosed with Alzheimer's, had deteriorated to the point where he needed twenty-four-hour care. His paranoia, tendency to wander, and increasingly combative personality took a profound toll on seventy-two-year-old Serena's

---

9. In California in 2004, the "need standard"—or the amount of monthly income that the state determined is necessary for an individual to meet monthly expenses, not including medical bills—was $600 a month or $934 a month for an elderly/disabled couple. Individuals could not qualify for state aid unless they had less than $2,000 in financial assets. Clothing, jewelry and furniture were generally exempt from consideration. Applicants were also permitted to keep a car, as long as they could show that the car is used for medical purposes. Generally, if an individual has an income above the "need standard" and a doctor determines that nursing home care is "medically necessary," the patient can qualify for Medicaid, but must pay a "share of cost" for his or her medical bills each month.

physical and emotional health. Having reached a point where she acknowledged she needed help, she looked into financial assistance: "Everything we tried, we were not eligible for," she recounted in her interview. "Everything, everything we tried, we were not eligible."

Face to face with a means test designed to screen out all but the very poor, many middle-class families with few other financial alternatives available to them actively sought out ways to arrange their affairs so that their care recipient ultimately qualified for Medi-Cal. This could be accomplished either by shifting assets or by "spending down." Family caregivers could take advantage of Medicaid asset transfer rules to shift assets to family members, reducing their "means" for purposes of the means test, but without losing ultimate command over their resources (Goodin and Le Grand 1986). Federal laws designed to prevent "artificial impoverishment" on the part of the non-poor disabled elderly impose a penalty period—during which applicants are denied Medicaid eligibility—for those who illegally divest or shelter assets for the purpose of qualifying for Medicaid. But to enforce these rules, states must prove that someone divested their assets for the sole purpose of obtaining Medicaid benefits. Because people can divest their wealth for a variety of reasons, this case can be difficult to make (Burwell 1991).

In fact, many forms of asset transfers are explicitly permitted under Medicaid rules. In particular, special rules—so-called "spousal impoverishment" protections—allow married couples to set aside income and assets for spouses who will remain living in the community after their loved one is institutionalized.[10] Those familiar with Medicaid rules can find a variety of ways to gain entry to Medicaid (Burwell 1991), and in this study, many middle- and upper-income caregivers sought the assistance of elder law attorneys to inquire into this option. Serena, who had been repeatedly denied eligibility for her husband, eventually hurt her back and needed to place her husband in a nursing facility. It was at this point that she sought the assistance of an attorney:

> So what she did was put things in my name, so that he could qualify. And she told me how to get my own checking account and the property tax and everything comes in my name. Because…in order for us to qualify, we would have to get down to like $2,000 apiece. And I was trying to do that, but then the taxes, the property taxes here is like

10. For many years, Medicaid rules required couples to spend down almost all of their assets and income before they could be eligible for nursing home aid. This left the partner still living in the community (typically the wife) with few resources on which to survive. The "spousal impoverishment" protections enacted by Congress in 1988 significantly increased the amount of income the community spouse can keep.

> $1,800 something and then we have another property, it was $1,600....Well there's no way that I could keep the bank account under $4,000 and have the taxes when it's time to pay. So she helped, the lawyer helped me do those things.

While for most caregivers like Serena, asset-shifting was the only way to obtain financing for necessary care services, a few caregivers were upfront about the fact that the primary reason for shifting assets was to preserve inheritances for their children. Karen, who lived in a large house in a wealthy neighborhood in Los Angeles, was quite clear about her motivations in this regard:

> I'm very interested in protecting assets, I won't deny that. I didn't spend all my life thinking about ways to acquire, to protect, to pass on to my children to now to think of passing it on to strangers...so yeah, I'm definitely interested in asset protection.

Media coverage often gives the impression that "artificial impoverishment" is a wide-spread phenomenon, but empirical evidence suggests that in fact most of the elderly with disabilities have too little wealth to warrant hiring an attorney to arrange an asset transfer.[11]

A second much more common way for non-poor families to gain access to Medi-Cal benefits is to "spend down" their assets until the care receiver is effectively impoverished, at which point he or she qualifies for Medi-Cal. At the time of this study—in 2004—approximately 40% of nursing home residents nationwide relied on Medicaid as their primary source of payment at admission—either because they were already poor or because they had previously "spent down" their assets due to high medical expenses (O'Brien and Elias 2004). Another 20% entered nursing homes and subsequently depleted all of their life savings until they qualified for Medicaid coverage (O'Brien and Elias 2004).

For some caregivers in this study, spending down a lifetime of savings to care for a spouse or parent was seen as the natural course of things—what else is money for, if not to take care of your family? Ida Mae, for example, spent the entirety of her parents' $1 million estate on in-home care assistance over a ten-year period. At the time of her interview, her mother had just obtained eligibility for Medi-Cal and had been placed in a nursing home. "We came from a more than comfortable family, and couldn't believe it when I had to resort to [Medi-Cal]," she said. "Because my parents just outlived their money. My mom is ninety today."

---

11. See O'Brien (2005) for a review of studies on estate planning and Medicaid.

But most participants in this study viewed the spend-down advice with resentment. They saw the advice as inverting the lessons they had learned about the value of work, individual responsibility, and the possibilities for upward mobility. They had been taught to work hard, pay their taxes, and save for their retirement; now the spend-down advice asked caregivers to spend their lifetime savings to move down the mobility ladder to poverty. Karen typifies the resentment expressed by many caregivers in the following angry commentary:

> [I]t's the middle class that's expected to work all its life, pay high taxes, plot and plan to save for their retirement and to pass on some of what they acquired to their children…[now] they're expected to drain themselves. I mean, lawyers will say to you go, spend down. Go on that cruise. Do this, do that. What do they mean?

Isadore, who at the time of this study was just acknowledging that he could no longer care for his wife on his own, expressed dismay that the government would want him to just "spend" a lifetime of savings he had earned through hard work and a "little bit of frugality."

> [T]o ask somebody to go into a nursing home and come up with $50,000 to spend down, you begin to wonder to yourself, well, was I right in my frugality or should I have bought a brand new Cadillac every three years like everybody else? And here the government is taking care of them anyway!

In much of the discourse around Medi-Cal eligibility, caregivers like Isadore compared those who had "done right" by working hard, saving, and paying their taxes, with those who had never worked and were getting help from the government anyway. Their references to "deservingness" in the context of the public assistance program were notable, given that it is typically social insurance beneficiaries who are characterized as deserving, not public assistance beneficiaries. As the following section shows, the discourse that non-poor caregivers used to talk about their Medi-Cal experiences reflected lessons learned from the contributory social insurance programs for which they were eligible: Social Security and Medicare.

NAVIGATING CONFLICTING POLICY MESSAGES

While the typical American has little contact with the Social Security Administration or the Centers for Medicare & Medicaid Services and knows very little about either program's scope or rules, he or she is often keenly aware of the taxes taken from every paycheck for the two contributory programs, as well as the "contractual" promise they represent: the govern-ment deducts taxes from every paycheck, and in return, the state guarantees retirement and health care benefits when the taxpayer reaches the requisite age. This simple understanding of social insurance—and the relationship between citizen and state it embodies—lay at the heart of virtually every argument made by non-poor caregivers in this study for why they should be entitled to Medi-Cal assistance.

In making a case for state assistance, caregivers like Reba typically pref-aced their arguments by emphasizing that they and their care receivers had always been hard-working, taxpaying citizens:

> I've been paying taxes all my life. [My husband's] been working and paying taxes all his life. I don't mean that we want to freeload, but the thing is, if you haven't got it, I want the people to have it, and I want there to be a place where you're not worried all the time about how you're going to go destitute.

Caregivers suggested that because they've worked hard over their life-times, and because they've paid taxes or "paid into the system," the help they wanted from the state has in some way been earned, in the same way they understood Social Security or Medicare to be earned benefits. Here of course, entitlements discourse did not refer to benefits actually granted by any state authority—again, Medi-Cal is not an entitlement program. Instead, caregivers relied on entitlements discourse in an aspirational sense, drawing on constructs of social citizenship learned from their participation in Social Security and Medicare to make a case for what kinds of benefits they felt were owed to them by the state. The following comments from Joe and Toni are illustrative of how caregivers imported this political logic into the context of long-term care:

> Middle America's the ones that pay in, so we should be entitled [to long-term care bene-fits]. . . . I don't think we'll have to have another Boston Tea Party, but [the government's] got to understand that they just can't say give me give me give me give me and not let the people know that okay, while I'm taking, I'm giving something back.

> I think it's awful that the amount of monies that they take from us over the years, that they can't have facilities or be able to put some of the money back to help people.

In addition to drawing on the logic of contributory social welfare programs to make a case for why they deserved public long-term care assistance, caregiv-ers frequently drew a distinction between themselves as "deserving" work-ers, taxpayers, or citizens, and "undeserving" Medi-Cal beneficiaries. In Los Angeles, where there is a significant immigrant population, constructions of "undeserving" Medi-Cal recipients were frequently laced with anti-immigrant rhetoric. Mary, a caregiver for both her parents, illustrates the combination of rhetorical strategies in the following commentary to her support group:

> I remember a long time ago when I got divorced. And I had two kids and I was working but...I was like two dollars over the limit [to qualify for Medi-Cal]! You know, I have worked, my parents have worked, they have put into the system, but all the people that were sitting there didn't speak English, they all qualified because...because. Because of whatever. I think we've neglected to care for our own and chosen to care for the people who...and I'm not saying they don't have rights. I'm not saying they don't have rights. But we've chosen to take care of them rather than take care of our own. And I think it's wrong....I think we the people who live here and have contributed and our ancestors have contributed, you know, our mothers, our fathers, our grandparents, we should have rights just like they do. And just because we've worked hard and made a *minimal* living shouldn't disqualify people from services.

Dora echoed this sentiment during a focus group discussion:

> [T]here are too many people, especially in California and some of the border states, where we've got people who are benefiting from Medicare and Medi-Cal that don't pay a thing. And our kids [who] were born in the United States, their parents and grandparents have all paid taxes, they aren't eligible for anything.

Soss (2005) observed a similar phenomenon in his study of AFDC recipients: Because the stigma of being on "welfare" poses a real threat to self-image, he argued, AFDC clients found ways to sustain the belief that they are "good" people. By contrasting an "undeserving" majority of AFDC clients with a smaller and more virtuous group that included themselves, AFDC recipients suggested that while negative stereotypes may be properly applied to the majority, they were not applicable to themselves. The "less deserving" reference group, in other words, was intended to make them look good by comparison.

While a similar type of stigma management (cf. Goffman 1986) may have been at work in this case, it was notable that non-poor caregivers very rarely made direct references to the stigma of Medi-Cal.[12] When participants did construct a reference group which made them look comparatively "deserving," it was typically in the context of critiquing Medi-Cal's stringent eligibility requirements. The reference group was used, in other words, to

---

12. While few caregivers mentioned the stigma of Medicaid, many caregivers did express concern about the poor quality and choice of services available to Medicaid beneficiaries.

suggest that if policymakers can give benefits "to undeserving people like *them*," then surely they should give benefits to "those of us who really earned them." Gina, for example, a caregiver for her mother, illustrates this well:

> I hate to say this, but we have people coming from other countries, and taking so many things that we are paying taxes for. Never had a day job in their life, you know, between food stamps, just automatically "well here's a check for you." And we're all paying for this. So I think...if the government can pay for that, then they can certainly help pay for some of the things that we're out there working to put our taxes in for.

Jackie was similarly critical of Medi-Cal's eligibility requirements:

> [M]ost of us are not poverty. We're almost there, but we're not eligible because of the way the system is written now....And sometimes I really feel, when I really want to think about it, it's not fair. Because the people who are $700 and below, don't pay taxes, and probably don't own property, and I could go on with what they don't have. And those of us who do "own property" or...pay taxes, we're not eligible. So where does our money go?

While the "undeserving" reference group for non-poor caregivers, then, may have been partly about stigma management, it was primarily an articulation of the expectation that the government should be responsive to the needs of its taxpaying citizens. Consistent with the political logic behind Social Security and Medicare, caregivers argued that the government had a responsibility to protect middle-income Americans from falling into poverty beyond their control. As one caregiver put it: "You shouldn't have to be poverty-stricken in order to get help....[P]eople did not arrive at that place in life...on their own. It wasn't anything they did....[W]hen they need help like that, they should be able to get it."

It's important to emphasize that by relying on the political logic of social insurance policies, caregivers were not necessarily endorsing a social insurance approach to state intervention.[13] As noted in Chapter 4, caregivers in this study were often uncomfortable with the idea of a social insurance model for care provision, fearing that the government would appear to be "taking over" care responsibilities that more properly belonged to the family. Even as they argued for state intervention in long-term care, caregivers like John and Jill expressed widespread skepticism about the efficacy of government programs.

---

13. Caregivers who explicitly identified as "liberal" Democrats—or in some cases "left of liberal"—were an exception to this rule. Self-identified liberals were strong advocates of universal benefits distributed to all Americans regardless of income.

The government is so involved in everything in so many parts of our lives. And every-thing that the government is involved with is, for the most part, poorly run.

There's so many problems like that where the government *does* get into it, you know, of accountability. It frightens me. It's kind of like a loose cannon, it could just go out of control.

The discourse of deservingness, then, may have signaled the expectation among caregivers that state assistance was due to them as "deserving" citizens, but the pervasive distrust of state programs suggested that for many caregivers, their support for state intervention was more about practical need than a principled desire to hand over more responsibility for social welfare to the state.

What was notable here, however, was the fact that non-poor caregivers were drawing on the lessons learned from "top tier" social insurance policies as they sought access to "bottom tier" public assistance programs. Rather than view themselves as inferior or stigmatized—the cues normally associated with Medicaid—applicants instead recast Medi-Cal as a middle-class entitlement. The civic lessons absorbed as participants in, or beneficiaries of, American social insurance programs simultaneously provided a certain resilience to the negative cues of Medi-Cal and a political logic for why the state "owed" them the long-term care benefits provided under Medi-Cal.

CONCLUSION

As we've seen before, most caregivers expect very little from the state when they first begin caring for a family member with a chronic illness. Even after they enter the market for supportive services, caregivers demonstrate a strong normative commitment to keeping the costs of long-term care within the family: they pay for supportive services out of pocket, with the assistance of family members, or in some cases with the help of one-time grants from nonprofit organizations, long-term care insurance, or reverse mortgages. But the costs of market-based care in the United States can often be prohibitive for families dealing with chronic illness, such that many working- and middle-income families simply lack the resources to meet the needs of their care receivers. Only when private-sector solutions failed to resolve their caregiving dilemmas did caregivers in this study look to the state's means-tested Medi-Cal program for assistance.

Those non-poor caregivers in this case who did seek assistance from Medi-Cal demonstrated a strong belief in themselves as good citizens, hard workers, taxpayers, and "deserving" beneficiaries of the American welfare state—all beliefs we associate with beneficiaries of "top tier" programs like

Social Security and Medicare. Their assertion of entitlement—that they were citizens who had earned the benefits they sought—not only preserved their self-conception as "deserving" citizens in the context of a public assistance program, but effectively redefined what constituted the social responsibility for care. Medicaid is not a contributory social insurance program, but these mostly middle-class caregivers treated it as if it were—reconceptualizing the means-tested program as an entitlement program by drawing on the more familiar tropes of hard work, paying taxes, and upward mobility. Like the role of Medicaid in grievance construction—providing caregivers with a model for what the state could do to assist families with long-term care provision—existing entitlement programs in this case played a powerful role in shaping caregivers' view of themselves as citizens deserving of state assistance. Embedded in their justifications for state assistance was a relatively coherent set of normative principles about the responsibilities of the state in ensuring the health and economic security of its citizens.

And yet the fact that caregivers primarily viewed the government as a place of last resort illustrates again the dominance of the ideology of family responsibility, suggesting that support for state intervention in this case had as much to do with the weaknesses of private-sector alternatives as it did with the strength of state solutions. It is true, as political conservatives have claimed, that these non-poor caregivers viewed Medicaid benefits as a "middle-class entitlement." But contrary to concerns that middle-class caregivers are gaming the Medicaid program to preserve their family assets, the data from this study showed caregivers of all classes to be doggedly persistent in their efforts to keep the costs of care provision within the family, in some cases endangering their own health or economic security as they struggled to provide requisite levels of care for their family members. For most caregivers, the turn to the state was a decision made out of desperation, and not as a prerogative. Indeed few caregivers in this study ever questioned this view of the state as a place of last resort, suggesting that their underlying views regarding who should be primarily responsible for long-term care provision remained intact.

Still, the combination of family responsibility and entitlement discourse did in some cases produce an understanding of long-term care that seemed to transcend existing cultural categories. The counterhegemonic potential of discursive integration lies in its capacity to recombine elements of the dominant ideology across cultural categories to construct something new. Caregivers in this case reaffirmed their commitment to taking care of their own, but they also constructed a role for the government that defied the rigid categories of the existing welfare state. They relied on a model of social provision that emphasizes family responsibility, and yet they sought long-term care security for a broad swath of the middle class. They justified their claims on the basis of need, and yet they understood their claims as entitlements due to them as hard-working citizens.

This model of social provision does not exist in the United States, nor is it even debated in American political discourse, but it forms the basis for many of the long-term care policies in Europe. Couched between Nordic models of long-term care based on social citizenship, where the state is the primary provider of care, and residualist models, where governments play a minor role in providing or paying for care services, are a set of social policies that emphasize the family as primarily responsible for care provision, but where the state plays an active role in supporting families. Britain, Germany, France, Belgium, and the Netherlands, for example, have all adopted such policies, providing families with free or subsidized in-home care assistance, respite care, and day care, while also granting cash allowances and tax credits for families providing long-term care at home, and offering paid family leave. Participants in this study did not seek to replicate these policies—indeed as Chapter 4 illustrates, the policy solutions of other countries very rarely resonated with caregivers—but instead constructed this model of state provision with the cultural resources provided by existing American social policy. Both residual and social insurance policies played a powerful interpretive role in shaping how American caregivers viewed the respective responsibilities of family and state in caring for the chronically ill. But in reconciling the cultural conflicts that contemporary caregiving produces, individuals transposed, extended, and refashioned the cultural resources at their disposal to imagine a new role for the American state entirely.

Contrary to what theory predicts, then, caregivers who sought assistance from the state did not lack for a sense of entitlement in communicating their demands for state intervention. They not only formulated political grievances, but they had a sense that they deserved the state's intervention. Why, then, do these grievances fail to emerge in public discourse as organized political demand? The following chapter examines the structural impediments to demand making. While there are many obvious reasons why caregivers might not participate in organized reform efforts—most notably, a lack of time or energy—many caregivers are deeply politicized by their experience in providing long-term care. The next chapter considers why caregivers who are both willing and able to press their claims on the state nevertheless rarely participate in organized efforts to do so.

CHAPTER 6

Communicating Grievances—
Obstacles to Activism

Citizen participation in political demand making is a product of not only the interpretive processes that shape political consciousness, but also the presence of structural opportunities for demand making. This chapter examines the conditions that shape how and under what conditions grievants choose to make their voices heard in the public arena as part of an organized reform effort. We have seen at each stage of politicization a range of reasons why caregivers might choose not to act to improve the conditions for families providing chronic care, and at each stage the pack of politicized individuals becomes thinner. But there are caregivers who, despite the odds, have become deeply politicized by their experiences seeking solutions to long-term care needs—individuals who are willing and able to participate in political demand making, yet have not found an opportunity to do so. This chapter seeks to understand why.

A substantial literature on political activism has shown that, regardless of the strength of political beliefs or expectations, individuals are unlikely to participate in political action without structural opportunities for doing so (McAdam 1986; McAdam 1988; McAdam 1989; Snow et al. 1980). We have long known that social relationships not only shape how we come to understand our individual problems as collective grievances (as we observed in Chapter 3), but they also affect the likelihood that we will participate in collective efforts to do something about those grievances (Curtis and Zurcher 1973; Gould 1991; McAdam 1988; McAdam and Paulsen 1993; Passy and Giugni 2001; Rosenstone and Hansen 1993; Skocpol 2003; Snow et al.1980). To participate in political activity, individuals need information about how and when and where to get involved (Rosenstone and Hansen 1993). They require leadership and organizational resources for coordinating their individual grievances into collective political demands (Snow et al. 1986). Traditional social movement models of politicization have long assumed that individuals are embedded in a web of social ties in which the relationships that facilitate the formulation of collective grievances are somehow connected to the social relationships that recruit individuals into organized political activity (McAdam 1988). But as the following discussion elaborates, long-term trends in the field of political organizations—in particular, the decoupling of social welfare organizations from organized politics and the shift in political mobilization technologies toward "targeted activation" (Schier 2000)—have attenuated the nexus between grievance construction and political mobilization in matters of social welfare. As a consequence, many individuals who experience unmet long-term care needs today lack the necessary ties to express their grievances as political demands.

GROUP TIES AND MOBILIZATION

One of the most durable findings in research on social movements and political participation is the key role of *organizational fields*—the system of overlapping memberships in political organizations, voluntary associations, and other more informal social groups—in shaping the development of political grievances and linking potential participants to organized political activity (Armstrong 2002; Curtis and Zurcher 1973; Evans and Kay 2008; Gould 1991; McAdam 1988; McAdam and Paulsen 1993; Passy and Giugni 2001; Snow et al. 1980). Within any organizational field, one can find small group settings or "free spaces" (Evans and Boyte 1986) that play a key part in collective attribution, shaping how we define our circumstances (Polletta 1999). As we saw in Chapter 3, we are more likely to attribute the cause of our problems to political or social structures when we have the opportunity to interact with others experiencing similar problems. History is replete with examples of politicization taking place in tenant associations, bars, union halls, student lounges and hangouts, churches, and women's living rooms (Evans 1979; Ferree and Hess 2000).[1]

If group relations within organizational fields play an important role in shaping processes of collective attribution, they also affect our conceptions of what to do about newly perceived grievances. Historical examples of group settings in which processes of attribution and organization came

---

1. For an excellent review of this literature—and a more critical analysis of "free spaces"—see Polletta (1999).

together to produce collective political action include the black churches of the 1950s and 1960s that formed the organizational heart of early civil rights organizing (McAdam 1982; Morris 1984); fraternal/service organizations which played a key role in the emergence of a local antipornography movement in Texas (Curtis and Zurcher 1973); the friendship networks on which the women's liberation movement was based (Ferree and Hess 2000; Freeman 1975); and the role of organizations and Parisian neighborhood ties in the emergence of the Paris Commune insurgency of 1871 (Gould 1991). In all of these cases, the perception of collective grievances served to "push" individuals in the direction of political participation, but structural opportunities were necessary to actually "pull" potential participants into organized activity (McAdam 1988).

The role of group relations in processes of politicization is so well established in the literature on social movements that researchers today often take for granted the presence of structural ties that link these two dimensions of politicization: we assume, in other words, that individuals are embedded in organizational fields in which the social relationships that "push" them toward the formulation of political grievances are somehow connected to the social relationships that "pull" them into organized political activity. This assumption, I suggest, is far more historically contingent than social movement theorists have so far allowed. Many of our analytical tools for understanding processes of politicization are based on studies of political mobilization that took place during periods of heightened activism, or "cycles of protest" (Tarrow 1994), when the field of political organizations looked quite different from more typical historical moments. In the 1960s and early 1970s, social movements were constituted by wide-ranging and diverse organizations (Ferree and Hess 2000; Minkoff 1994) in which overlapping memberships and social networks could easily connect individuals with grievances to opportunities for political demand making. Similarly, political parties and large, federated civic associations during that period provided dense networks of social ties to recruit people into political activity (Crenson and Ginsberg 2002; Skocpol 2003).

Consider, for example, the consciousness-raising groups of the feminist movement, often described as playing a key role in the politicization of the suburban housewife.[2] Participants in these groups challenged taken-for-granted assumptions about a whole range of issues—sex, marriage, domestic violence, rape, reproductive freedom, employment discrimination—and in doing so, reconceptualized their personal problems as political grievances. But to carry these grievances out of the living room

2. For more on consciousness-raising groups of the feminist movement, see Chapter 3.

and into the public arena, they required opportunities to participate in organized political action. And in the early 1970s, women enjoyed a wide array of organizational resources for doing so (Ferree and Hess 2000; Ferree and Martin 1995b; Minkoff 1995). The social networks through which women were recruited into consciousness-raising groups also connected participants with protest organizations ranging from the Women's International Terrorist Conspiracy from Hell (WITCH) (Rosen 2000) to the National Organization for Women (Freeman 1975). Women were similarly linked to collective efforts to start day care centers, battered women's shelters, rape clinics, women's bookstores, and newspapers and magazines, and to organize women's groups in labor unions and universities (Ferree and Hess 2000; Freeman 1975). In the early 1970s the social ties that "pushed" women into formulating political grievances substantially overlapped with the ties that "pulled" them into organized political action.

Changes in political organization in the period since the late 1960s, however, have reconfigured the organizational fields in which processes of politicization involving many social welfare issues take place. These changes have attenuated—and in some cases severed—the structural link between collective attribution and mobilization. Contemporary organizational fields may share the appearance of those of an earlier era in that there are wide-ranging group contexts in which collective attribution can potentially take place and a dense network of political advocacy organizations for mobilizing collective grievances. But the paths that once connected processes of collective attribution and mobilization in matters of social welfare often diverge in the contemporary context. This divergence has important implications for how individuals transform their experiences with unmet social welfare needs into political demands for new social policy.

THE CHANGING ORGANIZATIONAL FIELD FOR SOCIAL WELFARE PROVISION

Two long-term changes in political organizations are particularly relevant to processes of politicization in this case: (1) the expansion of the welfare state into community-based health and human service organizations, and (2) the shift in mobilization technologies used by advocacy organizations toward "strategic mobilization" (Rosenstone and Hansen 1993) or "targeted activation" (Schier 2000). The former trend has affected how individuals connect their personal social welfare struggles to political reform efforts (i.e., the "push") while the latter trend has changed how reform organizations seek out and recruit potential participants for mobilization (i.e., the "pull.") Both long-term trends have been well documented in the respective literatures on social work and political mobilization. Here I consider their consequences for the mobilization of contemporary social welfare grievances.

First, the dramatic expansion of the welfare state since the 1960s into community-based health and human service organizations has created a barrier—both professional and organizational—between processes of collective attribution involving matters of social welfare and the political organizations involved in mobilizing for social policy reform. Community-based social service organizations of the late 1960s and early 1970s—such as anti-poverty programs, legal aid services, rape crisis centers, battered women's shelters, and women's health clinics—were often overtly political organizations, providing not only social services, but also spaces in which political education and activism were encouraged (Davis 1993; Ferree and Martin 1995a; Kornbluh 2007; Martin 2005; Matthews 1994; Schechter 1982). Beginning with the implementation of President Johnson's Great Society programs, the federal government sought to dramatically expand social service delivery by partnering with community-based social service organizations (Crenson and Ginsberg 2002; Katz 1996). In 1967, federal legislation permitted state agencies to enlist nonprofit organizations in the delivery of services, and legislation over the subsequent decade funneled vast sums of federal monies into nonprofit organizations. By the late 1970s, the nonprofit sector had become the principal vehicle for the delivery of government-financed social services, and, equally importantly, the government had become the primary source of funding for nonprofit social services (Salamon 1995).

One of the most well documented consequences of the influx of federal dollars into the social welfare sector over the course of the 1970s was a sharp reduction in political activism. To qualify for federal money, social service organizations were required to formalize and professionalize their organizations: they legally incorporated, added boards of directors, and hired full-time staff to replace volunteers (Gornick et al. 1985; Smith and Lipsky 1993). Activists were replaced by social workers and other professionals who focused on individual casework rather than social activism (Katz 1996; Rothman 1985). Organizational leaders who had been recruited for their political ideals were supplanted by executives who possessed management skills that could more effectively meet new state requirements for program and fiscal accountability (Smith and Lipsky 1993). As nonprofit service organizations became more and more fiscally dependent on state contracts for funding, a proportionally greater share of their resources shifted to the provision of direct services and away from social reform efforts. Some abandoned political activism in order to meet the explicit demands of their funders; others toned down their activism in the hopes of increasing their prospects for winning public contracts (Campbell et al. 1998; Crenson and Ginsberg 2002; Gornick and Meyer 1998; Maier 2008; Schechter 1982).[3] But the net result was a broad-based shift away from an emphasis on societal transformation in social welfare provision and toward the provision of individual direct services.

Today, "consciousness-raising" groups have largely been replaced with self-help or support groups in which political activity—and even "political talk"—is often explicitly proscribed (Archibald 2007; Katz 1993).[4] While processes of collective attribution may still occur in such organizations—as the sharing of experiences in any group context can arguably lead to a structural understanding of one's individual problems—those processes often take place in an organizational context in which the links between social service and political organizations are attenuated. We should expect such a reconfiguration in the organizational field to affect how individuals confronting unmet social welfare needs connect their grievances to organized reform efforts.

If the reconfiguration of social welfare provision in the United States has altered the structural nexus between collective attribution and mobilization by transforming how individuals are "pushed" toward political participation, a second long-term trend—in mobilization technologies—has transformed how individuals get "pulled" into political activism. In the 1960s and early 1970s, mobilization by social movement organizations, labor unions, civic associations, and political parties was characterized by time- and labor-intensive methods of face-to-face recruitment, often through personal networks that connected newly politicized individuals to the political process (Schier 2000; Skocpol 2003). Such tactics hewed closely to the conventional wisdom in social movement theory that people are more likely to respond positively to recruitment attempts if invited by somebody they already know (Snow et al. 1980). Beginning in the 1970s, however, social change activities began to shift increasingly toward advocacy[5]—or efforts to change policies and secure collective goods through routine institutional

3. Other trends in social welfare provision contributed to the depoliticization of the social service sector, including the institutionalization of tax incentives for nonprofit social welfare organizations that limited their political activism (Sobieraj and White 2004), and the ascendance of group psychotherapy and self-help (Archibald 2007).

4. This is not to say that all self-help groups today are nonpolitical. Some self-help groups remain closely tied to social movements. Breast cancer support groups, for example, have roots in both the women's health movement and AIDS activism (Klawiter 2008). Support groups for women who suffer from postpartum depression are also closely linked to the women's movement (Taylor 1996; Taylor and Van Willigen 1996). In both cases, social service provision has remained closely linked to organized political activism.

5. Useful accounts of the "advocacy explosion" and its implications include Andrews and Edwards (2004), Berry (1977, 1999), Berry and Wilcox (1989), Walker (1991), Minkoff (1994; 1995), Skocpol (2003), Rosenstone (1993), McCarthy and Zald (1977; 1973), McCarthy (2005), Putnam (1995), and Schlozman et al. (1999).

means (Jenkins 1987:297). Organizations seeking to influence public policy in state and national legislative arenas or the judicial system turned to more efficient methods of securing resources in order to support the costs of hiring professional lobbyists, litigators, public relations experts, and other paid staff. These technologies included direct mail, telemarketing, online recruitment, paid canvassing, and more recently, payroll deductions and phone texting contributions (Oliver and Marwell 1992; Schier 2000). In contrast to 'old-style' mobilization tactics, these new "targeted activation" (Schier 2000) or "strategic mobilization" (Rosenstone and Hansen 1993) technologies depend for their success not on personal relationships, but on the identification of individuals who are most likely to respond to an organization's appeals (Fisher 2006; Goldstein 1999; Oliver and Marwell 1992; Rosenstone and Hansen 1993; Schier 2000). In other words, they are designed to "activate" people the organization already knows, as the cost is low and probability of success is high; people at the center of social networks, as they are easier to identify and because they are in a good position to mobilize others; people with political influence; and people who—because of their resources, interests, and beliefs—are more likely to participate in politics than others (Brady et al. 1999; Rosenstone and Hansen 1993; Walker 2008).[6] Larger, well-established organizations often have their own professionalized mailing operations for identifying such candidates, but lists of likely activists and voters are also available for purchase from marketing firms (Oliver and Marwell 1992; Walker 2009).

One of the most well documented consequences of these shifts in mobilization technologies is the stratification of political participation: the people who tend to be targeted for recruitment are those who are older, more educated, and who have higher levels of income (Brady et al. 1999; Rosenstone and Hansen 1993; Schier 2000; Skocpol 2003). But the data from this study suggest that the turn toward targeted activation has also constrained advocates' ability to mobilize citizens with an emergent or developing political consciousness. Because political consciousness is not a static entity—it is not a quality one either 'has' or 'doesn't have,' but is continually developed in concrete social action—it does not easily lend itself to measurement by practitioners of targeted activation, who tend to focus on relatively fixed attributes of groups (e.g., income, education level, or party affiliation) in assessing recruitability. Many contemporary social welfare

---

6. This is not to suggest that all organizations seeking to influence social policy rely on activation strategies. There are important exceptions: most notably, community-based activism that continues to draw on "old"-style mobilization strategies, particularly at the local level (Lopez 2004; Marwell 2004; McCarthy and Walker 2004; Taylor et al. 2009; Walker 2009; Wood 2002).

issues—such as health care, child care, unemployment—are temporary concerns in the lives of affected individuals: they last only for a matter of months or years and may be salient in individuals' political consciousness only for discrete periods. Without personal knowledge of the circumstances of these individuals—either their degree of politicization or their availability for participation—organizations that rely on targeted activation technologies are unlikely to expend scarce resources to mobilize them. As a consequence, even when affected individuals are available for recruitment, the mobilization technologies used by advocacy organizations are unlikely to "pull" them into organized political activity.

The expansion of the state into community-based social service organizations and the growth in targeted activation strategies together have potentially reconfigured the connections between the "push" and "pull" of politicization in matters of social welfare. To understand why families struggling with unmet long-term care needs have not transformed their grievances into political demands, we need to retrace these processes of politicization, identifying where once prevalent linkages between citizens and political organization no longer hold, and where, perhaps, new linkages have been forged.

LONG-TERM CARE (NON)MOBILIZATION

In order to identify what obstacles prevent caregivers from communicating their grievances to an official agency or perceived responsible party for action, the analysis of (non)mobilization here focuses on a specific group of family care providers: grievants who are willing and able to make demands on the state for policy reform and who are embedded in organizational fields that theoretically should facilitate participation in organized demand making. All of the support group participants in this study were embedded in a long-term care organizational field composed not only of support groups, but also city, county, and state health and human service agencies; for-profit and nonprofit social service organizations; and, importantly, local, state and national advocacy organizations seeking long-term care policy reform. Some advocacy organizations emphasize legislative advocacy in state or national policymaking arenas. Others target government agencies such as the Center for Medicare and Medicaid Services or the California Department of Social Services. Others focus on legal advocacy, and still others emphasize program advocacy, seeking to change organizational practices within service organizations, such as nursing homes. While some of the local advocacy organizations, such as Bet Tzedek Legal Services, are quite small, the field also includes some of the country's most influential advocacy groups: the AARP, for example, with over thirty-five million members, is one of the largest and most powerful membership organizations in the United States.

All of these organizations should theoretically provide opportunities for politicization. Social welfare organizations offer spaces where individuals can interact with similarly situated families and create the shared meanings and identities that social movement theory has long associated with emergent collective action. Advocacy organizations offer specific solutions to unmet long-term care needs and opportunities to help obtain them. But while many individuals embedded in this organizational field expressed grievances over unmet long-term care needs and demonstrated a willingness to participate in reform efforts, very few had actually participated in organized or collective action. Indeed, most caregivers were not aware of having policy advocates at all. The exception, highlighted as a case comparison at the end of the chapter, was the Association of Caregiver Resource Centers, an advocacy organization that relied partly on traditional recruitment tactics through support groups, thereby providing a concrete opportunity for politicized caregivers to act on their grievances.

The "Push" Toward Politicization: Collective Attribution and the Separation of Support and Politics

We saw in Chapter 3 that participation in support groups, caregiver classes, workshops and other forms of supportive services had a clear consciousness-raising effect on caregivers, highlighting similarities in the experiences of family caregivers, reframing their individual care struggles as collective problems, and emphasizing the underlying structural and sociocultural factors that make long-term care so difficult for contemporary American families. In contrast to caregivers who had little contact with supportive services—and who spoke of their long-term care problems in terms that reflected norms about care provision as a private, family responsibility—most participants in support groups and other caregiver services expressed a clear normative expectation that their collective long-term care problems ought to be redressed through policy intervention. Yet what distinguishes these support groups from the "free spaces" social movement scholars have long associated with collective attribution is that they were not connected to organizations engaged in political reform efforts. In contrast to the political consciousness-raising groups of the 1970s, support group facilitators were prevented from promoting an overt political agenda in their groups due to professional norms in social work and organizational rules for nonprofit organizations.

The social workers that facilitated the support groups in this study viewed their groups not as sites for political consciousness raising, but as tools for changing individual behaviors. They saw their primary role as providing information about diseases and resources in the community, and maintaining a safe, therapeutic space for caregivers to give and receive advice on alleviating feelings of stress, guilt, fear, and inadequacy. When asked whether support group conversations ever turned into political discussions, one social worker conceded that they did, but saw the facilitator's role as trying to contain, discourage, or avoid those conversations:

> I personally...will say...if it starts being completely focused on politics, that I don't think it's appropriate to discuss...particular personal politics. I definitely discourage that, because it takes the focus away from what we're really there for.

What caregivers were "really there for" was, according to social workers, emotional support and information. Asked if they were aware of ever introducing their own politics into the group, most facilitators responded that it would be inappropriate for a social worker to do so: "That is not professional," one facilitator responded indignantly. Another facilitator observed that it's "just Social Work 101, you know, we're not supposed to bring our own stuff into group."

Organizational rules similarly constrained how facilitators ran their groups. Some social workers noted that their status as a nonprofit organization prevented them from taking an overtly political role in support groups. "[W]e're a nonprofit organization and we're not allowed to make any kind of political stands," observed one social worker when asked why politics didn't come up more often in her group. Many of the Los Angeles dementia support groups were formally affiliated with the Alzheimer's Association, a national nonprofit organization with chapter affiliates located around the country. Part of the affiliation process involved formal training for support group facilitators. One social worker who had attended these trainings observed that they had been advised by the Alzheimer's Association to avoid introducing any form of overt politics into their groups:

> The training that the Alzheimer's Association gave us as facilitators was very clear: it's not up to us to give them the answers. And it's not up to us to decide what direction the group goes in. And I try very hard to observe those guidelines. Partly because that's part of the affiliation agreement, but partly because I agree with them.

Professional and organizational proscriptions against introducing politics into caregiver support groups meant that most facilitators of support groups actively avoided references to specific political issues involving long-term care, and when such issues did come up, they redirected conversations toward individual strategies for handling long-term care crises. Most facilitators studiously avoided promoting particular framings of long-term care problems or suggesting structural solutions for caregiver problems, nor did they give advice about how caregivers might get involved in organized activism.

The consequences of this were striking: collective attribution may have produced expectations among caregivers that public policy intervention was necessary to ameliorate long-term care dilemmas, but without organizational resources, most caregivers had no idea what they might do about their inchoate political grievances. Asked whether they had ever contacted an elected official about a long-term care issue, many caregivers made clear that the idea had simply never occurred to them. Others observed that they "should" contact an elected official or they "would" if they had the opportunity. Susan's response to an interview question about participation in collective action typifies these potential participants:

> I have researched the hell out of this [disease]. And made sure that we've seen the top specialists. But not on a political level. But I would. You want me? Call me.

Asked if she had ever contacted an elected official about a caregiving issue, Linda responded,

> No.... But you know what? I really should. I really should. It's just that I don't know what to ask for. You know, find a cure for Alzheimer's? ... Help us take care of our parents who have Alzheimer's? I don't know what to ask for.

Most people require information about when and how they might participate in political demand making. They need information about what to ask for. But grievants in this case had trouble identifying any organization they might join in an effort to participate in political demand making around issues of long-term care. When given a list of local, state, and national advocacy organizations, few could even say they'd heard of the organizations; even fewer could say that they had contacted them. Respondents were least likely to recognize caregiving-focused organizations: four out of five caregivers interviewed (80%) had never heard of the National Alliance for Caregiving; more than nine out of ten caregivers (92%) had never heard of the National Family Caregiver Association. Local advocacy organizations that were engaged at least partly in social service provision fared relatively better: just over half of the sample had heard of the Los Angeles Caregiver Resource Center (54%) and Bet Tzedek Legal Services (51%).

While nearly all of those interviewed recognized the much larger Alzheimer's Association and the AARP, few caregivers knew what these more well known organizations were doing to advance reforms around long-term care. In a peer group discussion about proposals for public policy supports for caregivers, for example, one caregiver, Lois, articulated concern over the absence of organizational advocates:

> It sounds like what we're talking about here is there's no grassroots movement, you know? We have the AARP, and they're certainly not a radical, get-out-the-vote group. And what happened to the Gray Panthers? For a while they were around, but I haven't heard of them. So there's...no organization, and I don't know why.

Isadore expressed a similar concern:

> I know there's lots of lobbyists in Washington that are tuned in to the special interests over there, such as tobacco and drugs and so forth....I don't know of anything that's up there that's really representing caregivers at all.

Those caregivers who had been politically active in the past made clear that they knew what kind of organized action might be effective, but in most cases, these activists, too, had not participated in any long-term care policy reform efforts. Miguel, for example, who had been active in the AIDS movement and who credited the movement with successfully pushing for the development of medications for managing HIV and AIDS, wondered why a similar mobilization had not occurred for Alzheimer's disease:

> [S]ome of us, we need to get involved. I don't know if you know ACT-UP....Maybe start a [similar] movement where we could send letters. Because that's the only way they're going to listen to us.

Another caregiver, who had been active in local politics about other issues, responded similarly to the question of whether she had ever contacted an elected official about a long-term care issue. "[T]hat is a very good question," she said, "because at the very least...a handwritten letter from me would have the force of 500 people. So, yeah, I should."

Regardless of their previous levels of activism, interactions with other caregivers in a group context clearly played a role in "pushing" caregivers along the path of politicization—helping reconceptualize "private" family responsibilities as political problems and to formulate political grievances. But for most caregivers in this study the path to politicization faded when they arrived at this point. If in the models of politicization posited by conventional analyses, individuals are linked to organized reform efforts through interactions with social movement and political actors who can orient them toward political activity, here we see that long-term care issues were deliberated within a social service sector which maintained rigid professional and organizational demarcations between service delivery and political activity. As a consequence, participants lacked the necessary structural ties to connect them to organized political reform efforts. As the following section elaborates, these newly politicized individuals were also unlikely to be recruited into collective reform efforts by political advocacy organizations.

The "Pull" Toward Politicization: Mobilization and the Limitations of Targeted Activation

Social movement theorists and political scientists have long observed that for individuals to mobilize their political grievances, they need to be recruited into political activity (Rosenstone and Hansen 1993). The high levels of political activism which characterized the 1960s and 1970s were facilitated by mobilization strategies that emphasized time- and resource-intensive tactics of face-to-face recruitment. Today, however, organizations seeking to influence public policy often rely on impersonal, media-driven "targeted activation" technologies designed to mobilize those constituents who are most likely to participate in political activity (Rosenstone and Hansen 1993; Schier 2000). In the absence of personal knowledge of potential recruits, advocates who rely exclusively on targeted activation technologies are poorly equipped to identify potential partici-pants who have been politicized by their experiences with long-term care. In this study, advocates widely dismissed caregivers as a constituency for being either too indifferent to long-term care policy or too overwhelmed by the responsibilities of caregiving to be likely participants in political reform initiatives. As a consequence, individuals who were both willing and able to participate in organized political activity were almost never recruited by advocacy organizations in the study, with just one notable exception discussed below.

Taken as a group, family caregivers do seem to make unlikely candidates for mobilization. Until "it happens to them," most families in the United States have little knowledge of long-term care. Many caregivers in this study admitted they had never heard of services like adult day care or respite care before their family members required such assistance. Nor were they aware of how much such services cost. "[P]eople don't want to talk about it," observed Margery Minney, Director of the Valley Caregiver Resource Center in California. "They don't want to hear about it, they don't want to deal with it, because at this time it's not affecting them. And they're saying it's not going to. *That's not going to be me.*" Rigo Saborio of AARP California observed that the public's reluctance to discuss issues of long-term care presented a difficult framing dilemma for advocacy groups:

[H]ow do you create a message, how do you couch it, how do you make long-term care sexy?...People don't want to talk about it, you know? And how do you do that so that then it resonates with not only the people who are in it, but also among people not [in it], but may be at some point? How do you make that connection? Because that's what it's going to take. That's what it's going to take to really push long-term care to the next level.

The challenge of mobilizing individuals who have not yet been affected by long-term care is made more difficult by the fact that Americans possess high levels of misinformation about the extent to which long-term care services are covered by Medicare or health insurance policies. Unless already retired, the typical American has little contact with Medicare administrators, and knows little about the scope of the program or its eligibility rules (Marmor et al. 1990). A 1995 survey conducted during the height of a Medicare reform debate—which ostensibly should have raised public awareness about the program—found that fewer than half of all Americans knew that Medicare did not cover long-term care in nursing homes (Blendon et al. 1995). Even in 2013, 44% of people forty or older believe that Medicare pays for licensed home health care[7] and 37% believe it pays for ongoing care in a nursing home (Tompson et al. 2013). The barriers to Medicare home health benefits and nursing home care are among the most incomprehensible of the many economic frustrations that caregivers confront. Advocates from a wide range of organizations described their constituents as being "stunned" and "shocked" when they realize that Medicare doesn't cover the costs of long-term care. "[T]hey just can't imagine," echoed Stephen McConnell, the Alzheimer's Association's Senior Vice President for Public Policy and Advocacy, "that something that expensive and that traumatic wouldn't be covered."

Advocates observed that until families are in the position of paying for long-term care supportive services, they're not aware that policy reform might be needed—but by the time families understand what limited

---

7. Medicare-funded home health care pays only for post-acute, short-term rehabilitation and management of conditions that are not resolved in a hospital.

sources of social supports are available, they are typically too enmeshed in care provision to participate in political demand making. "You're talking about mobilizing people primarily that are absolutely up to their eyeballs with care issues and financial problems and disruptions in their lives," noted McConnell. Diane Lifney, a lobbyist for the National Committee to Preserve Social Security & Medicare, made the same point about her sister, who at the time was caring for their mother:

> My sister's not about to be joining some group or advocating for some changes in the law. She's just trying to get through the day and make sure everything's in place, you know? She's just glad when the agencies come when they're supposed to and the aides aren't sick.

From the perspective of advocacy organizations seeking "likely" candidates for participation, family caregivers thus offer poor prospects for recruitment. And in fact, very few of the advocacy organizations in this study could point to instances in which they explicitly targeted newly politicized caregivers for recruitment. When advocates organized email actions—asking participants to send a letter or email to their elected representative, for example—they primarily utilized email distribution lists made up of individuals who had already contacted their organization to sign up for "action alerts." Advocates struggled with the question of how to identify and mobilize individuals who had not contacted a political advocacy organization. Gail Hunt, Executive Director of the National Alliance for Caregiving, observed:

> [T]here are lots of marketing people who are interested in trying to reach family caregivers because they have a product they're trying to sell. And we get calls all the time asking, "Do we have a mailing list?" ... *And there is no mailing list.* ... You can't mobilize the caregivers across the country by zip code or congressional district. ... In terms of advocacy, that's the issue. ... The fact that ... there's no easy way to reach them really makes it hard to make a case.

Asked how the AARP tries to overcome the challenges of mobilizing this constituency, Rigo Saborio of AARP California responded simply, "That's the million-dollar question! ... I think I'd probably be a millionaire if I knew the answer to that."

Saborio's million-dollar question raises an important point: Do family caregivers make poor recruits for any type of mobilization, or are the targeted activation technologies used by most advocacy organizations today particularly ill-equipped to mobilize this constituency? It could be the case, in other words, that even "old-style" face-to-face mobilization tactics would be insufficient to mobilize this nascent constituency. Here the evidence suggests that targeted activation technologies are too blunt a recruitment tool to identify individuals who have been newly politicized by their social welfare experiences.

Because targeted activation technologies rely on estimates of the likelihood of participation based on relatively stable characteristics of groups rather than personal knowledge of individuals, they lack a mechanism for discerning changes in political consciousness among individuals. Participation potential in fact varies dramatically over the course of caregiving, as individuals' information, interests, time, and commitment shift in response to concrete experiences in care provision. Contrary to advocates' characterization of caregivers as either too indifferent or too overwhelmed to participate in collective action, many individuals who have been politicized by their experiences with long-term care provision actively sought out ways to help other families deal with the strains of long-term care. But in the absence of opportunities to join an organized or collective campaign, these actions were largely idiosyncratic, highly individualized, and perhaps most importantly, they were not aimed at policymakers or other targets of policy reform efforts.

One individual, for example, responded to the closing of an adult day-care center in her neighborhood by starting a foundation that not only reopened the facility, but helped to subsidize day care for other families in her community. Others sought ways to assist caregivers by writing for caregiver newsletters and distributing literature about supportive services in doctor's offices, libraries, churches, and other settings. Two caregivers attended training sessions to become caregiver support group leaders themselves. Still others remained active in support groups even after their caregiver roles had ended with the explicit intention of helping new caregivers navigate the challenges of long-term care provision. "I would not like to see anybody else go through this," observed one typical caregiver, explaining why she hoped to help other families, even after the death of her husband. All of these actions were described by respondents as conscientious attempts to use their caregiving experience to help improve conditions for other families. But as valuable as these activities are, they lacked the kind of direction characteristic of organized political action. These were not coordinated efforts. Nor were they actions aimed at any "official agency or other perceived responsible party," as our definition of political demand making requires.

A closer analysis of caregivers' experiences suggests that the potential for participation fluctuates over the course of the caregiving career.[8]

---

8. Note that this model is merely a heuristic device and is not meant to be representative of all caregiving experiences. Caregiving situations, for example, which begin with a sudden incident such as stroke, would show virtually no space between points A and B in the caregiving trajectory.

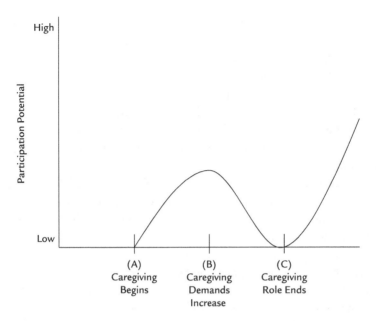

Figure 6.1
Participation Potential over the Caregiving Career

As Figure 6.1 illustrates, before the caregiving experience begins (point A) participation potential is, as advocates observed, typically very low, due largely to a lack of accurate information about or interest in long-term care issues.

But between the point at which caregiving begins (A) and the point at which caregiving demands have reached a "crisis" stage (B) (i.e., when individuals can handle nothing beyond care responsibilities) there is a period where individuals both obtain more knowledge about long-term care policies and have a vested interest in reforming such policies, increasing the likelihood they may participate in some form of activism. In this study, over half of the caregivers who described themselves as taking some form of conscious action to help other family care providers were stage A-B caregivers: they were active caregivers with a vested interest in obtaining long-term care assistance from the state, but were not overwhelmed by the emotional or physical responsibilities of caregiving.

As care provision demands more time and energy of caregivers, participation potential does in fact substantially decrease. A nonstatistical comparison between those caregivers who pursued some form of activism and those who had not illustrates the largely intuitive correlation between demands on time and participation potential:[9] activists tended to have fewer demands on their time than nonactivists. More than half of the nonactivist caregivers were providing care to people who needed assistance with more than three "activities of daily living," whereas only one-third of caregiver activists were providing comparable levels of care. Nonactivists were also more than twice as likely to be balancing care provision with full-time employment outside the home. These findings are consistent with the argument that as demands on time increase, we can expect participation potential to decrease.

But once the caregiving role has ended (C)—with the death or recovery of the care receiver, or termination of the caregiving role (i.e., when the caregiver hands over care responsibilities to someone else) the potential for participation again increases. As in the case of more famous caregivers who went on to become activists—Rosalyn Carter, Dana Reeve, Maria Shriver—the caregiving experience itself can be a politicizing one. Nearly a third of the caregivers who described themselves as taking some form of conscious action to help other family care providers were former caregivers who actively sought out ways to help other families even after their caregiving roles had ended. Indeed, it is this group, more than any other, that over time would seem to represent a significant constituency for mobilization. But without personal knowledge of the changing circumstances or shifting political consciousness of individual constituents, advocates who rely on targeted activation technologies have no way of identifying these potential participants.

CASE COMPARISON: ALZHEIMER'S ASSOCIATION VS. ASSOCIATION OF CAREGIVER RESOURCE CENTERS

The effects of new styles of mobilization on caregiver participation in organized demand making can be most clearly seen through a comparative case analysis of two advocacy organizations in the sample: the Alzheimer's Association, a 'new-style' advocacy organization, and the Association of

9. Notably, the likelihood of participating cannot be attributed to any traditional indicators associated with political participation such as higher levels of income, education, age, or history of activism. Indeed, nonactivists tended to have somewhat higher incomes than activists: 60% of nonactivists had incomes over $50,000, compared to just 41% of caregiver activists. Levels of education were roughly equal between both groups, and the average age of both groups was the same (63). Both groups had relatively similar histories of activism—42% of nonactivists and 50% of activists had engaged in any kind of collective or political actions (unrelated to long-term care) in the past.

Caregiver Resource Centers, the only advocacy organization to rely on 'old-style' mobilization tactics, and the only organization to successfully mobilize caregivers in this study. Both organizations have ties to social services and political advocacy. The Alzheimer's Association relies primarily on direct mail and internet technologies for mobilizing its constituents and draws a sharp line between the support groups it sponsors and organized politics. By contrast, the Association of Caregiver Resource Centers draws on personal contacts from their associated centers to identify participants and, within the bounds of nonprofit laws, actively encourages its clientele to participate in advocacy. In this study, the caregivers who were most likely to know about and take advantage of opportunities to participate in organized political activity were those associated with the Caregiver Resource Centers.

The Alzheimer's Association is a national advocacy organization that maintains chapters throughout the country, including the California Southland Chapter (which includes Los Angeles), a participant in this study. Each chapter provides information and referral services, education and training, Safe Return (a national registry program for people with memory loss), and support groups for family caregivers. With respect to political advocacy, the Alzheimer's Association relies primarily on targeted activation technologies to mobilize its constituency. Its website includes a page for "Advocacy," where it provides information on various legislative issues relating to Alzheimer's and long-term care. The web page also encourages visitors to sign up for its "E-Advocacy Network," an email distribution list that sends regular updates on legislative developments in Sacramento, as well as Action Alerts regarding specific phone or letter writing campaigns. These announcements, information, and Action Alerts are not announced in affiliated support group meetings. Indeed, because support group facilitators are advised by the Alzheimer's Association not to introduce any political subjects into group discussions, few caregivers in affiliated support groups were aware of what issues the Alzheimer's Association was promoting in state or national legislative arenas. In a peer group discussion with an affiliated support group about long-term care policy, for example, Tony, a caregiver and individual activist, expressed his frustration with the perceived disconnect between caregivers and policy advocates:

> How does the Alzheimer's Association view this, or have they been approached with the question of what would be best for caregivers? Has any national organization been approached or do they know about the problem?...I really don't think that besides us in this room, there's too many people know what's even going on here.

The Los Angeles Caregiver Resource Center (LACRC), by contrast, is part of a statewide system of eleven nonprofit Caregiver Resource Centers (CRCs) serving the entire state of California. The CRCs are primarily service organizations, providing support groups, counseling, family consultations, respite care, workshops, classes, caregiver retreats, and legal and financial consultations on long-term care provision. But in 1999, the directors of the CRCs formed their own nonprofit organization, the Association of Caregiver Resource Centers, to advocate for the caregivers in their respective regions in the California legislature. Like the Alzheimer's Association, the Association relies on the standard repertoire of direct mail and internet activation strategies, but it also draws on its connections to the social service sector to recruit participants. When the state legislature debates bills or budgetary matters that directly pertain to long-term care provision, the Association disseminates information about legislative proposals to clients through the CRC newsletters—available to all clients, and not just those who sign up for advocacy information—to "educate" them about how policies may potentially affect their families.[10] The Association also arranges "Advocacy Days" where advocates recruit clients, including caregivers from support groups, to travel to Sacramento and discuss their long-term care experiences with their elected representatives. When the California Senate Chair of the Aging and Long-Term Care Committee invited the Association to testify at a legislative hearing, they recruited caregivers to speak before the Committee.

For participants in the LACRC support group, the organization provided an important conduit between their support group and the political process. Dora, for example, was a former caregiver for her mother and a longtime member of the LACRC support group. Prior to her experience caring for her mother, she said, she was "interested" in political issues and "opinionated," but there had never been an issue for which she'd "actually gotten out and carried a banner." But, she said, after attending the support group at the LACRC, as well as the workshops and classes offered by the LACRC, she had become politicized. At the time of this study, Dora had attended a training class to lead her own support group, she had traveled to Sacramento twice for "Advocacy Days," had been asked to testify in a state legislative hearing on caregiving, and was poised to join an advisory council at a University of Southern California research center on Alzheimer's.

10. Service organizations which do not normally engage in advocacy on occasion play this role with their clientele when their resources are directly affected by state policy. The Wise Adult Day Care Center, for example, provided information to clients when state funding for adult day care was threatened, and a couple of support group participants reported writing letters to state representatives when provided with that information.

While Dora was unusual in the extent of her political involvement, other members of her support group had also made the trip to Sacramento, written their legislators about specific bills, and participated in other CRC initiatives. Importantly, none of the LACRC support group members who participated in this study complained, as other caregivers had done, about the lack of opportunities to participate in organized political demand making or the absence of information about specific legislative initiatives. In this regard, the LACRC offers a compelling illustration of how advocacy organizations can successfully recruit members of this new constituency into organized political activity.

While it is true, then, that some portion of family caregivers will always be too overwhelmed by the responsibilities of chronic care provision to be available for political mobilization, these obstacles to mobilization are particularly difficult to overcome for reform organizations relying exclusively on targeted activation technologies. An important consequence of the increase in targeted activation strategies is a further attenuation of the nexus between collective attribution and mobilization for individuals affected by long-term care. To the extent that individuals are politicized by the experience of providing chronic care, there are few structural opportunities for "pulling" them into the political process. To paraphrase Sidney Verba and his colleagues (1995), the absence of political demand making for long-term care policies may not be exclusively due to indifference or unavailability, but to the striking fact that potential participants have simply never been asked.

CONCLUSION

Social ties have long been understood to play a key role in shaping the formulation of political grievances and connecting grievants to organized opportunities for demand making (Diani and McAdam 2003). But as Figure 6.2 illustrates, social movement researchers have always assumed that there are structural ties that link these various dimensions of politicization. Here we find, to the contrary, that the social relationships that facilitate the formulation of political grievances involving long-term care are no longer clearly tied to the social relationships that recruit grievants into organized political activity.

The broad-based depoliticization of the social welfare sector that accompanied the expansion of the welfare state into community-based health and human service organizations has produced a social service sector in which individuals are actively discouraged from connecting their individual social welfare struggles to broader political reform efforts. Similarly, the dramatic

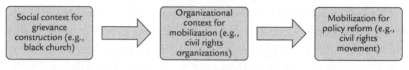

Conventional Social Movement Model
Positive Case Analysis: Social ties between grievance construction and mobilization assumed to connect

Contemporary Social Politics Model
Nagative Case Analysis: Social ties between grievance construction and mobilization severed due to changes in the field of political organizations

Figure 6.2
Consequences for Mobilization of Changes in the Field of Political Organizations

shift in political organization toward advocacy and the use of targeted activation technologies have limited the capacity of advocacy organizations to identify and mobilize newly politicized constituencies. As a consequence, those individuals who are politicized by their experiences with long-term care are nevertheless unlikely to be recruited into organized political activity.[11]

Earlier chapters demonstrated a number of ways in which existing social policies serve as important ideational resources in the process of politicization. The process of discursive integration—of synthesizing new and oppositional understandings of social welfare provision with more familiar

11. Whether these findings are generalizable to other social welfare issues—such as child care or job re-skilling—is a question ripe for future empirical investigation. Social welfare issues vary in the degree to which they are embedded in organizational fields that could potentially shape political grievances and link grievances to organized political demand making. Child care and other parenting needs, for example, are similar to elder care in that the affordability and quality of child care services are rarely discussed in political discourse as social policy priorities, despite well-documented social risks (Gornick and Meyers 2003). It may be that the shift toward treating child care as an "early education" issue (rather than a feminist or labor issue) has involved processes of depoliticization similar to those observed in the social welfare sector, attenuating the structural ties between collective attribution and political mobilization. The issue of job re-skilling, by contrast, looms large in the current economic crisis as a political solution to high—and potentially persistent—levels of unemployment. Despite a weakened labor movement, this issue more than any other would seem to possess the necessary structural linkages to draw affected constituencies into political mobilization: labor unions retain a firm presence in most states affected by trends in deindustrialization and continue to rely on 'old-style' methods of face-to-face mobilization (Lopez 2004). A comparative study of social welfare issues would help to illuminate the diverse ways in which long-term shifts in organizational fields are shaping the capacity of affected citizens to translate their personal grievances into political demands.

ways of talking and thinking about social welfare issues—may temper how radical political claims for reform may be, but it nevertheless does produce claims for social policy reform that challenge important elements of the ideology of family responsibility—most notably, the idea that families should be exclusively responsible for the costs and provision of care. Yet without institutional resources to connect grievants with organized opportunities for political demand making or to connect advocates with politicized caregivers, the possibilities of passing new social policies that respond to such claims remains dim.

CHAPTER 7

Caring for Our Own

The past several decades have witnessed remarkable changes in our society: women now participate in the paid labor force at rates equal to men, family forms have been reconfigured, and changes in health care and living standards have dramatically extended the life expectancy of the average citizen. But what is arguably most noteworthy about these transformations is what hasn't changed: traditional conceptions about family responsibility for care have persisted even as families find they can no longer meet those responsibilities on their own. In the case of long-term care, most Americans continue to believe that it is the sole responsibility of family to handle the costs and provision of chronic care. For most people, these beliefs are based on taken-for-granted expectations for how we should maintain our social welfare: *It's what families do.* As a consequence, despite the well-documented effects of contemporary care dilemmas on the economic security of families, the physical and mental health of family care providers, the bottom lines of businesses, and the financial health of existing social policies, American families have demonstrated little inclination for translating their private care problems into political demands for social policy reform. This book has sought to explain why the ideology of family responsibility for social welfare persists even in the face of unmet social welfare needs.

Ideology is invoked here in the social constructionist sense, as a process of meaning making in which meanings are constructed and used to establish and reinforce particular power relations or distribution of resources (Ewick and Silbey 1999). The power and durability of the ideology of family responsibility lies in its ability to inscribe itself in the rhythms of everyday life (Silbey 2005). By helping to constitute the way we routinely behave—by helping to naturalize "what families do"—the ideology of family responsibility not only legitimates particular norms and values, but it masks any alternatives. We can't even imagine how life could be structured in any other way.

This book has sought to understand the durability of norms and beliefs about family responsibility for care by looking at how ordinary people construct solutions to the everyday problems they encounter with contemporary long-term care provision. Under what conditions do families struggling with unmet needs reimagine the ideology of family responsibility for social welfare, and under what conditions do they merely reinforce it? What prevents oppositional understandings of new social welfare needs from developing into political demand for alternative social arrangements? The answer to these questions, this book has argued, lies in a better understanding of how the political imagination works.

OBSTACLES TO POLITICIZATION

To provide a way of dissecting the process by which individuals come to challenge taken-for-granted assumptions about social welfare provision, this book has utilized the concept of politicization. Politicization here refers to the processes by which individuals come to (1) view longstanding "private" needs as matters of legitimate public deliberation and decision making, (2) imagine solutions to their unmet needs, and (3) make claims to an official agency or other perceived responsible party for action. Analyses of these processes among family caregivers suggest three sets of obstacles to politicization in this case: the absence of social policies that provide both cultural and material resources, the role of discursive integration in reinforcing the ideology of family responsibility, and the absence of advocacy organizations to mobilize individual grievances into organized political demand making.

The Role of Existing Social Policy and Services in Politicization

While this study was ostensibly about the formation of political demand for new social policy, a recurring theme in the data involved the powerful role of existing social policies and services in politicizing caregivers. When imagining alternative social arrangements for care, individuals have available to them a limited cultural repertoire of meanings, practices, rules, and logics from which they can draw. Existing social policies and services proved to be a key source of these cultural tools, and caregivers were quite skilled at transposing or extending them to new contexts involving contemporary care provision.

In Chapter 3, we saw that when most caregivers began the experience of providing care to a family member with a chronic disease, they had little accurate information about what care provision would entail or what forms of assistance would be available. Few had any ideas about what kinds of public policies could ever be useful to them. Contact with social services was typically a crucial turning point for caregivers, and provided the context in which the process of politicization began. While these social services lacked an overtly political agenda, sustained exposure to the discourse of caregiving nevertheless had a consciousness-raising effect on caregivers, highlighting similarities in the experiences of family care providers, reframing individual care problems as collective problems, and emphasizing the underlying structural or sociocultural factors that make long-term care difficult for families in the United States. The physical spaces in which to share experiences and engage in the discourse of family caregiving proved to be important catalysts for politicization (see Evans and Boyte 1986).

Similarly, Chapter 4 showed the ways in which concrete social benefits—in this case from Medicaid—served as important models for what the state could do to assist families with the provision of chronic care. Because most caregivers had given very little thought to the state when they began caregiving, they required resources for the construction of political grievances—they needed a sense of who to blame for their unmet needs and some vision for how those needs could be ameliorated. The long-term care benefits provided to the poor through Medicaid may not have been available to most caregivers in this study, but they provided both a target for their frustration over the absence of long-term care assistance for the middle class, and a model for what they could ask of the state.

Finally, Chapter 5 demonstrated how the political logics of existing social insurance programs such as Social Security and Medicare helped caregivers formulate a view of themselves as citizens deserving of state long-term care assistance—even as they sought access to the material benefits of a means-tested public assistance program. The positive civic lessons learned from social insurance programs—encouraging a sense of entitlement and political efficacy—proved to be transposable to the context of long-term care, providing caregivers with a set of normative principles about the responsibilities of state in ensuring the health security of its citizens.

In each case, existing social policies provided key resources for imagining alternative social arrangements for care, and yet the capacity of existing social policies and services to serve as resources for families struggling with unmet social welfare needs was also limited by the paucity of the American welfare state. Many caregivers in this country lack access to the kinds of social services available to caregivers in this study—either because they live in rural or poorer parts of the country where there are few such services available, or because they face language or transportation barriers in accessing such services. And of course relative to other advanced democracies, the United States has very few social policies in place to offer material resources for families providing chronic care. Politicization in this regard involves a striking catch-22: the absence of social policies tends to mute political demand, and yet without political demand, new social policies are unlikely.

Discursive Integration

If existing social policies served as important cultural resources for imagining alternative social arrangements for care, discursive integration was the mechanism by which individuals transposed or extended those practices, models, and logics to the context of contemporary care provision. Synthesizing new models or political logics with more familiar ways of thinking and talking about social welfare has both the potential to legitimate existing ideologies and to challenge them. Discursive integration helps to explain why families struggling with new social needs can simultaneously seem to challenge the ideology of family responsibility even as they reproduce it. When oppositional beliefs are constructed with elements that are constitutive of the dominant ideology (Hunt 1990), they can easily be subsumed within the dominant ideology. Caregivers confronted heartbreaking struggles in this study. But even as they experienced the limitations of existing social services, long-term care insurance policies, Medicare, Medicaid, and family leave laws, the duty they felt to "care for our own" and the belief that this is "what families do," remained a powerful influence on how they viewed their circumstances.

In Chapter 3, for example, we saw how the family caregiver discourse used by social service providers helped to politicize individuals by separating the "normal" duties of family members from "caregiving" responsibilities. Yet by characterizing certain obligations of parents and adult children as "normal," the discourse of caregiving legitimized other dimensions of the ideology of family responsibility that are neither "natural" nor "normal" but are socially constructed—for example, the way caregiving responsibilities are often assigned to family members by gender, or the tendency of employers to assume caregivers are "bad workers" if they need time off or flexible hours. Similarly, Chapter 4 showed that even when individuals constructed concrete political claims for state intervention in long-term care, those claims were only as ambitious as their source: Because caregivers relied on a residualist model of social provision in imagining policy solutions for their unmet needs, their claims did little to transform understandings of citizenship, community, or social responsibilities for care. Instead they sought simply to ensure that our most basic needs are met by family, with help when absolutely necessary from the state. Likewise, Chapter 5 argued that while the process of discursive integration facilitated a normative expectation among caregivers that the government had an obligation to protect families providing long-term care from falling into destitution, virtually all families in this study still viewed the government as the place of last resort—a source of assistance only when family resources run out.

To those students of the welfare state who often point to other advanced welfare states as models of what the United States could do for American families, the data from this study re-emphasize Hunt's (1990) point that people always begin where they are at: In their search for alternative social arrangements in this case, individuals turned to those models that were most consistent with what they already knew. Rather than relying on European social welfare systems as models of what the government could do for families providing long-term care, caregivers in this study viewed the health care systems of other countries as too different or too unfamiliar to work in the United States. Indeed even Medicare, a highly respected social welfare program in the United States, failed to resonate with caregivers as a potential model for state intervention. The political logic of social insurance programs suggested to many caregivers that families would be "handing over" family care responsibilities to the state. Instead, they were drawn to Medicaid, with its familiar emphasis on family responsibility, as a model of state intervention.

How do we explain the power of the ideology of family responsibility to subsume new ideas, meanings, and political logics in this way? Under what circumstances is it possible for discursive integration to fundamentally challenge traditional norms and understandings? Here we see the crucial role of cultural categories in navigating the fine line between reinforcing and reimagining the social organization of care. Cultural distinctions reward those who follow the social norms of a society and stigmatize those who don't. People are invested in these distinctions because they reflect things like self-worth, status, and morality. In the case of long-term care provision, we've seen that people are deeply committed to being "dutiful" family members, not only for the personal satisfaction derived from meeting one's perceived obligations to family, but also because being a dutiful family member reflects well on who they are and what they stand for.

The demands of contemporary care provision threaten that status. Caregivers who, for physical, emotional, or economic reasons, cannot satisfy the chronic care needs of family members often see themselves—and are viewed by others—as "bad" partners or children. Their search for solutions to unmet needs are shaped in critical respects by the desire to restore or reinforce one's status as someone who properly cares for their own. In most cases, this discursive logic produced understandings of care and solutions for unmet needs that legitimated rather than challenged the ideology of family responsibility for care.

Discursive integration resulted in more counterhegemonic understandings of long-term care provision only when the process of reasserting the ideology of family responsibility threatened the status of other cultural identities. For example, when being a good spouse or child threatened one's status as a "good caregiver" or "deserving citizen," caregivers drew on and recombined cultural resources in ways that sought to retain a positive sense of self-worth across cultural categories. The cross-combination of cultural elements produced understandings of long-term care provision that seemed to transcend the traditional ideology of family responsibility for care.

We saw in Chapter 2, for example, how family care providers were introduced to the relatively new cultural category—caregiver—with its own set of normative expectations for what it means to be a "good" caregiver: good caregivers recognize that they are making an important social contribution in providing care for their family members, not simply "doing what families do," and their efforts ought to be supported through community services. This understanding of caregivers as entitled to community support directly contradicts what it means to be a "dutiful" spouse or daughter or son, caring for family on one's own no matter what the cost. Those individuals in this study who were invested in being both a "good" caregiver and a "dutiful" spouse or adult child needed a way to maintain a positive perception of self-worth across categories. Social workers and service providers aided this process by arguing that being a good caregiver by, for example, seeking out community services, was actually a more effective way of meeting one's obligations to family. By integrating new ideas about supportive services with deeply held beliefs about their obligations to family, discursive integration produced a much more oppositional understanding of long-term care provision, one that views care provision as a matter appropriate for state intervention.

Chapter 5 provides a second example of the oppositional potential of discursive integration. Residualist social welfare policies like Medicaid tend to reinforce the primacy of family responsibility and the status of care providers as "dutiful" spouses or children. As a result, caregivers in this study were often drawn to this model in imagining solutions to their family's unmet needs. But beneficiaries of public assistance programs are often stigmatized as supplicants in this country, the opposite of what it means to be a "deserving" citizen. Caregivers who were invested in maintaining a positive sense of self-worth across cultural categories drew on the key elements of "deservingness"—as hard workers, taxpayers, law-abiding citizens—to reassert their status as "deserving" citizens in the context of a public assistance program. Middle-class caregivers, in other words, treated Medicaid as if it were a social insurance program, emphasizing concepts such as entitlement and state obligation that lie at the heart of more interventionist models of social policy. This combination of entitlement discourse and the discourse of family responsibility produced understandings of chronic care provision that transcended existing political categories to imagine a new relationship between citizens and the state in matters of long-term care.

The Absence of Advocates

Finally, the third set of obstacles standing in the way of full-fledged politicization involved the absence of advocacy organizations to give voice to caregiver struggles. Unlike most social movement accounts of political mobilization, which assume a role for organizational actors in both collective attribution and mobilization, most individuals in this study lacked any connection to political advocacy organizations. Whereas researchers have long understood social movements as playing a key part in processes of collective identification and consciousness-raising, offering particular frames for understanding the problems of, for example, contemporary care provision as well as solutions and plans for action, here caregivers produced these understandings in a depoliticized social service sector, drawing from their own experiences and those of the caregivers they knew (rather than from social movement actors) for sources of meaning. But to communicate grievances as part of organized political demand making, individuals need information about how and when and where to get involved. They need leadership and other organizational resources for coordinating their individual grievances into collective political demands. As Chapter 6 illustrated, the decoupling of social welfare organizations from organized politics, together with the shift in mobilization technologies used by advocacy organizations toward "targeted activation," has severed the structural ties needed to communicate grievances to policymakers or other relevant political targets. Where those ties remained intact—as in the case of the California Caregiver Resource Centers—politicized caregivers were substantially more likely to personally participate in political demand making.

It's important here not to romanticize the potential of social movement organizations to pressure policymakers for political solutions that ameliorate the strains on contemporary families. Advocacy organizations seeking to influence public policy do not construct collective action frames in a political vacuum, but are themselves influenced by political institutions, power relations, and the terms of dominant political discourse (Ferree 2003; Steinberg 1999). Activists seeking long-term care public policy reform today confront bipartisan concerns about the financial viability of existing social programs (e.g., Social Security, Medicare) in the current economic context, as well as skepticism from the political right regarding any expansion of the state. Such a political environment sharply constrains the range of policy solutions advocacy organizations can credibly seek for a social problem such as long-term care provision. As a consequence, most advocacy organizations, including the AARP and Alzheimer's Association, are currently pursuing modest, incremental, market-based reforms[1] that bear little resemblance to the needs or expectations of caregivers for an expanded safety net for the middle class.

Nevertheless, there are at least two reasons why the work of such advocacy organizations is still vital to the politicization of family caregivers. First, from the perspective of caregivers, advocacy organizations represent a voice in policymaking arenas for advancing the interests of American families and a resource for communicating to caregivers opportunities for political demand making. Without organizational resources, most politicized caregivers in this case lacked any sense of what to do about their political grievances. Second, the transformative power of politicization lies in the nexus of social policy, discursive integration, and advocacy organizations. Understanding discursive integration as the recombination of already existing elements means that every adjustment in social policy changes the possibilities for future strategic action. Every transformation in official law changes the expectations for future law. The critical project at stake in unmasking the hegemonic power of family responsibility lies in helping to "construct anew" (Silbey and Sarat 1987:172)—to not just observe how ordinary citizens seek to solve problems or advance their interests in the world, but to actually demonstrate new configurations. New social welfare programs such as the Affordable Care Act provide not only concrete benefits that help meet the needs of American families, but also ideational resources for affected citizens to imagine new political solutions. In contemporary politics, advocacy organizations potentially serve as important sources of new models of social arrangements—either through the successful passage of new social policies or through public advocacy of particular policy proposals.

---

1. Most market-based policy reform proposals at the time of this study primarily focused on making long-term care insurance more available to the middle class by offering tax credits for individuals purchasing insurance policies.

In the context of long-term care, the passage of social policy that addresses any of the unmet needs of American families could serve as a bridge between longstanding beliefs about long-term care provision as a family responsibility and nascent understandings of long-term care as at least partly a social responsibility. State programs that do not "take over" the cost or provision of care, for example, but instead subsidize the ability of families to utilize adult day care or respite care or to take paid time off from work would be consistent with caregivers' search for solutions that permit them to meet their perceived obligations to family. Such programs, if enacted, would then establish a legitimate role for the state in long-term care policy, not as a residual safety net, but as a key partner in ensuring that families have every resource they need to provide high-quality care, and that patients have all the care they require as key rights of citizenship.

RETHINKING LEGAL CONSCIOUSNESS AND POLITICAL MOBILIZATION

In seeking to explain the durability of the ideology of family responsibility despite well-documented unmet social welfare needs, this book has sought to build on the work of socio-legal scholars who study legal consciousness and the durability of liberal legal ideology (Ewick and Silbey 1999; Sarat and Silbey 1988). Early legal consciousness scholars encouraged a shift away from the study of policy failures to focus instead on the ways in which law is effective—so effective, in fact, that we no longer notice its presence in everyday life. The legal consciousness literature that has grown out of the cultural turn to the study of law in everyday life is a vibrant and still growing area of study. But this book has argued that the move away from the study of social policy has hampered our ability to understand how individuals reproduce (or resist) dominant ideologies in their day-to-day lives. Studying law in everyday life has been largely divorced from the project of studying the policies that shape everyday living.

The laws and regulations, benefits, and services that constitute "social policy" in the United States serve as important resources in the American cultural repertoire and, as such, play a profound role in shaping the political imagination. The systems of provision intended for one constituency can be imagined for another. The rules and regulations that shape existing policy can be the source of the kind of righteous indignation that fuels political demand making. The lessons learned from social policies about self-worth and citizenship are transposable to new contexts. The incrementalism of social change in contexts involving highly institutionalized social practices and beliefs highlights the important point that that there will never be a radical break from what we know as the ideology of family responsibility. But it does underscore the subtle, yet powerful role that social policy can have in challenging the norms, beliefs, and practices that constitute that ideology.

With regard to social movements and political mobilization, this study points to the importance of understanding the absence of mobilization. In a study of nonmobilization, it is always easy to identify reasons why mobilization might not occur, such that nonmobilization seems to be virtually overdetermined. But there are important theoretical reasons for social movement scholars to make the effort. Social movement research has historically involved the study of how grievances which have been ignored by—or shut out of—institutional politics can be collectively mobilized to become a voice in American social politics. Identifying the conditions conducive to mobilization has been, in this regard, an important theoretical and political project. But by relying on positive cases of emergent action to illuminate conditions that facilitate mobilization, social movement researchers have given scant attention to obstacles to mobilization—those conditions that not only impede collective action, but that facilitate inaction. As this study has demonstrated, this includes examining individuals who are not affiliated with social movements, as shifts in their political consciousness are important indicators of their willingness and ability to participate in collective action.

Related to this, we cannot assume that the theories that explain collective action during periods of heightened activism will necessarily explain processes of politicization during periods of relative political calm. A negative case, where theoretical predictions have been contradicted in some way, forces researchers to rethink and potentially reconstruct existing theory to account for changing historical conditions. The case of long-term care offers an important example of how contemporary trends in social welfare and political advocacy are reconfiguring how ordinary citizens connect to the political process.

FROM POLITICAL CONSCIOUSNESS TO POLITICAL DEMAND

The analysis in this book has been largely focused on individual processes of politicization, and it's worth stepping back now to consider the broader politics in which these processes have been taking place and their implications for future social policy reform. As elaborated in Chapter 2, the gap between the long-term care needs of Americans and the capacity of Americans today to meet those needs has been caused not only by an aging population or smaller family sizes, but by the failure of existing social practices to change alongside these long-term social trends. More specifically, policymakers have failed to update social policies in ways that reflect and ameliorate contemporary strains on families, and, just as importantly, families themselves have been reluctant to consider ways of sharing the costs of chronic care provision beyond the domain of the family. These two forms of inaction have been mutually reinforcing: existing social policies reflect and reinforce normative assumptions about the responsibility of family members to provide care for free, and public beliefs in family responsibility for care provision legitimize government nonintervention. The ideology of family responsibility, in other words, maintains itself in the face of rapidly changing social conditions by minimizing demand for new social policies.

It would be naïve to argue that the politicization of family caregivers will necessarily lead to the passage of new social policies. In the current political context even the most powerful advocacy organizations are unlikely to successfully orchestrate a campaign for new entitlement programs. But what the politicization of family caregivers can do is remove the political cover for maintaining the status quo. The politics of nonintervention only work when the government can successfully claim that existing policies are congruent with public choice. As long as Americans continue to view family care provision as "natural" or "normal" and the exclusive prerogative of family, the state can continue to maintain the impression that nonintervention is justified. When public opinion shifts in favor of policy reform, then political contestation can really begin.

Since this study was conducted, the political landscape has changed very little. While the 2008 election of President Obama seemed to signal a move away from the antigovernment, antitax politics that have dominated Washington, D.C. for decades, the reality is that sharp fiscal constraints and partisan politics have tempered any hope for dramatic change. Policymakers continue to remain ambivalent about family caregivers— they want to support them enough to keep them on the job, but not so much to create a new entitlement program or to discourage unpaid family care. In the absence of a comprehensive long-term care policy, reform initiatives have been scarce, piecemeal, poorly funded, and, in some cases, temporary. The passage of three pieces of long-term care legislation illustrates this well: the National Family Caregiver Support Program (NFCSP) created in 2000 under the federal Older Americans Act and reauthorized in 2006; the Federal Lifespan Respite Care Act of 2006; and the Community Living Assistance Service and Supports (CLASS) Act, passed in 2010 as part of the Affordable Care Act.

The passage of the NFCSP was hailed as the federal government's first recognition of the work of informal caregivers. The NFCSP provides grants to states to work with area agencies on aging and with local service providers to develop support systems for family caregivers in five basic areas: information about available services, assistance to caregivers in gaining access to supportive services, individual counseling and support groups, respite care, and supplemental services such as home modifications (Feinberg and Newman 2006). These services are provided on a limited basis and are designed to complement the care provided by caregivers. Like other service programs under the Older Americans Act, however, the NFCSP was only modestly funded when Congress initially authorized it ($125 million in fiscal year 2001), and has continued to be funded at about $153 million per year for the past decade (Napili and Colello 2013), despite reports that the need for support services in all fifty states far exceeds what Congress appropriates every year (Feinberg and Newman 2006).

The reauthorization of the Older Americans Act in 2006 also created the Federal Lifespan Respite Care Program, which awards matching grants to eligible state agencies to develop or enhance respite care services at the state and local levels for family caregivers who are caring for children and adults with special needs. "Respite care" under the Act is defined as "planned or emergency care provided to a child or adult with a special need in order to provide temporary relief to the family caregiver of that child or adult" (Napili and Colello 2013). In 2011, the Lifespan Respite Care Program was funded at just under $2.5 million. Grants to eligible state agencies did not exceed $200,000 (Napili and Colello 2013). The program was due to be reauthorized by Congress in 2011, but the reauthorization bill died in committee. Since 2011, Congress has continued to appropriate funding for the program at just over $2 million a year. In contrast to the $450 billion (Feinberg et al. 2011) worth of unpaid care family members provide each year, the federal contributions to caregiver support systems are negligible. Agency officials have consistently described Congress's appropriations for these programs as wholly insufficient (Levine and Murray 2004).

In 2010, Congress passed the Community Living Assistance Service and Supports (CLASS) Act, as part of the Affordable Care Act. At the time of its passage, observers hailed the CLASS Act as the most significant change in the way the U.S. government finances long-term care since 1965. The CLASS Act called for the creation of a federally operated, voluntary, consumer-financed, long-term care cash benefit insurance program. The Act did not provide comprehensive benefits, nor did it provide universal coverage, but for the first time it defined long-term care needs as insurable events that should be addressed through public administration (Wolf 2012). Long-term care, the legislation suggested, is a social risk, a risk for which resources should be pooled and safeguarded, rather than a condition that individuals and families should face alone. The CLASS Act would have introduced non-means-tested cash benefits for the long-term care of chronically ill elders for the first time, responding to the widespread preference people have for consumer choice in the acquisition of long-term care services, and for community-based rather than institutional care (Hudson 2012).

But then, on October 14, 2011, Secretary Kathleen Sebelius announced that despite the Department of Health and Human Services' best efforts, she did not see "a viable way forward for CLASS implementation at this time" (Wolf 2012). The CLASS Act's provisions of voluntary enrollment, a minimum daily cash benefit, coverage of disabled workers after a short vesting period, and a requirement that the plan be sustained entirely by the premiums charged, all meant that the program would depend on unsustainably high premiums. Today, the CLASS Act remains in policy limbo: it has been suspended, but officially remains on the books. By most accounts it will almost certainly not be revived in its current form (Wolf 2012).

CONCLUSION

Congress's modest policy solutions for contemporary long-term care dilemmas have done little to improve conditions for care provision within American families since this study was conducted. As a result, many of this country's most vulnerable citizens are not receiving the amount or quality of care they need. One of the critical findings of this study is that the silence of the American public about the contemporary crisis in care does not signal assent to the yawning gap in social welfare provision, nor does it reflect indifference or apathy or the absence of need. The absence of political demand instead reflects how difficult it is to adjust to changing social conditions while simultaneously maintaining one's deep commitments to family. The absence of political demand highlights the challenges of imagining policy solutions to unmet needs that rise above (or between) the sharp dichotomies posed by the American welfare state, where neither the social insurance nor public assistance models fully accords with what families need and want and believe they deserve. And finally, the absence of political demand reflects how difficult it is for ordinary American families to communicate their grievances in ways that policymakers will hear.

Despite the wide-ranging impediments to demand making observed in this case, it's important to emphasize that this study found ample evidence of politicization among family caregivers. Notwithstanding strong norms to the contrary, family care providers are beginning to view themselves as members of a larger group or constituency, re-envision their care circumstances as political grievances, and justify their claims for state intervention with relatively sophisticated ideas about the relationship between care provision and the role of the state in social welfare provision. And while some family caregivers will always be too overwhelmed by the responsibilities of care provision to participate in social reform efforts, the study observed a growing constituency of current and former caregivers who would be both willing and able to participate in such reform efforts, if given the opportunity to do so. For an issue long domesticated as nonpolitical by the American public, the invocation of the state by caregivers marks an important shift in political consciousness. As the ranks of current and former caregivers continue to increase with the aging of the baby boomer generation, as social policies continue to be tested, refined, expanded or contracted, and as advocates continue to develop new strategies and technologies for mobilization, there is every reason to expect that this burgeoning wave of politicization could yet develop into full-fledged political demand.

Demographic Statistics for Family Caregiver Sample (n=176)

	Support Group Participants* (n=158)	Peer Group Participants (n=80)	Interview Subjects (n=79)
Sex of Caregiver	N=158	N=80	N=79
Female	104 (66%)	54 (67%)	57 (72%)
Male	54 (34%)	26 (33%)	22 (28%)
Race/Ethnicity	N=156	N=80	N=79
Black	24 (15%)	12 (15%)	17 (22%)
Hispanic	27 (17%)	18 (23%)	9 (11%)
Asian/Pacific Islander	4 (3%)	4 (5%)	4 (5%)
Caucasian	100 (64%)	46 (57%)	48 (61%)
Other	1 (1%)	0 (0%)	1 (1%)
Relationship to Care Receiver	N=158	N=80	N=79
Spouse or Partner	94 (60%)	47 (59%)	39 (49%)
Son or Daughter	52 (33%)	25 (31%)	36 (46%)
Other	12 (8%)	8 (10%)	4 (5%)
Median Age			N=78
			63
Income			N=75
<$30,000			18 (24%)
$31–50,000			17 (23%)
$51–70,000			11 (15%)
over $70,000			29 (39%)
Political Ideology			N=75
Liberal			33 (44%)
Moderate			21 (28%)
Conservative			9 (12%)
Other			12 (16%)
Party Usually Votes For			N=75
Democrat			54 (72%)
Republican			12 (16%)
Other			9 (12%)

*Membership in the three groups was partially, but not entirely, overlapping. Peer group and most interview participants were recruited from support groups. In all, 50 individuals participated in all three groups.

Demographic Statistics for Family Caregiver Sample (n=170)

Advocacy Organizations and Interview Subjects

NAME OF ORGANIZATION	TYPE OF ORGANIZATION	NAME AND POSITION OF INTERVIEW SUBJECT
Center for Health Care Rights	Administrative advocacy (Los Angeles)	Aileen Harper, executive director
Center for Medicare Advocacy	Administrative and legal advocacy (Washington, D.C.)	Alfred Chiplin, D.C. managing attorney Toby Edelman, senior policy attorney
Association of California Caregiver Resource Centers	Legislative advocacy (California)	Vicki Farrell, chairperson
Los Angeles Caregiver Resource Center	Service and administrative/program advocacy (California)	Donna Benton, director
Valley Caregiver Resource Center	Service and administrative/program advocacy (California)	Margery Minney, director
Redwood Caregiver Resource Center	Service and administrative/program advocacy (California)	Nancy Powers-Stone, director
Coast Caregiver Resource Center	Service and administrative/program advocacy (California)	Mary Sheridan, director
Mountain Caregiver Resource Center	Service and administrative/program advocacy (California)	Susanne Rossi, director
National Committee to Preserve Social Security and Medicare	Legislative advocacy (Washington, D.C.)	Diane Lifney, legislative representative Alison Bonebrake, legislative representative Sue Ward, director, grassroots advocacy
AARP California	Legislative advocacy (California)	Rigo Saborio, director of State Management Ernie Powell, advocacy representative
National Alliance for Caregiving	Legislative and program advocacy (Washington, D.C.)	Gail Hunt, executive director
Bet Tzedek Legal Services	Service and program advocacy (Los Angeles)	Janet Morris, director, Long-Term Care Program Kim Williams, caregiver advocate

(Continued)

(Continued)

NAME OF ORGANIZATION	TYPE OF ORGANIZATION	NAME AND POSITION OF INTERVIEW SUBJECT
National Respite Coalition	Legislative advocacy (Washington, D.C.)	Jill Kagan, co-founder
Alzheimer's Association of Los Angeles	Program and legislative advocacy	Judith Delaney, clinical manager Michelle Barclay, director, Patient, Family and Training Servs.
Alzheimer's Association (national office)	Legislative advocacy (Washington, D.C.)	Stephen McConnell, senior vp for public policy and advocacy
Family Caregiver Alliance	Program and legislative advocacy (California)	Kathleen Kelly, executive director
National Center on Caregiving	Legislative and program advocacy (California)	Lynn Feinberg, deputy director
California Advocates for Nursing Home Reform	Administrative and legislative advocacy (California)	Patricia McGinnis, executive director Michael Connors, long-term care advocate
AARP Foundation (Legal Advocacy)	Legal advocacy (Washington, D.C.)	Stuart Cohen, director of legal advocacy
National Family Caregiver Alliance	Program and legislative advocacy (Washington, D.C.)	Susanne Mintz, co-founder and president
LA Council on Aging	Administrative and program advocacy (Los Angeles)	Ed Woods, president

REFERENCES

Abel, Emily K. 1990. "Family Care of the Frail Elderly." Pp. 65–91 in *Circles of Care: Work and Identity in Women's Lives,* edited by E. K. Abel and M. K. Nelson. Albany: State University of New York Press.

——. 1991. *Who Cares for the Elderly? Public Policy and the Experiences of Adult Daughters.* Philadelphia: Temple University Press.

Abramovitz, Mimi. 1996. *Regulating the Lives of Women: Social Welfare Policy from Colonial Times to the Present.* Boston: South End Press.

Administration on Aging. 2012. *A Profile of Older Americans: 2012.* Washington, DC: Administration on Aging, U.S. Department of Health & Human Services,

Albiston, Catherine R. 2005. "Bargaining in the Shadow of Social Institutions: Competing Discourses and Social Change in Workplace Mobilization of Civil Rights." *Law & Society Review* 39(1):11–50.

Albrecht, Terrance, Gerianne Johnson, and Joseph Walther. 1993. "Understanding Communication Processes in Focus Groups." Pp. 51–64 in *Successful Focus Groups: Advancing the State of the Art,* edited by D. L. Morgan. Newbury Park: Sage Publications.

Alzheimer's Association & National Alliance for Caregiving. 1999. *Who Cares? Families Caring for Persons with Alzheimer's Disease.* Washington, DC: Alzheimer's Association & National Alliance for Caregiving,

Anderson, Perry. 1977. "The Antinomies of Antonio Gramsci." *New Left Review* 100:5–78.

Andrews, Kenneth T. and Bob Edwards. 2004. "Advocacy Organizations in the U.S. Political Process." *Annual Review of Sociology* 30:479–506.

Archibald, Matthew E. 2007. *The Evolution of Self-Help: How a Health Movement Became an Institution.* New York: Palgrave Macmillan.

Armingeon, Klaus and Giuliano Bonoli. 2006. *The Politics of Post-Industrial Welfare States: Adapting Post-War Social Policies to New Social Risks.* New York: Routledge.

Armstrong, Elizabeth A. 2002. *Forging Gay Identities: Organizing Sexuality in San Francisco, 1950-1994.* Chicago: University of Chicago Press.

Arras, John D, ed. 1995. *Bringing the Hospital Home: Ethical and Social Implications of High-Tech Home Care.* Baltimore, MD: Johns Hopkins University Press.

Arras, John D. and Nancy Neveloff Dubler. 1995. "Introduction: Ethical and Social Implications of High-Tech Home Care." Pp. 1–31 in *Bringing the Hospital Home: Ethical and Social Implications of High-Tech Home Care,* edited by J. D. Arras. Baltimore, MD: Johns Hopkins University Press.

Auletta, Ken. 1982. *The Underclass: A First-Hand Account of America's New Social Dropouts.* New York: Random House.

Aumann, Kerstin, Ellen Galinsky, Kelly Sakai, Melissa Brown, and James T. Bond. 2010. "The Elder Care Study: Everyday Realities and Wishes for Change." Families and Work

Institute, New York, http://familiesandwork.org/site/research/reports/elder_care.pdf (accessed July 27, 2013).

Auyero, Javier and Debora Alejandra Swistun. 2009. *Flammable: Environmental Suffering in an Argentine Shantytown.* New York: Oxford University Press.

Bachrach, Peter and Morton S. Baratz. 1962. "Two Faces of Power." *American Political Science Review* 56(4): 947–952.

Balbo, Laura. 1982. "The Servicing Work of Women and the Capitalist State." *Political Power and Social Theory* 3:251–270.

Barker, Rodney. 1990. *Political Legitimacy and the State.* New York: Oxford University Press.

Barrett, Michelle and Mary McIntosh. 1982. *The Anti-Social Family.* London: Verso.

Benford, Robert D. 1997. "An Insider's Critique of the Social Movement Framing Perspective." *Sociological Inquiry* 67(4): 409–430.

Berry, Jeffrey M. 1977. *Lobbying for the People: The Political Behavior of Public Interest Groups.* Princeton, NJ: Princeton University Press.

———. 1999. "The Rise of Citizen Groups." Pp. 367–393 in *Civic Engagement in American Democracy,* edited by Theda Skocpol and Morris P. Fiorina. Washington: Brookings Institution Press.

Berry, Jeffrey M. and Clyde Wilcox. 1989. *The Interest Group Society.* Glenview, IL: Scott, Foresman.

Blendon, Robert J., Drew E. Altman, and John Benson. 1995. "The Public's View of the Future of Medicare." *JAMA* 274(20): 1645–1648.

Bonoli, Giuliano. 2006. "New Social Risks and the Politics of Post-Industrial Social Policies." Pp. 3–26 in *The Politics of Post-Industrial Welfare States: Adapting Post-War Social Policies to New Social Risks,* edited by K. Armingeon and G. Bonoli. New York: Routledge.

Bonoli, Giuliano, Vic George, and Peter Taylor-Gooby. 2000. *European Welfare Futures: Towards a Theory of Retrenchment.* Cambridge, UK: Polity Press.

Boris, Eileen and Jennifer Klein. 2012. *Caring For America: Home Health Workers in the Shadow of the Welfare State.* New York: Oxford University Press.

Brady, Henry E., Kay Lehman Schlozman, and Sidney Verba. 1999. "Prospecting for Participants: Rational Expectations and the Recruitment of Political Activists." *American Political Science Review* 93(1): 153–168.

Britt, Lory and David Heise. 2000. "From Shame to Pride in Identity Politics." Pp. 252–268 in *Self, Identity, and Social Movements,* edited by S. Stryker, T. J. Owens, and R. W. White. Minneapolis: University of Minnesota Press.

Brodaty, Henry, Brian Draper, Dania Saab, Lee-Fay Low, Vicki Richards, Helen Paton, and David Lie. 2001. "Psychosis, Depression and Behavioural Disturbances in Sydney Nursing Home Residents: Prevalence and Predictors." *International Journal of Geriatric Psychiatry* 16(5):504–512.

Brody, Elaine M. 2004. *Women in the Middle: Their Parent Care Years.* New York: Springer.

Brooks, Clem and Jeff Manza. 2007. *Why Welfare States Persist: The Importance of Public Opinion in Democracies.* Chicago: University of Chicago Press.

Bruch, Sarah K., Myra Marx Ferree, and Joe Soss. 2010. "From Policy to Polity: Democracy, Paternalism, and the Incorporation of Disadvantaged Citizens." *American Sociological Review* 75(2): 205–226.

Bumiller, Kristin. 1988. *The Civil Rights Society: The Social Construction of Victims.* Baltimore, MD: Johns Hopkins University Press.

Burawoy, Michael. 1992. "The Extended Case Method." Pp. 271–287 in *Ethnography Unbound: Power and Resistance in the Modern Metropolis,* edited by M. Burawoy. Berkeley: University of California Press.

Burwell, Brian. 1991. *Middle-Class Welfare: Medicaid Estate Planning for Long-Term Care Coverage.* Cambridge, MA: SysteMetrics.

Bussiere, Elizabeth. 1997. *(Dis)Entitling the Poor: The Warren Court, Welfare Rights, and the American Political Tradition*. University Park: Pennsylvania State University Press.

Campbell, Andrea Louise. 2003. *How Policies Make Citizens: Senior Political Activism and the American Welfare State*. Princeton, NJ: Princeton University Press.

Campbell, R., C. Baker, and T. L. Mazurek. 1998. "Remaining Radical? Organizational Predictors of Rape Crisis Centers' Social Change Initiatives." *American Journal of Community Psychology* 26(3): 457–483.

Carrerra, Francesca, Emmanuele Pavolini, Costanzo Ranci, and Alessia Sabbatini. 2013. "Long-Term Care Systems in Comparative Perspective: Care Needs, Informal and Formal Coverage, and Social Impacts in European Countries." Pp. 23–52 in *Reforms in Long-Term Care Policies in Europe*, edited by Costanza Ranci and Emmanuele Pavolini. New York: Springer.

Clark, Phillip G. 1993. "Public Policy in the United States and Canada: Individualism, Familial Obligation, and Collective Responsibility in the Care of the Elderly." Pp. 13–48 in *The Remainder of Their Days: Domestic Policy and Older Families in the United States and Canada*, edited by J. Hendricks and C. J. Rosenthal. New York: Garland Publishing.

Clemens, Elisabeth S. 1997. *The People's Lobby: Organizational Innovation and the Rise of Interest Group Politics in the United States, 1890-1925*. Chicago: University of Chicago Press.

Coltrane, Scott and Justin Galt. 2000. "The History of Men's Caring: Evaluating Precedents for Fathers' Family Involvement." Pp. 15–36 in *Care Work: Gender, Labor, and the Welfare State*, edited by M. Harrington Meyer. New York: Routledge.

Cook, Fay Lomax and Edith J. Barrett. 1992. *Support for the American Welfare State: The Views of Congress and the Public*. New York: Columbia University Press.

Crenshaw, Kimberle Williams. 1988. "Race, Reform, and Retrenchment: Transformation and Legitimation in Antidiscrimination Law." *Harvard Law Review* 101(7): 1331–1387.

Crenson, Matthew A. 1971. *The Un-Politics of Air Pollution: A Study of Non-Decisionmaking in the Cities*. Baltimore, MD: Johns Hopkins University Press.

Crenson, Matthew and Benjamin Ginsberg. 2002. *Downsizing Democracy: How America Sidelined Its Citizens and Privatized Its Public*. Baltimore: Johnson Hopkins University Press.

Crowther, M.A. 1982. "Family Responsibility and State Responsibility in Britain Before the Welfare State." *Historical Journal* 25(1): 131–145.

Csikszentmihalyi, Mihaly. 1996. *Creativity: Flow and the Psychology of Discovery and Invention*. New York: HarperCollins.

Curtis, Russell L., Jr. and Louis A. Zurcher, Jr. 1973. "Stable Resources of Protest Movements: The Multi-Organizational Field." *Social Forces* 52(1): 53–61.

Dahl, Robert. 1963. *Who Governs? Democracy and Power in an American City*. New Haven, CT: Yale University Press.

Dalley, Gillian. 1988. *Ideologies of Caring: Rethinking Community and Collectivism*. London: Palgrave MacMillan.

Daly, Mary. 1997. "Welfare States under Pressure: Cash Benefits and European Welfare States over the Last Ten Years." *Journal of European Social Policy* 7(2): 129–146.

——. 2001a. "Care Policies in Western Europe." Pp. 33–55 in *Care Work: the Quest for Security*, edited by Mary Daly. London: International Labour Office.

——. 2001b. *Care Work: the Quest for Security*. London: International Labour Office.

——. 2005. "Changing Family Life in Europe: Significance for State and Society." *European Societies* 7(3): 379–398.

Daly, Mary and Katherine Rake. 2003. *Gender and the Welfare State: Care, Work and Welfare in Europe and the USA*. Malden, MA: Blackwell Publishing.

Davis, Martha F. 1993. *Brutal Need: Lawyers and the Welfare Rights Movement, 1960-1973*. New Haven, CT: Yale University Press.

Diani, Mario and Doug McAdam. 2003. *Social Movements and Networks: Relational Approaches to Collective Action*. New York: Oxford University Press.

Donelan, Karen, Craig A. Hill, Catherine Hoffman, Kimberly Scoles, Penny Hollander Feldman, Carol Levine, and David Gould. 2002. "Challenged to Care: Informal Caregivers in a Changing Health System." *Health Affairs* 21(4): 222–231.

Doty, Pamela. 2010. "The Evolving Balance of Formal and Informal, Institutional and Non-Institutional Long-Term Care for Older Americans: A Thirty-Year Perspective." *Public Policy & Aging Report* 20(1): 3–9.

Douglas, Mary. 1966. *Purity and Danger: An Analysis of the Concepts of Pollution and Taboo*. New York: Routledge.

Duffy, Mignon. 2011. *Making Care Count: A Century of Gender, Race, and Paid Care Work*. New Brunswick, NJ: Rutgers University Press.

Dunham, Charlotte Chhorn and Bernadette E. Dietz. 2003. " "If I'm Not Allowed to Put My Family First": Challenges Experienced by Women Who Are Caregiving for Family Members with Dementia." *Journal of Women & Aging* 15(1): 55–69.

Ehrenreich, Barbara and Arlie Hochschild. 2002. *Global Woman: Nannies, Maids, and Sex Workers in the New Economy*. New York: Metropolitan Books.

Emigh, Rebecca Jean. 1997. "The Power of Negative Thinking: The Use of Negative Case Methodology in the Development of Sociological Theory." *Theory and Society* 26(5): 649–684.

Engel, David M. 1980. "Legal Pluralism in an American Community: Perspectives on a Civil Trial Court." *Law and Social Inquiry* 5(3): 425–454.

Engel, David M. and Frank W. Munger. 2003. *Rights of Inclusion: Law and Identity in the Life Stories of Americans with Disabilities*. Chicago: University of Chicago Press.

England, Paula and Nancy Folbre. 1999. "The Cost of Caring." *ANNALS, AAPSS* 561:39–51.

Epp, Charles R. 2009. *Making Rights Real: Activists, Bureaucrats, and the Creation of the Legalistic State*. Chicago: University of Chicago Press.

Epstein, Steven. 1996. *Impure Science: AIDS, Activism, and the Politics of Knowledge*. Berkeley: University of California Press.

Esping-Anderson, Gosta. 1990. *The Three Worlds of Welfare Capitalism*. Princeton, NJ: Princeton University Press.

Estes, Carroll L. and James H. Swan. 1993. *The Long-Term Care Crisis: Elders Trapped in the No-Care Zone*. Newbury Park, CA: Sage Publications.

Evans, Rhonda and Tamara Kay. 2008. "How Environmentalists "Greened" Trade Policy: Strategic Action and the Architecture of Field Overlap." *American Sociological Review* 73(6): 970–991.

Evans, Sara. 1979. *Personal Politics: The Roots of Women's Liberation in the Civil Rights Movement and the New Left*. New York: Knopf.

Evans, Sara M. and Harry C. Boyte. 1986. *Free Spaces: The Sources of Democratic Change in America*. New York: Harper & Row.

Ewick, Patricia and Susan Silbey. 1992. "Conformity, Contestation, and Resistance: An Account of Legal Consciousness." *New England Law Review* 26:731–749.

———. 1995. "Subversive Stories and Hegemonic Tales: Toward a Sociology of Narrative." *Law and Society Review* 29(2): 197–226.

———. 1999. "Common Knowledge and Ideological Critique: The Significance of Knowing That the "Haves" Come Out Ahead." *Law & Society Review* 33(4): 1025–1041.

Ewick, Patricia and Susan S. Silbey. 1998. *The Common Place of Law: Stories from Everyday Life*. Chicago: University of Chicago Press.

Family Caregiver Alliance. November 9, 2006. "Family Caregiving Valued at $306 Billion." Family Caregiver Alliance News Release.

Feinberg, Lynn Friss and Sandra L. Newman. 2006. "Preliminary Experiences of the States in Implementing the National Family Caregiver Support Program: A 50-State Study." *Journal of Aging & Social Policy* 18(3–4): 95–113.

Feinberg, Lynn, Susan C. Reinhard, Ari Houser, and Rita Choula. 2011. "Valuing the Invaluable: 2011 Update—The Growing Contributions and Costs of Family Caregiving." Washington, DC: AARP Public Policy Institute

Felstiner, William, Richard L. Abel, and Austin Sarat. 1980–1981. "The Emergence and Transformation of Disputes: Naming, Blaming, Claiming…" *Law & Society Review* 15(3–4):631–654.

Ferree, Myra Marx. 2003. "Resonance and Radicalism: Feminist Framing in the Abortion Debates of the United States and Germany." *American Journal of Sociology* 109:304–344.

Ferree, Myra Marx, William Anthony Gamson, Jurgen Gerhards, and Dieter Rucht. 2002. *Shaping Abortion Discourse: Democracy and the Public Sphere in Germany and the United States.* New York: Cambridge University Press.

Ferree, Myra Marx and Beth B. Hess. 2000. *Controversy and Coalition: The New Feminist Movement Across Four Decades of Change.* New York: Routledge.

Ferree, Myra Marx and Patricia Yancey Martin. 1995a. *Feminist Organizations: Harvest of the New Women's Movement.* Philadelphia: Temple University Press.

Ferree, Myra Marx and Patricia Yancey Martin. 1995b. "Doing the Work of the Movement: Feminist Organizations." Pp. 3–23 in *Feminist Organizations: Harvest of the New Women's Movement,* edited by M. M. Ferree and P. Y. Martin. Philadelphia: Temple University Press.

Ferree, Myra Marx and Frederick D. Miller. 1985. "Mobilization and Meaning: Toward an Integration of Social Psychological and Resource Perspectives on Social Movements." *Sociological Inquiry* 55(1): 38–61.

Finch, Janet. 1989. *Family Obligations and Social Change.* Cambridge, UK: Polity Press.

Fisher, Dana. 2006. *Activism, Inc.: How the Outsourcing of Grassroots Campaigns Is Strangling Progressive Politics in America.* Stanford: Stanford University Press.

Folbre, Nancy and Julie A. Nelson. 2000. "For Love or Money—Or Both?" *Journal of Economic Perspectives* 14(4): 123–140.

Foucault, Michel. 1978. *The History of Sexuality, Volume I: An Introduction.* Translated by Robert Hurley. New York: Vintage Books.

Fraser, Nancy. 1989. *Unruly Practices: Power, Discourse and Gender in Contemporary Social Theory.* Minneapolis: University of Minnesota Press.

——. 1997. *Justice Interruptus: Critical Reflections on the "Postsocialist" Condition.* New York: Routledge.

Fraser, Nancy and Linda Gordon. 1992. "Contract Versus Charity: Why Is There No Social Citizenship in the United States?" *Socialist Review* 22(3): 45–67.

——. 1994. "A Genealogy of Dependency: Tracing a Keyword of the U.S. Welfare State." *Signs* 19(2): 309–336.

Frease, Dean E. 1975. "A Politicization Paradigm: the Case of Yugoslavia." *The Sociological Quarterly* 16(1): 33–47.

Freeman, Jo. 1975. *The Politics of Women's Liberation.* New York: David McKay.

Futrell, Robert. 2003. "Framing Processes, Cognitive Liberation, and NIMBY Protest in the U.S. Chemical-Weapons Disposal Conflict." *Sociological Inquiry* 73(3): 359–386.

Gamson, William A. 1992a. "The Social Psychology of Collective Action." Pp. 53–103 in *Frontiers in Social Movement Theory,* edited by A. Morris and C. M. Mueller. New Haven, CT: Yale University Press.

——. 1992b. *Talking Politics.* New York: Cambridge University Press.

——. 1995. "Constructing Social Protest." Pp. 85–106 in *Social Movements and Culture,* edited by Hank Johnston and Bert Klandermans. Minneapolis: University of Minnesota Press.

Gamson, William A., Bruce Fireman, and Steven Rytina. 1982. *Encounters with Unjust Authority*. Chicago: Dorsey Press.

Gamson, William A. and Andre Modigliani. 1989. "Media Discourse and Public Opinion on Nuclear Power: A Constructionist Approach." *American Journal of Sociology* 95(1): 1–37.

Garey, Anita Ilta, Karen V. Hansen, Rosanna Hertz, and Cameron L. MacDonald. 2002. "Care and Kinship." *Journal of Family Issues* 23(6): 703–715.

Gaventa, John. 1982. *Power and Powerlessness: Quiescence & Rebellion in an Appalachian Valley*. Urbana: University of Illinois Press.

George, L.K. and L.P. Gwyther. 1986. "Caregiver Well-Being: A Multidimensional Examination of Family Caregivers of Demented Adults." *Gerontological Society of America* 26(3): 253–259.

Georgetown University Long-Term Care Financing Project. 2007. "National Spending for Long-Term Care." Washington, DC: Georgetown University,

Gilligan, Carol. 1982. *In a Different Voice: Psychological Theory and Women's Development*. Cambridge, MA: Harvard University Press.

Gilliom, John. 2001. *Overseers of the Poor: Surveillance, Resistance, and the Limits of Privacy*. Chicago: University of Chicago Press.

Glazer, Nona Y. 1988. "Overlooked, Overworked: Women's Unpaid and Paid Work in the Health Services' 'Cost Crisis.'" *International Journal of Health Services* 18(1): 119–137.

——. 1990. "The Home as Workshop: Women as Amateur Nurses and Medical Care Providers." *Gender and Society* 4(4): 479–499.

——. 1993. *Women's Paid and Unpaid Labor: The Work Transfer in Health Care and Retailing*. Philadelphia: Temple University Press.

Glenn, Evelyn Nakano. 2000. "Creating a Caring Society." *Contemporary Sociology* 29(1): 84–94.

——. 2010. *Forced to Care: Coercion and Caregiving in America*. Cambridge: Harvard University Press.

Goffman, Irving. 1986. *Stigma: Notes on the Management of Spoiled Identity* New York: Touchstone.

Goldman, Connie. 2002. *The Gifts of Caregiving: Stories of Hardship, Hope, and Healing*. Minneapolis: Fairview Press.

Goldstein, Kenneth M. 1999. *Interest Groups, Lobbying, and Participation in America*. New York: Cambridge University Press.

Gonyea, Judith G. 2005. "The Oldest Old And a Long-Lived Society: Challenges for Public Policy." Pp. 157–180 in *The New Politics of Old Age Policy*, edited by R. B. Hudson. Baltimore, MD: The Johns Hopkins University Press.

Goodin, Robert E. and Julian Le Grand. 1986. "Creeping Universalism in the Welfare State: Evidence from Australia." *Journal of Public Policy* 6(3): 255–274.

Gordon, Linda. 1994. *Pitied but Not Entitled: Single Mothers and the History of Welfare, 1890-1935*. New York: Free Press.

Gornick, Janet, Martha R. Burt, and Karen J. Pittman. 1985. "Structure and Activities of Rape Crisis Centers in the Early 1980s." *Crime & Delinquency* 31(2): 247–268.

Gornick, Janet C. and D. S. Meyer. 1998. "Changing Political Opportunity: The Anti-Rape Movement and Public Policy." *Journal of Policy History* 10(4): 367–398.

Gornick, Janet C. and Marcia K. Meyers. 2003. *Families That Work: Policies for Reconciling Parenthood and Employment*. New York: Russell Sage Foundation.

Goss, Kristin A. 2006. *Disarmed: The Missing Movement for Gun Control in America*. Princeton, NJ: Princeton University Press.

Gould, Roger V. 1991. "Multiple Networks and Mobilization in the Paris Commune, 1871." *American Sociological Review* 56(6): 716–729.

Gramsci, Antonio. 1971. *Selections from the Prison Notebooks*. New York: International Publishers.

Greenhouse, Carol. 1986. *Praying for Justice: Faith, Order, and Community in an American Town.* Ithaca: Cornell University Press.

Grogan, Colleen M. and Christina M. Andrews. 2010. "The Politics of Aging Within Medicaid." Pp. 275–306 in *The New Politics of Old Age Policy*, edited by R. B. Hudson. Baltimore: Johns Hopkins University Press.

Grogan, Colleen and Eric Patashnik. 2003a. "Between Welfare Medicine and Mainstream Entitlement: Medicaid at the Political Crossroads." *Journal of Health Politics, Policy and Law* 28(5): 821–858.

——. 2003b. "Universalism within Targeting: Nursing Home Care, the Middle Class, and the Politics of the Medicaid Program." *Social Service Review* 77(1): 51–71.

Hacker, Jacob S. 2002. *The Divided Welfare State: The Battle over Public and Private Social Benefits in the United States.* New York: Cambridge University Press.

——. 2006. *The Great Risk Shift: The Assault on American Jobs, Families, Health Care, and Retirement and How You Can Fight Back.* New York: Oxford University Press.

Hacker, Jacob S. 2004. "Privatizing Risk without Privatizing the Welfare State: The Hidden Politics of Social Policy Retrenchment in the United States." *American Political Science Review* 98(2): 243–260.

Haines, Herbert. 1979. "Cognitive Claims-Making, Enclosure, and the Depoliticization of Social Problems." *Sociological Quarterly* 20(1): 119–130.

——. 1984. "Black Radicalization and the Funding of Civil Rights: 1957-1970." *Social Problems* 32(1): 31–43.

Hall, Peter A. 1986. *Governing the Economy: The Politics of State Intervention in Britain and France.* New York: Oxford University Press.

Harrington Meyer, Madonna and Pamela Herd. 2007. *Market Friendly or Family Friendly? The State and Gender Inquality in Old Age.* New York: Russell Sage Foundation.

Harrington Meyer, Madonna and Michelle Storbakken. 2000. "Shifting the Burden Back to Families? How Medicaid Cost-Containment Reshapes Access to Long Term Care in the United States." Pp. 217–228 in *Care Work: Gender, Class, and the Welfare State*, edited by M. Harrington Meyer. New York: Routledge.

Harrington, Mona. 2000. *Care and Equality: Inventing a New Family Politics.* New York: Routledge.

Hartog, Hendrik. 2012. *Someday All This Will Be Yours: A History of Inheritance and Old Age.* Cambridge: Harvard University Press.

Hay, Colin. 2007. *Why We Hate Politics.* Malden, MA: Polity Press.

Hayward, Mark D., Toni P. Miles, Eileen M. Crimmins, and Yu Yang. 2000. "The Significance of Socioeconomic Status in Explaining the Racial Gap in Chronic Health Conditions." *American Sociological Review* 65:910–930.

Health & Human Services. 1998. "Informal Caregiving: Compassion in Action." Washington, DC: Department of Health and Human Services.

Hellman, R., C. Copeland, and J. Van Derhei. 2012. "The 2012 Retirement Confidence Survey: Job Insecurity, Debt Weigh on Retirement Confidence, Savings." Washington, DC: Employee Benefit Research Institute,

Hochschild, Arlie. 1983. *The Managed Heart: Commercialization of Human Feeling.* Berkeley: University of California Press.

——. 2003. *The Commercialization of Intimate Life: Notes from Home and Work.* Berkeley: University of California Press.

Hochschild, Arlie R. 1997. *The Time Bind: When Work Becomes Home and Home Becomes Work.* New York: Metropolitan Books.

Holtz-Eakin, Douglas. 2005. "The Cost and Financing of Long-Term Care Services." In testimony before the Subcommittee on Health and Committee on Energy and Commerce, U.S. House of Representatives. Washington, DC: Congressional Budget Office.

Hondagneu-Sotelo, P. 2001. *Domestica: Immigrant Workers Cleaning and Caring in the Shadows of Influence*. Berkeley: University of California Press.

Hooyman, Nancy R. and Judith Gonyea. 1995. *Feminist Perspectives on Family Care: Policies for Gender Justice*. Thousand Oaks, CA: SAGE Publications.

House, James S., Ronald C. Kessler, and A. Regula Herzog. 1990. "Age, Socioeconomic Status, and Health." *The Milbank Quarterly* 68(3): 383–411.

Huber, Evelyne, Charles Ragin, and John Stephens. 1993. "Social Democracy, Christian Democracy, Constitutional Structure, and the Welfare State." *American Journal of Sociology* 99(3): 711–749.

Huber, Evelyne and John D. Stephens. 2001. *Development and Crisis of the Welfare State: Parties and Policies in Global Markets*. Chicago: University of Chicago Press.

Huber, Evelyne and John D. Stephens. 2006. "Combating Old and New Social Risks." Pp. 143–168 in *The Politics of Post-Industrial Welfare States: Adapting Post-War Social Policies to New Social Risks*, edited by K. Armingeon and G. Bonoli. New York: Routledge.

Hudson, Robert B. 2012. "The CLASS Promise in the Context of American Long-Term Care Policy." Pp. 61–199 in *Universal Coverage of Long-Term Care in the United States: Can We Get There from Here?* edited by D. Wolf and N. Folbre. New York: Russell Sage Foundation.

Hull, Kathleen E. 2001. "The Political Limits of the Rights Frame: The Case of Same-Sex Marriage in Hawaii." *Sociological Perspectives* 44(2): 207–232.

——. 2006. *Same-Sex Marriage: The Cultural Politics of Love and Law*. New York: Cambridge University Press.

Hunt, Alan. 1990. "Rights and Social Movements: Counter-Hegemonic Strategies." *Journal of Law and Society* 17(3): 309–328.

Hunt, Scott A. and Robert D. Benford. 2004. "Collective Identity, Solidarity, and Commitment." Pp. 433–457 in *The Blackwell Companion to Social Movements*, edited by D. A. Snow, S. A. Soule, and H. Kriesi. Oxford: Blackwell Publishing.

Jacobs, Jerry A. and Kathleen Gerson. 2004. *The Time Divide: Work, Family, and Gender Inequality*. Cambridge, MA: Harvard University Press.

Jacobs, Lawrence R. 1993. *The Health of Nations: Public Opinion and the Making of American and British Health Policy*. Ithaca, NY: Cornell University Press.

Jalbert, Jessica J., Lori A. Daiello, and Kate L. Lapane. 2008. "Dementia of the Alzheimer Type." *Epidemiologic Reviews* 30(1): 15–34.

Jasper, James M. 1997. *The Art of Moral Protest: Culture, Biography and Creativity in Social Movements*. Chicago: University of Chicago Press.

——. 1998. "The Emotions of Protest: Affective and Reactive Emotions in and Around Social Movements." *Sociological Forum* 13(3): 397–424.

Jenkins, J. Craig. 1987. "Nonprofit Organizations and Policy Advocacy." Pp. 296–318 in *The Non-Profit Sector*, edited by W. W. Powell. New Haven: Yale University Press.

Jones, Lynn. 2006. "The Haves Come out Ahead: How Cause Lawyers Frame the Legal System for Movements." Pp. 182–196 in *Cause Lawyers and Social Movements*, edited by A. Sarat and S. A. Scheingold. Stanford: Stanford University Press.

Katz, Alfred H. 1993. *Self-Help in America: A Social Movement Perspective*. New York: Twayne.

Katz, Michael B. 1996. *In the Shadow of the Poorhouse: A Social History of Welfare in America*. New York: Basic Books.

Kaye, H. Stephen, Charlene Harrington, and Mitchell P. LaPlante. 2010. "Long-Term Care: Who Gets It, Who Provides It, Who Pays, And How Much?" *Health Affairs* 29(1): 11–21.

Kelly, Erin. 2010. "Failure to Update: An Institutional Perspective on Noncompliance With the Family and Medical Leave Act." *Law & Society Review* 44(1): 33–66.

Kiecolt-Glaser, J., J.R. Dura, and C.E. Speicher. 1991. "Spousal Caregivers of Dementia Victims: Longitudinal Changes in Immunity and Health." *Psychosomatic Medicine* 53(4): 345–362.

King, A.C., R.K. Oka, and D.R. Young. 1994. "Ambulatory Blood Pressure and Heart Rate Responses to the Stress of Work and Caregiving in Older Women." *Journal of Gerontology: Medical Sciences* 49(6): M239–M245.

Kittay, Eva Feder and Diana T. Meyers. 1987. *Women and Moral Theory*. Totowa, NJ: Rowman & Littlefield.

Klandermans, Bert. 1984. "Mobilization and Participation: Social-Psychological Expansions of Resource Mobilization Theory." *American Sociological Review* 49:583–600.

———. 1988. "The Formation and Mobilization of Consensus." Pp. 173–196 in *From Structure to Action: Comparing Social Movement Research Across Cultures*, Vol. 1, *International Social Movement Research*, edited by B. Klandermans, H. Kriesi, and S. Tarrow. Greenwich, CT: JAI Press.

Klandermans, Bert, and Marga Weerd. 2000. "Group Identification and Political Protest." Pp. 68–90 in *Self, Identity, and Social Movements*, edited by S. Stryker, T. J. Owens, and R. W. White. Minneapolis: University of Minnesota Press, 2000.

Klawiter, Maren. 2008. *The Biopolitics of Breast Cancer: Changing Cultures of Disease and Activism*. Minneapolis: University of Minnesota Press.

Koren, M.J. 1986. "Home Care—Who Cares?" *New England Journal of Medicine* 314(14): 917–920.

Kornbluh, Felicia. 2007. *The Battle for Welfare Rights: Politics and Poverty in Modern America*. Philadelphia: University of Pennsylvania Press.

Kutner, Gail. 2001. "AARP Caregiver Identification Study." Washington, DC: AARP Research

Levine, Carol. 2012. "Long-Term Care and Long-Term Family Caregivers: Outdated Assumptions, Future Opportunities." Pp. 11–36 in *Universal Coverage of Long-Term Care in the United States: Can't We Get There from Here?*, edited by D. Wolf and N. Folbre. New York: Russell Sage Foundation.

Levine, Carol and Thomas H. Murray. 2004. "Conclusion: Building on Common Ground." Pp. 171–182 in *The Cultures of Caregiving: Conflict and Common Ground among Families, Health Professionals, and Policy Makers*, edited by C. Levine and T. H. Murray. Baltimore, MD: Johns Hopkins University Press.

Levitsky, Sandra R. 2008. " "What Rights?" The Construction of Political Claims to American Health Care Entitlements." *Law & Society Review* 42(3): 551–590.

Litowitz, Douglas. 2000. "Gramsci, Hegemony and the Law." *Brigham Young University Law Review* MM/2: 515–551.

Lopez, Steven Henry. 2004. *Reorganizing the Rust Belt: An Inside Study of the American Labor Movement*. Berkeley: University of California Press.

Lowi, Theodore J. 1964. "American Business, Public Policy, Case Studies, and Political Theory." *World Politics* 16(4): 677–715.

———. 1972. "Four Systems of Policy, Politics, and Choice." *Public Administration Review* 32(4): 298–310.

Lyketsos, C. G., O. Lopez, B. Jones, A. L. Fitzpatrick, J. Breitner, and S. DeKosky. 2002. "Prevalence of neuropsychiatric symptoms in dementia and mild cognitive impairment: Results from the cardiovascular health study." *JAMA* 288(12): 1475–1483.

Macaulay, Stewart. 1963. "Non-Contractual Relations in Business: A Preliminary Study." *American Sociological Review* 28(1):55–68.

MacDonald, Cameron L. and David A. Merrill. 2002. " "It Shouldn't Have to Be a Trade": Recognition and Redistribution in Care Work Advocacy." *Hypatia* 17(2): 67–83.

Maier, Shana L. 2008. "Are Rape Crisis Centers Feminist Organizations?" *Feminist Criminology* 3(2): 82–100.

Mann, Michael. 1986. *The Sources of Social Power, Volume 1: A History of Power from the Beginning to AD 1760*. New York: Cambridge University Press.

Mansbridge, Jane. 2001. "The Making of Oppositional Consciousness." Pp. 1–19 in *Oppositional Consciousness: The Subjective Roots of Social Protest*, edited by J. Mansbridge and A. Morris. Chicago: Chicago University Press.

Mansbridge, Jane and Aldon Morris. 2001. *Oppositional Consciousness: The Subjective Roots of Social Protest*. Chicago: University of Chicago Press.

Manza, Jeff and Fay Lomax Cook. 2002. "A Democratic Polity? Three Views of Policy Responsiveness to Public Opinion in the United States." *American Politics Research* 30(6): 630–667.

Marks, N., J.D. Lambert, and H. Choi. 2002. "Transitions to Caregiving, Gender, and Psychological Well Being: A Prospective U.S. National Study." *Journal of Marriage and the Family* 64(3): 657–667.

Marmor, Theodore R. 2000. *The Politics of Medicare*. New York: Aldine de Gruyter.

Marmor, Theodore R., Jerry L. Mashaw, and Philip L. Harvey. 1990. *America's Misunderstood Welfare State: Persistent Myths, Enduring Realities*. New York: Basic Books.

Marshall, Anna-Maria. 2003. "Injustice Frames, Legality, and the Everyday Construction of Sexual Harassment." *Law and Social Inquiry* 28(3): 659–689.

———. 2005. *Confronting Sexual Harassment: The Law and Politics of Everyday Life*. Burlington, VT: Ashgate Publishing.

Marshall, T.H. [1950] 1992. *Citizenship and Social Class*. London: Pluto Press.

Martin, Patricia Y. 2005. *Rape Work: Victims, Gender and Emotions in Organization and Community Context*. New York: Routledge.

Marwell, Nicole P. 2004. "Privatizing the Welfare State: Nonprofit Community-Based Organizations as Political Actors." *American Sociological Review* 69(2): 265–291.

Mather, Lynn and Barbara Yngvesson. 1981. "Language, Audience, and the Transformation of Disputes." *Law & Society Review* 15(3–4):775–782.

Matthews, Nancy 1994. *Confronting Rape: The Feminist Anti-Rape Movement and the State*. London: Routledge.

McAdam, Doug. 1982. *Political Process and the Development of Black Insurgency, 1930-1970*. Chicago: University of Chicago Press.

———. 1986. "Recruitment to High-Risk Activism: The Case of Freedom Summer." *American Journal of Sociology* 92(1): 64–90.

———. 1988. "Micromobilization Contexts and Recruitment to Activism." *International Social Movement Research* 1:125–154.

———. 1989. "The Biographical Consequences of Activism." *American Sociological Review* 54(5): 744–760.

McAdam, Doug and Ronnelle Paulsen. 1993. "Specifying the Relationship between Social Ties and Activism." *American Journal of Sociology* 99(3): 640–667.

McCann, Michael. 1994. *Rights at Work: Pay Equity Reform and the Politics of Legal Mobilization*. Chicago: University of Chicago Press.

McCarthy, John D. 2005. "Persistence and Change Among Nationally Federated Social Movements." Pp. 193–225 in *Social Movements and Organization Theory*, edited by G. Davis, D. McAdam, W. R. Scott, and M. N. Zald. New York: Cambridge University Press.

McCarthy, John D. and Mayer N. Zald. 1973. *The Trend of Social Movements in America: Professionalization and Resource Mobilization*. Morristown, NJ: General Learning Press.

———.1977. "Resource Mobilization and Social Movements: A Partial Theory." *American Journal of Sociology* 82(6): 1212–1241.

McCarthy, John D. and Edward T. Walker. 2004. "Alternative Organizational Repertoires of Poor People's Social Movement Organizations." *Nonprofit and Voluntary Sector Quarterly* 33(3) (Supplement): 97S–119S.

McConnell, Stephen. 2004. "Advocacy in Organizations: Elements of Success." *Generations* 28(1): 25-30.

Merrill, Deborah. 1997. *Caring for Elderly Parents: Juggling Work, Family, and Caregiving in Middle and Working Class Families.* Westport, CT: Auburn House.

Merry, Sally Engle. 1990. *Getting Justice and Getting Even: Legal Consciousness Among Working-Class Americans.* Chicago: University of Chicago Press.

MetLife Mature Market Institute and National Alliance for Caregiving. 2006. "The MetLife Caregiving Cost Study: Productivity Losses to U.S. Business." New York: MetLife Mature Market Institute.

Mettler, Suzanne. 2005. *Soldiers to Citizens: The G.I. Bill and the Making of the Greatest Generation.* Oxford: Oxford University Press.

Mettler, Suzanne and Joe Soss. 2004. "The Consequences of Public Policy for Democratic Citizenship: Bridging Policy Studies and Mass Politics." *Perspectives on Politics* 2(1): 55–73.

Meyer, Madonna Harrington. 1994. "The Impact of Family Status on Income Security and Health Care in Old Age: A Comparison of Western Nations." *International Journal of Sociology and Social Policy* 14(1–2): 53–73.

Miller, Edward Alan, Susan M. Allen, and Vincent Mor. 2009. "Navigating the Labyrinth of Long-Term Care: Shoring Up Informal Caregiving in a Home—and Community-Based World." *Journal of Aging and Social Policy* 21(1): 1–16.

Mills, C. Wright. [1959] 2000. *The Sociological Imagination.* New York: Oxford University Press.

Minkoff, Debra C. 1994. "From Service Provision to Institutional Advocacy: The Shifting Legitimacy of Organizational Forms." *Social Forces* 72(4): 943–969.

——. 1995. *Organizing for Equality: The Evolution of Women's and Racial Ethnic Organizations in America, 1955-1985.* New Brunswick: Rutgers University Press.

Montgomery, Rhonda J.V. 1999. "The Family Role in the Context of Long-Term Care." *Journal of Aging & Health* 11(3): 401–434.

Montgomery, Rhonda J.V. and Karl D. Kosloski. 2001. *Change, Continuity and Diversity Among Caregivers.* Washington, DC: Administration on Aging.

——. 2013. "Pathways to a Caregiver Identity and Implications for Support Services." Pp. 131–156 in *Caregiving Across the Lifespan: Research, Practice, Policy,* edited by R. C. Talley and R. J. V. Montgomery. New York: Springer.

Moon, Marilyn and Pamela Herd. 2002. *A Place at the Table: Women's Needs and Medicare Reform.* New York: Century Foundation.

Moore, Barrington, Jr. 1978. *Injustice: The Social Bases of Obedience and Revolt.* White Plains, NY: M.E. Sharpe.

Morel, Nathalie. 2006. "Providing Coverage Against New Social Risks in Bismarckian Welfare States: The Case of Long-Term Care." Pp. 227–247 in *The Politics of Post-Industrial Welfare States: Adapting Post-War Social Policies to New Social Risk,* edited by K. Armingeon and G. Bonoli. New York: Routledge.

Morris, Aldon D. 1984. *The Origins of the Civil Rights Movement: Black Communities Organizing for Change.* New York: Free Press.

——. 1992. "Political Consciousness and Collective Action." Pp. 351–373 in *Frontiers in Social Movement Theory,* edited by A. Morris and C. M. Mueller. New Haven, CT: Yale University Press.

Moses, Stephen A. 1993. "The Case for Long-Term Care Insurance (And How to Make It)." *Nursing Homes* 42(1): 28–32.

—— 1996. "Medicaid Stifles LTC Ins. Purchases." *National Underwriter,* Aug. 5, pp. S9.

Napili, Angela and Kirsten J. Colello. 2013. "Funding for the Older Americans Act and Other Aging Services Programs." Washington, DC: Congressional Research Service

National Alliance for Caregiving and AARP. 2009. "Caregiving in the U.S." Washington, DC: National Alliance for Caregiving.

Nelson, Julie A. 1999. "Of Markets and Martyrs: Is it OK to Pay Well for Care?" *Feminist Economics* 5(3): 43–59.

Nelson, Julie A. and Paula England. 2002. "Feminist Philosophies of Love and Work." *Hypatia* 17(2): 1–18.

Nielsen, Laura Beth. 2000. "Situating Legal Consciousness: Experiences and Attitudes of Ordinary Citizens about Law and Street Harassment." *Law & Society Review* 34(4): 1055–1090.

——. 2004. *License to Harass: Law, Hierarchy, and Offensive Public Speech*. Princeton NJ: Princeton University Press.

Noddings, Nel. 1984. *Caring: A Feminine Approach to Ethics and Moral Education*. Berkeley: University of California Press.

O'Brien, Ellen. 2005. "Medicaid's Coverage of Nursing Home Costs: Asset Shelter for the Wealthy or Essential Safety Net?" Long-Term Care Financing Project, Georgetown University. Washington, DC: Georgetown University Health Policy Institute.

O'Brien, Ellen and Risa Elias. 2004. "Medicaid and Long-Term Care." Kaiser Commission on Medicaid and the Uninsured, Washington, DC: The Henry J. Kaiser Family Foundation.

O'Connor, Deborah L. 1999. "Living with a Memory-Impaired Spouse: (Re)Cognizing the Experience." *Canadian Journal on Aging* 18(2): 211–235.

Oberlander, Jonathan. 2003. *The Political Life of Medicare*. Chicago: University of Chicago Press.

Oliver, Pamela and Gerald Marwell. 1992. "Mobilizing Technologies for Collective Action." Pp. 251–272 in *Frontiers in Social Movement Theory*, edited by A. Morris and C. M. Mueller. New Haven, CT: Yale University Press.

Orloff, Ann Shola. 1999. "Motherhood, Work and Welfare: Gender Ideologies and State Social Provision in Australia, Britain, Canada and the United States." Pp. 291–320 in *State/Culture*, edited by G. Steinmetz. Ithaca, NY: Cornell University Press.

Ory, Marcia G., Richard R. Hoffman, Jennifer L. Yee, Sharon Tennstedt, and Richard Schulz. 1999. "Prevalence and Impact of Caregiving: A Detailed Comparison between Dementia and Nondementia Caregivers." *The Gerontologist* 39(2): 177–185.

Padamsee, Tasleem J. 2009. "Culture in Connection: Re-Contextualizing Ideational Processes in the Analysis of Policy Development." *Social Politics* 16(4): 413–445.

Parker, Kim and Eileen Patten. 2013. "The Sandwich Generation: Rising Financial Burdens for Middle-Aged Americans." Pew Research Social and Demographic Trends. Washington, DC: Pew Research Center, http://www.pewsocialtrends.org/2013/01/30/the-sandwich-generation/ (accessed November 22, 2013).

Passy, Florence and Marco Giugni. 2001. "Social Networks and Individual Perceptions: Explaining Differential Participation in Social Movements." *Sociological Forum* 16(1): 123–153.

Perrin, Andrew J. 2006. *Citizen Speak: The Democratic Imagination in American Life*. Chicago: University of Chicago Press.

Pierson, Paul. 1993. "When Effect Becomes Cause: Policy Feedback and Political Change." *World Politics* 45(4): 595–628.

——. 1994. *Dismantling the Welfare State? Reagan, Thatcher, and the Politics of Retrenchment*. Cambridge, UK: Cambridge University Press.

——. 2001a. *The New Politics of the Welfare State*. New York: Oxford University Press.

——. 2001b. "Postindustrial Pressures on the Mature Welfare States." Pp. 80–104 in *The New Politics of the Welfare State*, edited by P. Pierson. New York: Oxford University Press.

Pinquart, M. and S. Sorensen. 2003. "Differences Between Caregivers and Noncaregivers in Psychological Health and Physical Health: A Meta-Analysis." *Psychology & Aging* 18(2): 250–267.

Pitt-Catsouphes, Marcie, Ellen E. Kossek, and Stephen Sweet. 2006. *The Work and Family Handbook: Multi-Disciplinary Perspectives and Approaches*. Mahwah, NJ: Lawrence Erlbaum Associates.

Piven, Frances Fox and Richard Cloward. 1993. *Regulating the Poor: The Functions of Public Welfare*. New York: Vintage.

Piven, Frances Fox and Richard A. Cloward. 1979. *Poor People's Movements: Why They Succeed, How They Fail*. New York: Vintage.

Polletta, Francesca. 1999. " "Free Spaces" in Collective Action." *Theory and Society* 28(1): 1–38.

———. 2000. "The Structural Context of Novel Rights Claims: Southern Civil rights Organizing, 1961-1966." *Law & Society Review* 34:367–406.

Polletta, Francesca and James M. Jasper. 2001. "Collective Identity and Social Movements." *Annual Review of Sociology* 27:283–305.

Poulshock, S.W. and G.T. Deimling. 1984. "Families Caring for Elders in Residence: Issues in the Measurement of Burden." *Journal of Gerontology* 39(2): 230–239.

Primus, Richard A. 1999. *The American Language of Rights*. New York: Cambridge University Press.

Putnam, Robert D. 1995. "Bowling Alone: America's Declining Social Capital." *Journal of Democracy* 6(1): 65–78.

Quinn, Beth. 2000. "The Paradox of Complaining: Law, Humor, and Harassment in the Everyday Work World." *Law and Social Inquiry* 25(4):1151–1185.

Rampell, Catherine. 2010. "Women Now a Majority in American Workplaces." *The New York Times*, February 5, p. A10.

Rice, Thomas, Katherine Desmond, and Jon Gabel. 1990. "The Medicare Catastrophic Coverage Act: A Post-Mortem." *Health Affairs* 9(3): 75–87.

Rosen, Ruth. 2000. *The World Split Open: How the Modern Women's Movement Changed America*. New York: Penguin.

Rosenstone, Steven J. and John Mark Hansen. 1993. *Mobilization, Participation, and Democracy in America*. New York: Macmillan.

Rothman, Gerald C. 1985. *Philanthropists, Therapists and Activists: A Century of Ideological Conflict in Social Work*. Cambridge, MA: Schenkman Publishing Co.

Rubin, L.B. 2001. "Getting Younger While Getting Older: Family-Building at Midlife." Pp. 42–57 in *Working Families: The Transformation of the American Home*, edited by R. Hertz and N. Marshall. Berkeley: University of California Press.

Rubin, Rose M. and Shelley I. White-Means. 2009. "Informal Caregiving: Dilemmas of Sandwiched Caregivers." *Journal of Family Economic Issues* 30:252–267.

Salamon, Lester M. 1995. *Partners in Public Service: Government-Nonprofit Relations in the Modern Welfare State*. Baltimore, MD: Johns Hopkins University Press.

Sarat, Austin. 1990. "…The Law is All Over": Power, Resistance, and the Legal Consciousness of the Welfare Poor." *Yale Journal of Law and Humanities* 2(2): 343–379.

Sarat, Austin and Susan Silbey. 1988. "The Pull of the Policy Audience." *Law & Policy* 10(2/3): 97–166.

Saunders, Cynthia M. 2006. "Insuring the Uninsured: Reducing the Barriers to Public Insurance." *The Qualitative Report* 11(3): 499–515.

Scharlach, Andrew, Nancy Giunta, Teresa Dal Santo, and Pat Fox. 2003. "California's Family Caregiver Support System: Findings and Recommendations." Berkeley, CA: Center for the Advanced Study of Aging Services, University of California.

Schechter, Susan. 1982. *Women and Male Violence: The Visions and Struggles of the Battered Women's Movement*. Boston: South End.

Scheingold, Stuart A. 1974. *The Politics of Rights: Lawyers, Public Policy, and Political Change*. New Haven: Yale University Press.

(198) *References*

Schier, Steven E. 2000. *By Invitation Only: The Rise of Exclusive Politics in the United States*. Pittsburgh: University of Pittsburgh Press.

Schlozman, Kay Lehman, Sidney Verba, and Henry E. Brady. 1999. "Civic Participation and the Equality Problem." Pp. 427–459 in *Civic Engagement in American Democracy*, edited by T. Skocpol and M. Fiorina. Washington: Brookings Institution Press.

Schmall, Vicki L., Marilyn Cleland, and Marilynn Sturdevant. 2000. *The Caregiver Helpbook: Powerful Tools for Caregiving*. Portland: Legacy Health System.

Schneider, Anne and Helen Ingram. 1993. "Social Construction of Target Populations: Implications for Politics and Policy." *The American Political Science Review* 87(2): 334–347.

———. 1997. *Policy Design for Democracy*. Lawrence: University of Kansas Press.

Schulz, Richard and Scott Beach. 1999. "Caregiving as a Risk Factor for Mortality: The Caregiver Health Effects Study." *JAMA* 282(23): 2215–2219.

Schulz, R., J. Newsom, M. Mittelmark, L. Burton, C. Hirsch, and S. Jackson. 1997. "Health and Effects of Caregiving." *Annals of Behavioral Medicine* 19(2): 110–116.

Scott, James C. 1990. *Domination and the Arts of Resistance: Hidden Transcripts*. New Haven, CT: Yale University Press.

Sewell, William H., Jr. 1992. "A Theory of Structure: Duality, Agency, and Transformation." *American Journal of Sociology* 98(1): 1–29.

Shaw, W.S., T.L. Patterson, S.J. Semple, S. Ho, M.R. Irwin, R.L. Hauger, and I. Grant. 1997. "Longitudinal Analysis of Multiple Indicators of Health Decline Among Spousal Caregivers." *Annals of Behavioral Medicine* 19(2): 101–109.

Silbey, Susan. 2005. "After Legal Consciousness." *Annual Review of Law and Social Science* 1:323–368.

Silbey, Susan and Austin Sarat. 1987. "Critical Traditions in Law and Society Research." *Law & Society Review* 21(1): 165–174.

———. 1989. "Reconstituting the Sociology of Law: Beyond Science and the State." Pp. 150–172 in *The Politics of Field Research: Sociology Beyond Enlightenment*, edited by D. Silverman and J. Gubrium Beverly Hills, CA: Sage.

Skrentny, John D. 2002. *The Minority Rights Revolution*. Cambridge, MA: Harvard University Press.

Skocpol, Theda. 1988. "The Limits of the New Deal System and the Roots of Contemporary Welfare Dilemmas." Pp. 293–311 in *The Politics of Social Policy in the United States*, edited by M. Weir, A. S. Orloff, and T. Skocpol. Princeton: Princeton University Press.

———. 1992. *Protecting Soldiers and Mothers: The Political Origins of Social Policy in the United States*. Cambridge, MA: Harvard University Press.

———. 2003. *Diminished Democracy: From Membership to Management in American Civic Life*. Norman, OK: University of Oklahoma Press.

Smith, Steven Rathgeb and Michael Lipsky. 1993. *Nonprofits for Hire: The Welfare State in the Age of Contracting*. Cambridge: Harvard University Press.

Smith, Suzanna D. 1999 (rev. 2005). "What is Caregiving?" Institute of Food and Agricultural Sciences, University of Florida, Florida Cooperative Extension Office. Gainesville, FL: University of Florida Digital Collections, http://ufdc.ufl.edu/IR00002518/00001 (accessed November 22, 2013)

Snow, David and Robert D. Benford. 1988. "Ideology, Frame Resonance, and Participant Mobilization." Pp. 197–217 in *From Structure to Action: Comparing Social Movement Research Across Cultures*, Vol. 1, *International Social Research*, edited by B. Klandermans, H. Kriesi, and S. Tarrow. London: JAI Press.

———. 1992. "Master Frames and Cycles of Protest." Pp. 133–155 in *Frontiers in Social Movement Theory*, edited by A. D. Morris and C. M. Mueller. New Haven: Yale University Press.

Snow, David A., Jr., Daniel M. Cress, Liam Downey, and Andrew W. Jones. 1998. "Disrupting the 'Quotidian': Reconceptualizing the Relationship Between Breakdown and the Emergence of Collective Action." *Mobilization: An International Journal* 3:1–22.

Snow, David A., Jr., E. Burke Rochford, Steven K. Worden, and Robert D. Benford. 1986. "Frame Alignment Processes, Micromobilization, and Movement Participation." *American Sociological Review* 51(4): 464–481.

Snow, David A., Jr., Louis A. Zurcher, and Sheldon Ekland-Olson. 1980. "Social Networks and Social Movements: A Microstructural Approach to Differential Recruitment." *American Sociological Review* 45(5): 787–801.

Snow, David A., and Doug McAdam. 2000. "Identity Work Processes in the Context of Social Movements: Clarifying the Identity/Movement Nexus." Pp. 41–67 in *Self, Identity, and Social Movements,* edited by S. Stryker, T. J. Owens and R. W. White. Minneapolis: University of Minnesota Press.

Sobieraj, Sarah and Deborah White. 2004. "Taxing Political Life: Reevaluating the Relationship Between Voluntary Association Membership, Political Engagement, and the State." *Sociological Quarterly* 45:739–764.

Somers, Margaret R. and Fred Block. 2005. "From Poverty to Perversity: Ideas, Markets, and Institutions over 200 Years of Welfare Debate." *American Sociological Review* 70(2): 260–288.

Soss, Joe. 2002. *Unwanted Claims: The Politics of Participation in the U.S. Welfare System.* Ann Arbor: University of Michigan Press.

——. 2005. "Making Clients and Citizens: Welfare Policy as a Source of Status, Belief, and Action." Pp. 291–328 in *Deserving and Entitled: Social Constructions and Public Policy,* edited by A. Schneider and H. Ingram. Albany: State University of New York Press.

Soss, Joe and Sanford F. Schram. 2007. "A Public Transformed? Welfare Reform as Policy Feedback." *American Political Science Review* 101(1): 111–127.

Starr, Paul and Ellen Immergut. 1987. "Health Care and the Boundaries of Politics." Pp. 221–254 in *Changing Boundaries of the Political: Essays on the Evolving Balance Between the State and Society, Public and Private in Europe,* edited by C. S. Maier. New York: Cambridge University Press.

Steensland, Brian. 2006. "Cultural Categories and the American Welfare State: The Case of Guaranteed Income Policy." *American Journal of Sociology* 111:1273–1326.

——. 2007. *The Failed Welfare Revolution: America's Struggle over Guaranteed Income Policy.* Princeton, NJ: Princeton University Press.

Steensland, Brian and Christi M. Smith. 2012. "Culture, State and Policy." Pp. 229–239 in *The Wiley-Blackwell Companion to Political Sociology,* edited by E. Amenta, K. Nash, and A. Scott. Malden, MA: Blackwell Publishing, Ltd.

Steinberg, Marc W. 1999. "The Talk and Back Talk of Collective Action: A Dialogic Analysis of Repertoires of Discourse among Nineteenth-Century English Cotton Spinners." *American Journal of Sociology* 105(3): 736–780.

Steinmo, Sven, Kathleen Thelen, and Frank Longstreth. 1992. *Structuring Politics: Historical Institutionalism in Comparative Analysis.* Cambridge, MA: Cambridge University Press.

Steinmo, Sven and Jon Watts. 1995. "It's the Institutions, Stupid! Why Comprehensive National Health Insurance Always Fails in America." *Journal of Health Politics, Policy and Law* 20(2): 329–372.

Stone, Deborah. 2000. "Why We Need a Care Movement." *The Nation,* March 13, pp. 13–16.

Stuber, Jennifer and K. Kronebusch. 2004. "Stigma and Other Determinants of Participation in TANF and Medicaid." *Journal of Policy Analysis and Management* 23(3): 509–530.

Stuber, Jennifer and Mark Schlesinger. 2006. "Sources of Stigma for Means-Tested Government Programs." *Social Science & Medicine* 63(4): 933–945.

Swidler, Ann. 1986. "Culture in Action: Symbols and Strategies." *American Sociological Review* 51(2): 273–286.

Tarrow, Sidney. 1994. *Power in Movement: Social Movements, Collective Action, and Politics.* Cambridge, UK: Cambridge University Press.

Taylor, Verta. 1996. *Rock-A-By Baby: Feminism, Self-Help, and Postpartum Depression.* New York: Routledge.

———. 2000. "Emotions and Identity in Women's Self-Help Movements." Pp. 271–299 in *Self, Identity, and Social Movements,* edited by S. Stryker, T. J. Owens, and R. W. White. Minneapolis: University of Minnesota Press.

Taylor, Verta, Nella Van Dyke, Katrina Kimport, and Ellen Ann Anderson. 2009. "Culture and Mobilization: Tactical Repertoires, Same-Sex Weddings, and the Impact on Gay Activism." *American Sociological Review* 74:865–890.

Taylor, Verta and Marieke Van Willigen. 1996. "Women's Self-Help and the Reconstruction of Gender: The Postpartum Support and Breast Cancer Movements." *Mobilization: An International Journal* 1:123–142.

Taylor, Verta and Nancy Whittier. 1992. "Collective Identity in Social Movement Communities: Lesbian Feminist Mobilization." Pp. 104–129 in *Frontiers in Social Movement Theory,* edited by A. Morris and C. M. Mueller. New Haven, CT: Yale University Press.

Teles, Steven M. 2008. *The Rise of the Conservative Legal Movement: The Battle for the Control of the Law.* Princeton, NJ: Princeton University Press.

Title III-E. 2000. "Older Americans Act Amendments of 2000," Public Law 106-501. November 13, 2000. Washington, DC: Administration on Aging, http://history.nih.gov/research/downloads/PL106-501.pdf (accessed November 22, 2013).

Tompson, Trevor, Jennifer Benz, Jennifer Agiesta, Dennis Junius, Kim Nguyen, and Kristina Lowell. 2013. "Long-Term Care: Perceptions, Experiences, and Attitudes among Americans 40 and Older." Chicago: Associated Press-NORC Center for Public Affairs Research.

Tronto, Joan C. 1994. *Moral Boundaries: A Political Argument for an Ethic of Care.* London: Routledge.

Turner, Ralph and Lewis M. Killian. 1957. *Collective Behavior.* Englewood Cliffs: Prentice-Hall.

Ungerson, Clare. 1987. *Policy is Personal: Sex, Gender and Informal Care.* New York: Tavistock.

Ungerson, Clare and Sue Yeandle. 2007. *Cash for Care in Developed Welfare States.* New York: Palgrave Macmillan.

Verba, Sidney, Kay Lehman Schlozman, and Henry E. Brady. 1995. *Voice and Equality: Civic Voluntarism in American Politics.* Cambridge, MA: Harvard University Press.

Voyer, Philippe, Rene Verreault, Ginette Azizah, Johanne Desrosiers, Nathalie Champoux, and Annick Bedard. 2005. "Prevalence of physical and verbal aggressive behaviours and associated factors among older adults in long-term care facilities." *BMC Geriatrics* 5:13.

Waldron, Jeremy. 1996. "Rights and Needs: The Myth of Disjunction." Pp. 87–109 in *Legal Rights: Historical and Philosophical Perspectives,* edited by A. Sarat and T. R. Kearns. Ann Arbor: University of Michigan Press.

Walker, Alan. 1991. "The Relationship Between the Family and the State in the Care of Older People." *Canadian Journal on Aging* 10(2): 94–112.

Walker, Edward T. 2008. "Contingent Pathways from Joiner to Activist: The Indirect Effect of Participation in Voluntary Associations on Civic Engagement." *Sociological Forum* 23(1): 116–143.

———. 2009. "Privatizing Participation: Civic Change and the Organizational Dynamics of Grassroots Lobbying Firms." *American Sociological Review* 74(1): 83–105.

Walker, Jack. 1991. *Mobilizing Interest Groups in America: Patrons, Professions, and Social Movements.* Ann Arbor: University of Michigan Press.

White, Lucie E. 1990. "Subordination, Rhetorical Survival Skills, and Sunday Shoes: Notes on the Hearing of Mrs. G." *Buffalo Law Review* 38(1): 1–58.

Wiener, Joshua M., Raymond J. Hanley, Robert Clark, and Joan F. Van Nostrand. 1990. "Measuring the Activities of Daily Living: Comparisons Across National Surveys." *Journal of Gerontology* 45(6): S229–S237.

Williams, Joan. 2000. *Unbending Gender: Why Family and Work Conflict and What to Do About It.* New York: Oxford University Press.

Williams, Joan C. and Heather Boushey. 2010. "The Three Faces of Work-Family Conflict: The Poor, the Professionals, and the Missing Middle." Washington, DC: Center for American Progress and WorkLife Law.

Williams, Patricia. 1987. "Alchemical Notes: Reconstructing Ideals From Deconstructed Rights." *Harvard Civil Rights-Civil Liberties Law Review* 22:401–433.

Williams, Rhys H. 1982. *The Sociology of Culture.* New York: Schocken Books.

Wilson, James Q. 1973. *Political Organizaitons.* New York: Basic Books.

Wolf, Douglas. 2012. "Introduction." Pp. 1–59 in *Universal Coverage of Long-Term Care in the United States: Can We Get There from Here?*, edited by D. Wolf and N. Folbre. New York: Russell Sage Foundation.

Wolf, Rosalie S. 1996. "Elder Abuse and Family Violence: Testimony Presented Before the U.S. Senate Special Committee on Aging." *Journal of Elder Abuse & Neglect* 8(1): 81–96.

Wood, Richard L. 2002. *Faith in Action: Religion, Race, and Democratic Organizing in America.* Chicago: University of Chicago Press.

Zarit, Steven. 2006. "Assessment of Family Caregivers: A Research Perspective." Pp. 12–37 in *Caregiver Assessment: Vol. 2, Voices and Views from the Field*, edited by National Center on Caregiving. San Francisco: Family Caregiver Alliance.

Zelizer, Viviana A. 2005. *The Purchase of Intimacy.* Princeton, NJ: Princeton University Press.

INDEX

Page numbers followed by *t* or *f* indicate tables or figures, respectively. Numbers followed by "n" indicate notes.